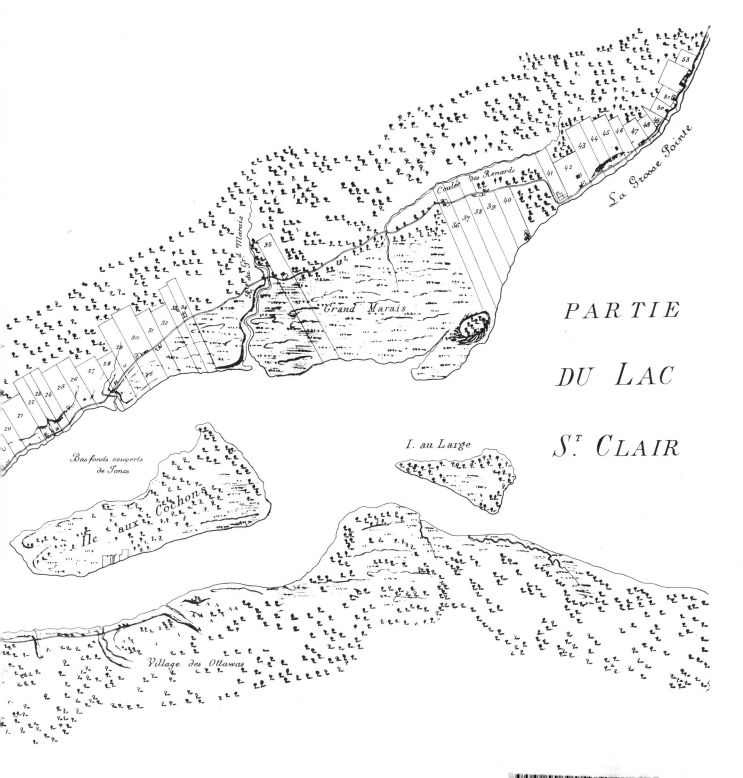

PARTIE

DU LAC

S.ᵗ CLAIR

TONNANCOUR

Life in
GROSSE POINTE
and along the Shores of
LAKE ST. CLAIR

ABOUT TONNANCOUR

A French word meaning "Thunder Court," used to identify the Theodore Parsons Hall summer estate built in 1880 near present-day Provencal Road in Grosse Pointe Farms. A retired commodities broker, Hall was married to Alexandrine Godefroy, a descendent of Detroit's first settlers. Hall named the estate after the seigneurie of her ancestor, Godefroy de Tonnancour, at Trois Rivieres in Quebec. In the late nineteenth century, visitors like Detroiters Caroline Hamlin and Silas Farmer made the estate a local cultural center. Among Hall's literary endeavors was the following poem, found by one of his daughters, Mrs. Marie Hall Fuger Delbos, in a family album.

By St. Clair's classic water
    On her low, meandering shore
Here a sleepy old French hamlet,
    Stands Chateau de Tonnancour.

When the voyagers sailed long ago,
    A hundred years or more,
Came with LaSalle's heroic band
    Godefroi de Tonnancour.

So, with bright memories of the past
    and tales of ancient lore,
His grandchildren here reared a home
    and called it Tonnancour.

Now, as ships float swiftly by,
    Each sail viewed from the shore
Recalls the Griffin's fateful voyage,
    LaSalle and Tonnancour.

Old inhabitants drive past to church
    in French Charrettes of yore,
and still respectfully salute
    St. Clair and Tonnancour.

The mournful bell has ceased its toll,
    They gather, rich and poor,
And never in their prayers forget
    Godefroi de Tonnancour.

Tonnancour, various views, from Silas Farmer's **History of Detroit and Wayne County.**

TONNANCOUR

Life in
GROSSE POINTE
and along the Shores of
LAKE ST. CLAIR

Volume 2

Edited
by
ARTHUR M. WOODFORD

Omnigraphics, Inc.

Penobscot Building
Detroit, MI 48226

* * *

ISBN 0-7808-0099-0

∞

This book is printed on acid-free paper meeting the ANSI Z39.48
Standard. The infinity symbol that appears above indicates that the
paper in this book meets that standard.

Printed in the United States of America

Contents

Tonnancour, Volume 2

Editor's Preface

The year 1996 is an important date in the history of the Detroit River region. It is the 200th anniversary of the arrival of the first American troops at Fort Detroit, and it is the 100th anniversary of the automobile. It is these two events that form the central theme of this second volume of *Tonnancour*.

On July 11, 1796, the American flag was first raised over Detroit as the British garrison evacuated the fort and town and moved across the river to Canada and the newly established Fort Malen and village of Amherstburg. To tell this story we have F. Clever Bald's fine history of the arrival of the American from his classic volume *Detroit's First American Decade*. In the fall of 1796 a young British traveler, Isaac Weld, visited Detroit and left a firsthand account of this frontier village. His fascinating narrative is reprinted here. Just days after the American soldiers arrived at Detroit, the civil government of the United States, in the person of the Territorial Secretary, arrived here. One of his first tasks was to establish a formal governmental structure, and on August 15, 1796, Wayne County was formed and from it the Township of Grosse Pointe. It is from the writings of historian Clarence Monroe Burton that we follow this event.

One hundred years later, a horseless carriage first traveled the streets of Detroit, and within a decade the city was on its way to becoming the world's motor capital. Although this first motor car never traveled the streets of Grosse Pointe, the impact of this new industry was soon felt here. In 1901 the Grosse Pointe Race Track was converted for motor car racing, and Mark Patrick, curator of the National Automotive History Collection Detroit Public Library, recounts those exciting days in his article, "Gentleman — Start Your Engines!" The story continues with Mike Mengden's survey of early Grosse Pointe gas stations, Jack Schramm's and Bill Henning's "The Motor Bus Comes to Grosse Pointe," and John Polacsek's article detailing the fabulous motor yachts built for the auto barons — the men who amassed their fortunes in the new auto industry.

Our story continues with a look back to the first French settlers of the Grand Marais, and the legends lore, and poetry of the habitants. Here we have the story of the Hall family of "Tonnancour," Friend Palmer's reminiscences of nineteenth-century Grosse Pointe, and the Civil War letters of George Frederick Neff.

As in Volume One, the reader will find here essays, poetry, and legends of Lake St. Clair. Here are the stories of the tug *Champion* and her tow of eight sailing vessels; the lighthouses of the lake; Belle Isle, that grand island park; the building of the Grosse Pointe Yacht Club; and a trip abroad an excursion steamer on a hot summer's day, up the lake to the Flats.

Prohibition and rum running, architecture, the game of golf, the Children's Home, and movies at the Punch — they are all here, helping to tell the story of life in Grosse Pointe and along the shores of Lake St. Clair.

Once again I was most fortunate in having the help of a number of knowledgeable people in preparing this volume. This includes, of course, the Advisory Board with their ideas, expertise, and in several instances their writings: Thomas A. Arbaugh, Thomas W. Brunk, Jean Dodenhoff, Michael W. Dixon, Philip P. Mason, Hudson, Mead, and Anne Lile Musial.

Thanks as well to David Poremba, Burton Historical Collection, and Jeff Tong, History and Travel Department, Detroit Public Library, both fine librarians. And thanks to Ralph Kliber, Past Commodore, and Jack Sullivan, Manager, Grosse Pointe Yacht Club; Roseann McKean, *Detroit Free Press*; Bob Edgar for his pictures of the Punch and Judy Theater; Judy Piatek of Lakeside Investment; Tom Franks and Tom Sherry for their help in photo reproduction; Diane Cusimano, Children's Home of Detroit; Ted Mecke, Judy Holmes, and Michelle Walker, St Paul's Church; Suzanne Kent, Grosse Pointe Woods Historical Commission; the ladies in the office of the Friends of Belle Isle; and to Frank Kerwin, sailor and friend, for his introduction.

The staff of Omnigraphics also deserve thanks — Publisher Frederick G. Ruffner, Jr., production manager Matt Barbour, publicity coordinator David Bianco, designer and typographer Mary Ann Stavros-Lanning, indexer Barry Puckett, cover designer Dick Golobic. And finally a special thank you to Laurie Lanzen Harris, Editorial Director. Without her support and ideas, this volume could never have been published—she is indeed an editor's editor.

Here then is Volume Two of *Tonnancour*, and again it is our hope that you, the reader, will find in this collection an interest that will lead you to read further and to enjoy these stories of life in Grosse Pointe and along the shores of Lake St. Clair.

Arthur M. Woodford
September, 1996

———————————— ❦ ————————————

Arthur M. Woodford, a native Detroiter, is director of the St. Clair Shores Public Library. Formerly, he held administrative positions with the Grosse Pointe Public Library and the Detroit Public Library. Woodford attended the University of Wisconsin studying civil engineering, received a BA in history from Wayne State University, and a MA in library science from the University of Michigan.

He co-authored with his father, the late Frank B. Woodford, All Our Yesterdays: A Brief History of Detroit *in 1969. In 1974 he published* Detroit and Its Banks: The Story of Detroit Bank and Trust, *and in 1979* Detroit: American Urban Renaissance. *In 1994 his fourth book,* Charting the Inland Seas: A History of the U.S. Lake Survey *was published. In addition to these books, Woodford has written several articles dealing with the history of Michigan and the Great Lakes.*

Introduction

The end plates of this volume are maps (or more properly, charts), printed two centuries apart, in 1796 and 1996. Together they represent two hundred years of the evolution of life along the shores of Lake St. Clair and the Detroit and St. Clair Rivers. To the cartographer and the mariner, these charts are more than two-dimensional representations of geography. You could navigate the waters of Lake St. Clair with the 1796 chart, albeit in slower-moving vessels. The modern chart contains a wealth of information, not only for navigation, but also for the characteristics of the shoreline that give imagery to the sailor. So too, from these flat pages of the second volume of *Tonnancour*, the reader will perceive the form, the shape, and the color of life along the shore of these fresh water seas.

The commercial and social life of our region has always been tempered by the presence of the waterways. The benign quality of the lakes, as opposed to the more foreboding oceans, led to the formation of the first yacht clubs. The Detroit Boat Club, founded in 1839, was the first organization in the United States devoted solely to pleasure boating. The celebration of water sports is evidenced in the Venetian architectural style of the club houses for the Detroit Boat Club and the Detroit Yacht Club, both on Belle Isle, and, of course, the Grosse Pointe Yacht Club at Vernier and Lakeshore Roads.

The commercial sailing vessels that plied the lake in the nineteenth century gave way to the steam packets and excursion vessels. As the lake freighters grew to the length of two football fields, the lighter and more versatile internal combustion engine led to the production of many types of private power vessels, from the grand yachts of the auto barons to the smallest naphtha fueled runabout.

From the Detroit River to the St. Clair Flats, the people that transformed the area of ribbon farms into cities were shaped by the water, as were their institutions and the structures that housed them. It is this story that is told in *Tonnancour*.

The water allowed the confluence of coal, timber, iron ore, and other mineral riches to fuel the vast industrial complex that developed along the shoreline of the Detroit River. This in turn produced the wealth that allowed the pursuit of a more genteel and reserved life style. The wealthy attempted to capture the refined tastes of European architecture in their homes, and the sense of purposeful gentility in their social world.

All of the twentieth century has been dominated by the automobile, but the industrial barons who built the automobiles did not allow the machine to overpower their residential areas. The result along the shores of Lake St. Clair was the orderly progression of streets and cul-de-sacs built for the pedestrian as well as the motor car. Commercial areas were deliberately understated first by philosophy and later by zoning.

It is the history and way of life of this region, tempered by the waterways and transformed by the men and women who have made it their home, that you will find in this volume of *Tonnancour*. We hope it will inform, amuse, and even edify you, as it relates stories of the arrival of the first Americans two centuries ago, to the arrival of the automobile a century ago, to today. Time may be a moving stream to the historian, but to the chronicler of social mores and institutions, it is more like a series of transparent overlays, each overlay a snapshot of its time, the more distant seen more dimly through the layers, but each one aligned with the index lines that are the shorelines of Lake St Clair, the Detroit and St. Clair Rivers.

Frank J. Kerwin
Past President of the Michigan Map Society
Instructor in Navigation (U.S.P.S.N)
Attorney at Law

Bird's Eye View: U.S. Government Canal and the St. Clair Flats, Circa 1885.

Located at the head of Lake St. Clair, the delta area popularly known as the "Flats" has been an obstacle to navigation since the first Native Americans explored the region by canoe. During the nineteenth century, as commerce developed on the Great Lakes, it became obvious that improvements were needed at the Flats. These improvements included the dredging of shipping channels and the building of lighthouses.

This "Bird's Eye View" shows an excursion steamer entering the lake from the Ship Canal, which was opened on July 25, 1871. At the ends of the dike are the twin lighthouses that went into operation in the fall of 1871. To the left of the Ship Canal can be seen the front and rear lights of the old South Channel. The story of the Canal and these lighthouses will be found in an article by Cynthia Bieniek on pages 109-117.

In addition to its importance for shipping, the St. Clair Flats became a nationally acclaimed summer resort during the later part of the nineteenth century. This "Bird's Eye View" also shows the location of some of the "Flats" most popular clubs and hotels. The story of this community at the "Flats" and an account of a trip aboard the White Star Line excursion steamer, "Owana," will be found in an article by Michael Dixon on pages 118-123. Illustration courtesy of Michael M. Dixon.

KEY TO " BIRD'S EYE VIEW"

1. St. Clair Hunting & Fishing Club
2. Rushmere
3. Butler's
4. Star Island Hotel
5. Boydell's
6. Peninsular Fishing & Shooting Club
7. Bedore's
8. Canadian Club House
9. North Channel Club House

Publisher's Letter

Welcome to the second volume of *Tonnancour*. I am encouraged by the warm response to the first volume, and I hope you will also enjoy this second excursion into the history and legend of Grosse Pointe. As in the first volume, this collection of essays celebrates the historical and cultural background of Grosse Pointe and the communities that border Lake St. Clair. The articles chosen reflect some of the most memorable events of our past. From an overview of the first French families to settle in Grosse Pointe, to articles celebrating the 100th anniversary of the automobile, to a history of one of our area's finest philanthropic institutions, the Children's Home of Detroit, this volume of *Tonnancour* tells the stories of the people who have given our community its rich cultural heritage.

I hope you enjoy this volume of *Tonnancour*, and I look forward to your comments.

Peter E. Ruffner
Publisher, *Tonnancour*
Omnigraphics, Inc.

September, 1996

R. N. Rice. *Color lithograph, 16⁷/8 x 28³/4 in.*

In Detroit during the later part of the nineteenth century, one of the most popular forms of illustration was the lithograph, particularly those produced by the Calvert Lithographing Company. This view of the side-wheel steamer R.N. Rice by Detroit artist Charles W. Norton (1848-1901), produced by Calvert, is a fine example of the earlier style of ship portraiture that preceded Seth Whipple's Tug Champion, the cover illustration of this volume. The story of this art form, and the Calvert Company, will be found in an article by Jennifer Williams on pages 91-96.

The R.N. Rice was built in Detroit in 1867 for the Detroit & Cleveland Steam Navigation Company. This 238-foot steamer was designed as a passenger and freight boat. After sailing the lakes for only ten years, the Rice was severely damaged by fire on June 10, 1877. She was salvaged and rigged as a schooner barge. She continued on the lakes until October 1889, when she foundered and was beached on Lake Michigan near the city of Holland. From the Collection of the Detroit Institute of Arts.

Articles to Appear in Forthcoming Volumes of *Tonnancour*

"Charles H. Haven: Windmill Pointe's Last Lighthouse Keeper," by Cynthia Bieniek

"Plan Topographique du Détroit: A Map of Early Detroit and the Grand Marais"

"Beverly Road Nominated to the National Register of Historic Places," from the *Detroit News*, Sept. 6, 1994

"Traveling Through Time: Grosse Pointe's Historical Markers," by Laura R. Ashlee

"Art Objects in the New Central Library," by W. Hawkins Ferry

"The Habitant's Lament Over the Gradual Decay of Old Grosse Pointe," by Jean Jae

"The Victorian Summer Cottages of Grosse Pointe," by Silas Farmer

"The Drive Out Grosse Pointe Way," by T.P. Hall

More Old French Verses by William Baubie

"Chronology of Grosse Pointe Woods," from the Grosse Pointe Woods Historical Commission

"Alexander Grant: The Commodore of Grosse Pointe," by Milo M. Quaife

"A Brief History of Grosse Pointe," by Kenneth Moore

"Atlas and Plat Book of Wayne County: Grosse Pointe, 1927"

"La Salle and the *Griffin*: The Discovery of Lake St. Clair," by Arthur M. Woodford

"*Legends of le Détroit*," continued, by Marie Caroline Watson Hamlin

"Faith, Fellowship, Fidelity: A Brief History of St. Paul's Parish," by Theodore H. Mecke, Jr.

"The Rebuilding of Chateau de Tonnancour," by Thomas W. Brunk

"Sisters of Bon Secours, 1909-1989," by Margaret Cronin Fisk

"The Country Club of Detroit, 100 Years"

"Henry B. Joy and the Packard Automobile"

"Grosse Pointe's Neighborhood Club"

"The Opening of the Grosse Pointe Club, 1888"

"Elise Dufresne Says Grosse Pointe Life is Dull and Uninteresting—Some Members of the Country Club Think Elise Dufresne is Dreadful," *Detroit Sunday News Tribune*, 1901

Detail from a painting "The Surrender of Fort Mackinac" by Robert Thom.

After Detroit was occupied, only Fort Mackinac on Mackinac Island remained in British hands. To complete their task, U.S. Army Major Henry Burbeck with 110 officers and men headed for Mackinac reaching the island on September 1, 1796, The American force marched up the steep path and entered the fort through the main gate. The major presented his orders to Lieutenant Andrew Foster, the British commandant. The Union Jack was lowered, the flag of the United States was raised, and at last all of Michigan was finally part of the United States. Detail from a painting "The Surrender of Fort Mackinac," by Robert Thom, text by F. Clever Bald, from the series "A History of Michigan in Paintings."

The Americans Arrive

by F. Clever Bald

On July 11, 1796 the American flag was first raised over "the ramparts of Detroit."
The treaty formally ending the Revolutionary War had been signed in 1783, yet it was to be
13 years before the Americans arrived at this frontier outpost to take over the fort and town
from the British. The causes of this delay and the story of the arrival of the Americans are
here ably told by historian F. Clever Bald.

IN THE SPRING of 1796 Detroit was in the hands of the British. Although the Treaty of Paris, formally terminating the Revolutionary War, had established a boundary which placed the town on American soil, British magistrates still administered the law, and a garrison of redcoats occupied Fort Lernoult. Repeated demands by the United States Government for transfer to its jurisdiction had been of no avail. Alleging failure of the Americans to fulfill certain treaty obligations, Great Britain continued to hold all the western forts. Only in the fall of 1794 did the British Government promise to deliver the posts on or before June 1, 1796.

The commandant of Fort Lernoult, which dominated Detroit from its position on higher ground behind the town, was Lieutenant Colonel Richard England. A man of gigantic stature, standing six feet six inches tall, the Colonel was a very capable officer, with more than thirty years of service to his credit. During the Revolutionary War he had served in Sir Guy Carleton's regiment; now he was in command of the Twenty-fourth Infantry. Jacob Lindley, an American Quaker who visited Detroit in 1793, described him as "a cheerful, open countenanced, masculine soldier, who received us like a gentleman, and kindly offered civilities to us."

In anticipation of the evacuation of Detroit Colonel England, during the spring of 1796, directed the building of a new British post near the mouth of the Detroit River, on the Canadian side. This was the beginning of Fort Malden at Amherstburg. Sheds for the storage of supplies which would be removed from Detroit were erected, and the construction of blockhouses was begun. After he was certain that the project was proceeding in a satisfactory manner, there was nothing further for the Colonel to do but await orders to deliver Fort Lernoult to the Americans.

June 1, the date set for the American occupation, came and passed; but neither orders nor Americans appeared. On June 5, however, Captain Bartholomew Shaumburgh arrived bearing a rather pompous note from General James Wilkinson asking when the Fort would be evacuated. Colonel England answered politely that he would inform the American general as soon as he received his orders.

It was not until the evening of June 30 that the order to evacuate, issued on the first day of the month, arrived at Detroit. On the same ship that brought it came Captain Henry De Butts, aide to General Anthony Wayne.

Colonel England immediately wrote to inform General Wilkinson that he was preparing to withdraw, and that he had directed vessels to sail for Fort Miamis at the foot of the rapids of the Maumee River, a few miles above the present city of Toledo, Ohio, to remove the garrison there under the command of Captain Shortt. He mentioned the arrival of Captain De Butts and added: "I shall have much pleasure in affording him every assistance in my power, in hiring or procuring Vessels to bring your Troops here." This letter and De Butts' of the same date to General Wayne, who was on his way to Detroit to take command, were sent off by Colonel England's own courier.

Captain De Butts, in his letter, promised to "dispatch three vessels to the Miamis immediately; all that I can possibly procure at this place." On July 2 he chartered from James May, of Detroit, the schooner *Swan* for £140 a month, the owner promising to provide the crew and all necessary supplies. De Butts also hired the schooner *Weazell* from John Askin, and purchased the sloop *Detroit* from Meldrum and Park.

At this time Lieutenant Colonel John Francis Hamtramck was at Camp Deposit on the Maumee River, a short distance above Fort Miamis and not far from the present town of Waterville, Ohio. There he had arrived on June 6, with his command of about five hundred American soldiers—infantry, riflemen, artillery, and light dragoons—ready to advance when the British should retire from Fort Miamis and Detroit.

From June 6 to July 7, 1796, Colonel Hamtramck remained in his camp on the left bank of the Maumee River, awaiting orders to advance to Detroit and means to transport his expeditionary force. The delay this time was the fault of the Government of the United States. In spite of the tension along the border the British Government in London and its agents in Canada and in the United States had cooperated cordially with the Americans in arranging for the abandonment of the posts. In May Lord Dorchester had offered to order an immediate evacuation. Captain Lewis, however, who had gone to Quebec to receive the documents which the American officers commanding the occupying forces were to present to the British commandants, asked him for time to permit the United States troops to prepare for the advance. Further delay was caused by the failure of James McHenry, Secretary of War, to forward these papers at once. It was not until June 28 that he sent them "by express" from Philadelphia.

Finally, on July 7, two small ships from Detroit arrived at the camp on the Maumee. They were the schooners which Captain De Butts had chartered: the *Weazell*, Captain

Louis Derineau, master, and the *Swan*, under the command of Captain Joseph May, brother of the owner. The first was a ship of sixteen tons burden and carried a crew of three. The other was probably of about the same size, for she also carried three men.

On these two schooners Colonel Hamtramck embarked sixty-five men commanded by Captain Moses Porter of the artillery, an officer who had served during the War for Independence, from the battle of Bunker Hill to the end of the conflict. Now he would have the honor of leading the first American troops into Fort Lernoult.

Carrying ammunition and cannon for arming the fort, the little vessels sailed down the Maumee River past Fort Miamis, still occupied by Captain Shortt and his British regulars, out into Lake Erie and northward toward their destination, a two days' sail, if wind and weather favored.

A short while after they had entered the mouth of the Detroit River a number of wooded islands loomed ahead as if to block their passage. The most notable were Grosse Ile, reaching far up the river, and, by its side, a smaller Bois Blanc. On the eastern bank of the river stood a few traders' houses, the beginning of the present town of Amherstburg. A little way above, a blockhouse appeared, with red-coated guards on duty. Soldiers were still engaged in erecting ramparts and other works of Fort Malden.

> "To the American soldiers this was a strange new world into which they were silently intruding."

On Bois Blanc Island, popularly known today as Bob-Lo, there were a small blockhouse and a detachment of British troops. Suspicious of the Yankees to the end, Lieutenant Governor Simcoe had warned Lord Dorchester that they might seize this island on their passage. The Commander in Chief expressed the opinion that the United States would carry out the terms of the Jay Treaty in good faith. Nevertheless, to humor Simcoe he ordered a sergeant and eight men stationed there as a guard.

The *Weazell* and the *Swan* sailed ever northward between low-lying meadows rank with rushes and marsh grass. Gradually the river banks began to rise, and houses appeared. On both sides of the stream they became more and more numerous and stood so close together that now it seemed as if the stream were bordered by two continuous villages.

To the American soldiers this was a strange new world into which they were silently intruding. Everything looked different from the scenes to which they were accustomed. The houses, built of wood, had steeply sloping roofs into which one or two dormer windows were set. All of them faced upon the river and each had a picket fence in front.

Behind the houses there were orchards of peach and apple trees, and the narrow fields of nearly ripened wheat or of half-grown Indian corn stretched back to the virgin forest beyond. These slender French farms, often only four or five hundred feet in width, each with its front on the river bank, or rather, just back of the river road, were unlike the isolated clearings in the woods with which the Americans were familiar. In Ohio, or Kentucky, or in western Pennsylvania the nearest neighbors might be miles away. Here they fairly touched elbows.

There were other strange sights, too. Here and there along the shore appeared windmills, the base of stone, the upper part of wood surmounted by a conical shingled roof, there long gaunt spars with white flapping sails revolving slowly in the breeze to turn the stone that ground the grain. Sometimes, when the ships edged in near shore, a wayside shrine was visible—a tall weather-beaten cross by the side of the road, or a gaunt crucifix.

And now, on the left, the Americans could see the banner of Great Britain waving above the ramparts of Fort Lernoult, which overlooked the close-ranged roof tops of the town below. The western wall of palisades reaching from the southwest angle of the Fort, the blockhouse over the open West Gate, the long Government wharf, the shorter merchants' wharf with the water blockhouse between, the ships at anchor in front of the town—all were now plainly spread before their curious eyes.

When Captain Porter landed at Detroit on July 11, 1796, he carried no copy of Lord Dorchester's order for the evacuation; for the one sent by Secretary McHenry was still on the way. In fact, it reached General Wayne at Greenville only on July 16. Colonel England, apparently, felt that it was not necessary. Undoubtedly Captain De Butts had already inspected the Fort and the other public works and had signed the required report.

Since Colonel England had long been awaiting the arrival of the Americans, he needed little time to arrange for the embarkation of his troops, and when they marched down to their transports, Captain Porter's little army of occupation was ready to enter Fort Lernoult.

Captain De Butts, who witnessed the transfer of sovereignty, described it simply: ". . . on the 11th inst. about noon, the flag of the United States was displayed on the ramparts of Detroit, a few minutes after the works were evacuated by Col. England and the British troops under his command, and with additional satisfaction I inform you that the exchange was effected with much propriety and harmony by both parties." He reported that "every attention was paid by the British and inhabitants to our troops."

1796
Fort Mackinac

DIRK GRINGHUIS

A Private of Artillery, Wayne's Legion, 1796.

In 1796 the American Army was known as the Legion of the United States and General Anthony Wayne was the commander-in-chief. The legion was divided into four sub-legions corresponding to regiments, although each was composed of infantry, artillery, and cavalry. The 1st Sub-Legion, (later to become the 1st Infantry Regiment) was commanded by Colonel Francis Hamtramck. The 1st Sub-Legion was assigned the duty of taking over Detroit from the British. Illustration courtesy of the Mackinac Island State Park Commission.

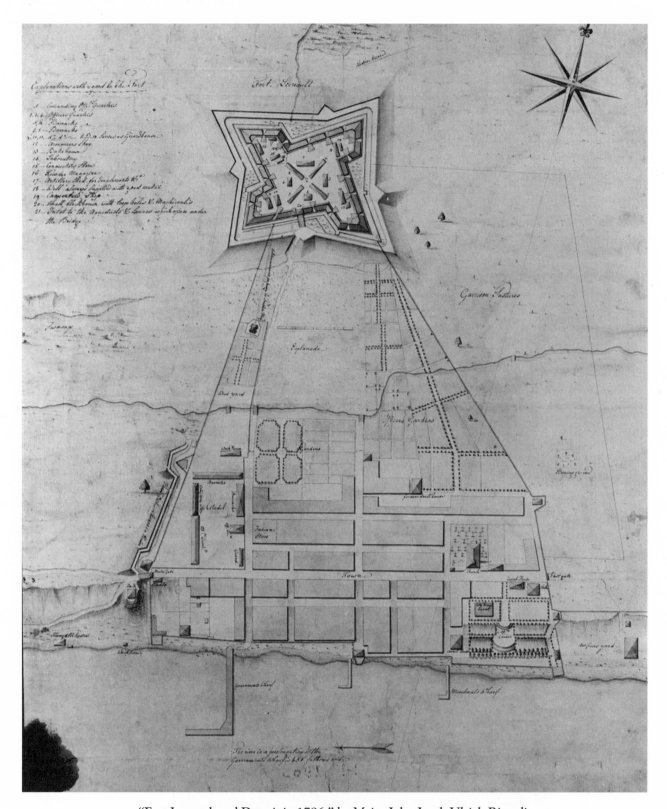

"Fort Lernoult and Detroit in 1796," by Major John Jacob Ulrich Rivardi.

Rivardi, a Frenchman serving in the Corps of Artillerists and Engineers of the U.S. Army, was stationed in Detroit from 1796 to 1797. During his stay here, Rivardi superintended the repair of Fort Lernoult. Photograph courtesy of the William L. Clements Library, University of Michigan.

On Wednesday, July 13, Colonel John Francis Hamtramck arrived with the remainder of his force. The sloop *Detroit*, commanded by Captain Peter Curry, had reached Swan Creek on the Maumee on July 9; and two days later the British evacuated Fort Miamis. Leaving a garrison there of fifty-nine soldiers under Captain Andrew Marschalk, Colonel Hamtramck embarked his men and supplies on eleven bateaux and the sloop, and sailed for Detroit.

The arrival of the Colonel with the main body of troops now gave the post a respectable force of about four hundred men. They were housed in the barracks of the Fort and of the Citadel, and the Commandant established his headquarters within the latter enclosure. Unlike Colonel England, his predecessor, he had no family with him. His wife had died less than two months before, while she was traveling from Fort Wayne to visit her parents at Vincennes. Two small daughters, Julienne, not yet four years old, and a younger one named Henriette, were left to the care of their father, but they did not accompany him.

The inhabitants of Detroit must have been surprised at the appearance of the new commandant. Accustomed to the huge bulk of Colonel England, they were probably disappointed by the diminutive figure of the man who now replaced him at the Fort.[1] Colonel Hamtramck was only five feet five inches tall, but, to compensate for his light stature, he had vigor and years of experience. A peppery temper and an imperious manner kept his subordinates attentive to their duties. Severe in discipline but ready to recognize merit, he was loyally supported by his officers.

Born in Quebec in 1756, Hamtramck was the son of a native of Luxemburg who had emigrated to Canada in 1749. When the Revolutionary War began, John Francis left his native land and espoused the cause of the Americans. He joined Montgomery's army in the fall of 1775, and he was a captain in the Fifth New York Regiment in November, 1776. After having fought throughout the war, he became one of the officers of the tiny army which was maintained after the Treaty of Paris.

Hamtramck was promoted to the rank of major on October 20, 1786. Serving under General Josiah Harmar in the Ohio country, he built Fort Knox at Vincennes in 1787. There he married Marie Edeline Perrot, widow of the late Nicholas Perrot, a merchant of the town. On February 18, 1793, he was commissioned lieutenant colonel and given command of the 1st Sub-Legion. General Wayne cited Hamtramck for personal bravery

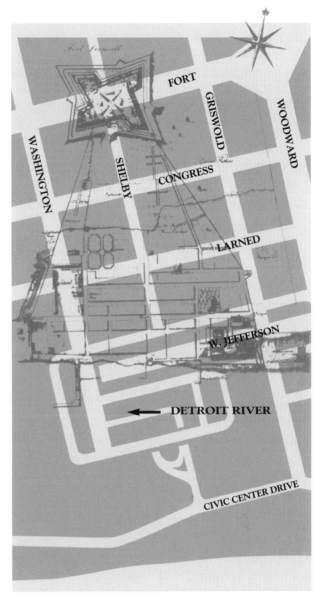

This overlay shows the location of Fort Lernoult and the town of Detroit in relationship to the present day city. Illustration from Philip P. Mason, Detroit, Fort Lernoult, and the American Revolution, *(Detroit, 1964).*

and for inspiring his men in action at the battle of Fallen Timbers. During the autumn of 1794, he built Fort Wayne and was in charge there until May, 1796, when he advanced to take possession of the posts about to be evacuated by the British. Canadian by birth and Roman Catholic in faith, Hamtramck was well qualified to command at Detroit.

---

[1] Hamtramck was nicknamed *Le Crapaud à cheval* ("The Frog on Horseback") because of "his singular appearance when riding." Louise Rau, manuscript biographical sketch of Hamtramck (1933), p. 11, Burton Hist. Coll., Detroit.

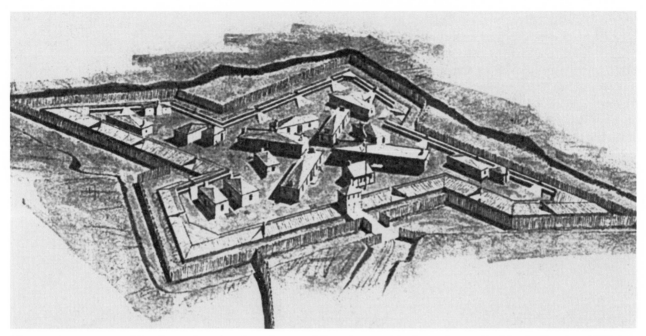

This artist's conception of Fort Lernoult is taken from the original Rivardi map of the fort and town. Built by the British in 1779 during the Revolutionary War, this fort was named in honor of the British officer commanding the army garrison, Captain Richard B. Lernoult. While the British remained in Detroit, the fort continued to be called Fort Lernoult. Following the arrival of the Americans, it was renamed Fort Detroit. After the War of 1812, it became Fort Shelby, in honor of the governor of Kentucky, who led an army of Kentuckians to the relief of Detroit. In 1827, no longer needed, and in a sad state of disrepair, the fort was torn down. Illustration from Philip P. Mason, Detroit, Fort Lernoult, and the American Revolution, (Detroit, 1964).

The Citadel, in which the Colonel established his headquarters, was an area enclosed by palisades of oak posts ten or eleven feet high. The southern line of pickets ran along the north side of Ste Anne Street from Lernoult Street to the western wall of the town, which formed a side of the enclosure. The eastern line of pickets extended along Lernoult Street north to Savoyard Creek. Within these palisades there were two-story barracks for officers and soldiers, a guardhouse, the hospital, and the commissary provision store surrounding an open square which served as a parade ground. As the two western bastions of the town were within this area, troops were always at hand to man them in case of attack.

Colonel Hamtramck inspected the defenses of his new post at the first opportunity. The Fort, of course, was of primary importance. To reach it from his quarters in the Citadel he took Lernoult Street and, proceeding north, crossed Savoyard Creek by a bridge, skirting the Grand Parade to his right. Before him bristled the abattis — felled trees with the sharpened branches pointing outward — protruding from the eastern bank of the glacis, the most advanced defensive work. Both the abattis and the glacis were in great need of repair because of neglect, and damage caused by the weather.

Through an opening in the glacis the Colonel reached the ditch before the rampart. Rains had washed earth into it from the inner face of the glacis and from the outer face of the rampart, so that it was too shallow to be of much service for defense. In the middle of the ditch stood a palisade of logs about nine feet high. These were badly decayed, and some of them had fallen from their places. Beyond rose the rampart, which faced toward the river. Halfway up the slope was a fraise of pointed stakes driven horizontally into the earth. At the top the parapet was notched with embrasures, from which the muzzles of newly planted cannon grimly surveyed the river and the town. Hamtramck crossed the ditch on a bridge and entered the Fort through the main gate, which was surmounted by a blockhouse.

Within there were wooden barracks for officers and men, and shops for the armorer, the baker, and the carpenter. By means of a ladder Hamtramck ascended the inside slope of the south rampart to the banquette behind the parapet. From this point of vantage he could look across the river and follow its course for some distance in both directions; and the village lay just below in perfect detail.

The Commandant must have been impressed by the view. What he thought of the town and its surrounding country is nowhere recorded; but others had described the settlement and its environs in glowing terms. Father Pierre Jean de Bonnecamps, who was there in 1749 with Céloron wrote: ". . . its situation appeared to me charming. A beautiful river runs at the foot of the Fort; vast plains, which only ask to be cultivated extend beyond the sight." Nearly forty years later Major Robert Matthew, lieutenant governor at Detroit, thus expressed his aversion to abandoning the place; "Had Mr. Oswald, or even Lord Lansdane [Lord Shelburne, Marquis of Landsdowne] seen this delightful settlement, they surely never could have signed away the right of the nation to it. In point of climate, soil, situation & the beauties of nature, nothing can exceed it."[2]

The gazetteers of the period were unanimous in asserting that "Its situation is delightful, and in the center of a pleasant and fruitful country." This was also the first impression of Dr. Charles Brown, surgeon of the regiment of artillerists and engineers, who arrived with the first American troops. To a friend in Philadelphia he wrote that "the country is beautiful & healthy."

Looking out from his position on the south rampart of the Fort, Colonel Hamtramck surveyed the panorama that lay before him. On the Canadian shore directly opposite, narrow French farms reached back to the woods. On the river all sorts of craft — sloops, schooners, bateaux, pirogues, and canoes — lay quietly at anchor or passed up and down. Just below was the town encircled by its defenses, which appeared as an irregular hexagon, the palisade along the river bank forming the longest side. It was pierced by two gates leading to the wharves, which were guarded by the water blockhouse between them. At each extremity of the palisade, raised above the pickets, a water battery completed the defense works of the river front.

The shortest side of the hexagon was the south rampart of the Fort. From the salient angles at its extremities the east wall and the west wall of palisades reached away in a southeasterly and a southwesterly direction respectively; then, to form the fifth and sixth sides of the hexagon, each, with a dog's leg angle turned south to meet the ends of the river wall at the water batteries. Two blockhouses guarded each of these long lines of pickets between the Fort and the river; and cannon mounted on the parapet commanded the river, the town, and the adjacent countryside.

Beyond the palisades, to the east, Isle aux Cochons (Belle Isle) with its defense forest stood in the strait, dividing its waters in two. Along the shore the River Road stretched away past the Côte du Nord-Est and the Grand Marais to Grosse Pointe.[3] About a mile and a half from the Fort, Hamtramck could see Parent's Creek spanned by Bloody Bridge, the site of Captain Dalyell's disastrous encounter with Pontiac's braves in the early morning of July 31, 1763. Behind the road the ribbon farms, enclosed by high picket fences, stood side by side, the farmhouses nestling in their gardens and orchards seeming to form half of a village street. Between the nearest farm and the eastern palisade an open space extended from the woods to the river. This was the Common; and at the foot of it, on the river bank, were the shipyard with its sail loft and the artificers' yard surrounded by a line of pickets.

To the west the River Road, between the edge of the high bank and the close-set farmhouses, led from the gate of the town along the Côte du Sud-Ouest toward the settlements at River Rouge and the River Raisin. Just outside the wall a narrow wagon track branched off to the left and sidled down the steep slope to the beach at the water's edge.

From his point of vantage Colonel Hamtramck could look down upon the roof tops of the village entrusted to his care. Lying cramped within the circuit of the palisades on three sides and Savoyard Creek on the fourth, its houses — there were fewer than a hundred of them[4] — along with stores, sheds, stables, warehouses, and some public buildings, appeared as groups of rectangular masses set off by

> "... its situation appeared to me charming. A beautiful river runs at the foot of the Fort; vast plains, which only ask to be cultivated extend beyond the sight."

---

[2] Oswald was the British agent who negotiated the Treaty of 1783; Shelburne was Prime Minister. This quotation is from a letter to General Frederick Haldimand, August 3, 1787, *Mich, Pio. and Hist. Soc. Colls.*, 26, 287. Haldimand was governor general of Quebec.

[3] This was the name given by the *habitants* to the region east of the town. The region west of the town was called the Côte du Sud-Ouest.

[4] The number of houses in Detroit was said by various writers to be 100, 150, or 300.
A report drawn up by Patrick McNiff on August 19, 1796, for Acting Governor Winthrop Sargent, however, gives the number of dwelling houses as 72. He also listed 77 stores and gave the total number of privately owned buildings as 149. Winthrop Sargent Papers, August 19, 1796, Ohio State Archaeological and Historical Society, Columbus.

unequally spaced streets. Ste Anne Street was the principal thoroughfare. It was a continuation of the River Road, which entered at the West Gate and continued through the Pontiac Gate in the eastern palisade. Within the walls there were buildings on both sides instead of on only one. It was only about twenty feet wide; the other streets were narrower. South of Ste Anne, St. Louis ran parallel with it; and to the north St. Jacques and St. Joseph completed the tale of east and west streets.

Leading north from the water blockhouse, St. Honoré Street cut through the center of the town and reached the Savoyard, where a bridge connected it with a path that angled to the left and led to the Fort. To the east Campau Alley, or St. Antoine Street, ran north from the merchants' wharf to the creek; and to the west Lernoult Street stretched from the Government wharf north to the Savoyard, where a bridge across the stream joined it with a road along the west side of the Esplanade that reached to the Fort. Between St. Honoré and Lernoult streets, and parallel to them, McDougall Alley extended from the river wall to St. Jacques Street. Just within the circuit of the palisades an open space called Le Chemin du Ronde gave room for defending troops to move from point to point inside the walls and served as a terminal communication for the several streets.

Among the buildings of the town Ste Anne's Church was the most conspicuous. Not far inside the Pontiac Gate and on the north side of Ste Anne Street, it stood almost surrounded by the cemetery. Just beyond and across the street was the commanding officer's garden, with tree-lined walks and formal garden beds. A vacant space in it marked the site of the governor's house, which had been destroyed by fire. In the southwest corner of this area, in the angle formed by Campau Alley and Le Chemin du Ronde, stood the Indian council house and the officers' mess.

At the other end of Ste Anne Street the buildings of the Citadel dominated the scene. North of it and across the creek was the barrack master's garden, laid out as a parallelogram with diagonal walks meeting in a circle at the center. Next to the garden, and closer to the Fort, was the squat powder magazine of stone, its "arch turned by good English masons," connected by a subterranean passage with the ditch between the glacis and the rampart of the Fort. The Esplanade or parade ground north of the creek occu-

pied a central position; and on the east the officers' mess garden, with its tree-lined paths, filled in the space between the east and the west walls above the town.

The Commandant was, of course, interested principally in the defenses and the public buildings entrusted to his charge. There were also, however, private residences, stores and taverns in the town, which, for a time at least, were his responsibility; and there were civilian residents with whom he would become more or less intimately acquainted.

As he rode through the narrow streets of the village to inspect the public buildings and to survey the exterior defense works, Colonel Hamtramck noticed many interesting details. The houses were "generally from One story to two stories & a half high — many of them well finished." Some were "Frame buildings." Others were "Built of Loggs & Covered with Boards of about an Inch Thick, Cut at a Saw Mill." The Commandant could not but be impressed by the superiority of these Detroit houses to those of the French at Vincennes, where he had formerly been stationed. There the walls were of hewn logs standing "erect with one end set well in the ground." The first buildings in Detroit had been constructed in the same manner.

Many of the houses had porches that encroached on the narrow streets. The front doors were made in two sections, so that the upper half could be left open in warm weather, while the lower part kept out vagrant animals and prevented small children from straying. The windows were glazed with tiny panes of glass, and every house had an enormous chimney or two built of stone, or brick, or simply of sticks and clay.

The streets were dusty in dry weather. After a heavy rain they were seas of mud. Then the half-wild horses of the *habitants* needed all their energy to draw a loaded cart into town. At the sides of most of the streets there were footways "of square logs, laid transversely close to each other." Stables, open drains, the slaughterhouse at the water's edge just outside the western line of palisades, packs of raw furs, John Askin's tan yard operated by Jacob Clemens, and offal which had been carelessly thrown into the streets — all contributed to the racy odor of the summer air. These smells were probably not noticed by the inhabitants, who

> "The Commandant could not but be impressed by the superiority of these Detroit houses to those of the French at Vincennes. . ."

were used to them; and they likewise accepted mosquitoes, flies, fleas, and other insects as pests which could not be escaped.

The town was well supplied with hostelries where travelers might lodge and where convivial Detroiters could quench their thirst. Thomas Smith, James Donaldson, George Sharp, Matthew Dolson, and John Dodemead were tavern keepers. There were several large stores, most of them on Ste Anne Street, kept by Angus Mackintosh, George McDougall, Meldrum and Park, James Abbott, John Askin, William Robertson, and Joseph Campau. Sometimes the living quarters for the family were in the same buildings, at the back, or upstairs. These merchants dealt in a bewildering variety of commodities, for which they were more likely to be paid in skins and produce than in coin.

The people whom the Commandant passed on the streets were dressed like those he had known in Vincennes. It was the costume brought by the French from Lower Canada. The men wore brightly colored shirts, trousers supported by a leather belt or a cloth sash, and straw hats or colored handkerchiefs on their heads. Some wore moccasins instead of shoes, and many enjoyed the luxury of bare feet. The women wore short gowns reaching only to their knees, with petticoats to their ankles. Broad-brimmed straw hats protected their heads and faces from the sun. The important merchants and other gentry wore brocaded waistcoats, lace jabots, long-tailed coats, and breeches with buckles at the knee. Their hair was powdered and done up in a queue, or clubbed at the back. Ladies dressed in the style of London, a little late, perhaps, but authentic nevertheless.

The population of Detroit at this time was probably about five hundred. As the figures given by men who were in the town in 1796 vary widely, it is impossible to know just how many there were. Whatever the exact number may have been, Detroit was only a village. Nevertheless, it was cosmopolitan. There was not the narrow provincialism which usually characterized a frontier settlement. Established by express sanction of Louis XIV, it had always been an important post. The commandant, an officer of the King's army, maintained his miniature court; and the traders, through their agents, were in communication with Montreal, Quebec, and even Paris. Officials of Church or State visiting the place, or pausing on their journeys to more distant posts, brought with them some of the glamor of the Old World.

After the British occupation the military element was still of consequence; and Scottish merchants, vigorously pursuing their vocation, imported their own culture as well as merchandise. War and commerce attracted all sorts of people to Detroit. As Joseph Moore, a Quaker visitor from Philadelphia in 1793, remarked: "The inhabitants of the town are as great a mixture, I think, as ever I knew in any one place. English, Scotch, Irish, Dutch, French, Americans from different states, with black and yellow, and seldom clear of Indians of different tribes in the daytime." This statement was not an exaggeration. The author could easily have pointed out representatives of every nation and race which he mentioned.

———————— ❦ ————————

EDITOR'S NOTE: When the Americans took control of the Detroit River region from the British in 1796, one of their first tasks was a survey of property up and down the river from the fort and town. The surveyor hired for this project was Patrick McNiff. Of particular interest is McNiff's recording of the original French claims and farms of the area that is today Grosse Pointe. Reprinted on pages 49-54 of Volume 1 of *Tonnancour* is that portion of McNiff's report with a description of the survey and map in an essay "Patrick McNiff's Plan of the Settlements at Detroit, 1796," by Dr. F. Clever Bald.

———————— ❦ ————————

SOURCE: *Detroit's First American Decade: 1796 to 1805.* (Ann Arbor: University of Michigan Press, 1948.).

———————— ❦ ————————

Frederick Clever Bald (1897-1970) received his BA degree from the University of Michigan in 1920 and his Master's degree from Wayne State University in 1937, where he studied under Milo M. Quaife. He received his PhD from U of M. A major figure in the promotion of state and local history, Bald wrote Michigan in Four Centuries, *(1954, rev. ed. 1962), which became the standard text in its field. He taught at the U of M and served as director of the University's Michigan Historical Collections from 1960 until his retirement in 1967.*

Detroit in 1796

By Isaac Weld

From 1795 to 1797 young British traveler Isaac Weld traveled throughout the eastern United States and the provinces of Upper and Lower Canada. During the fall of 1796, his journeys took him west to the frontier town of Detroit. Just three months earlier, the British army had turned over the fort at Detroit to the Americans, evacuated the town, and moved across the river to the newly established Fort Malden and village of Amherstburg. Weld was a keen observer, and from this account of his visit here we have this fascinating view of Detroit in 1796.

DETROIT IS AT present the head-quarters of the western army of the States; the garrison consists of three hundred men, who are quartered in barracks.

About two-thirds of the inhabitants of Detroit are of French extraction, and the greater part of the inhabitants of the settlements on the river, both above and below the town, are of the same description. The former are mostly engaged in trade, and they all appear to be much on an equality. Detroit is a place of very considerable trade; there are no less than twelve trading vessels belonging to it, brigs, sloops, and schooners, of from fifty to one hundred tons burthen each. The inland navigation in this quarter is indeed very extensive, Lake Erie, three hundred miles in length, being open to vessels belonging to the port, on the one side; and lakes Michigan and Huron, the first upwards of two hundred miles in length, and sixty in breadth, and the second, no less than one thousand miles in circumference, on the opposite; not to speak of Lake St. Clair and Detroit River, which connect these former lakes together, or of the many large rivers which fall into them. The stores and shops in the town are well furnished, and you may buy fine cloth, linen & c. and every article of wearing apparel, as good in their kind, and nearly on as reasonable terms, as you can purchase them at New York or Philadelphia.

The inhabitants are well supplied with provisions of every description; the fish in particular, caught in the river and neighbouring lakes, are of a very superior quality. The fish held in most estimation is a sort of large trout called the Michillimakinac white fish, from its being caught mostly in the straits of that name. The inhabitants of Detroit and the neighbouring country, however, though they have provisions in plenty, are frequently much distressed for one very necessary concomitant, namely, salt. Until within a short time past they had no salt but what was brought from Europe; but salt springs have been discovered in various parts of the country from which they are now beginning to manufacture that article for themselves. The best and most profitable of the springs are retained in the hands of government, and the profits arising from the sale of the salt, are to be paid into the treasury of the province. Throughout the western country, they procure their salt from springs, some of which throw up sufficient water to yield several hundred bushels in the course of one week.

There is a large Roman catholic church in the town of Detroit, and another on the opposite side, called the Huron church from its having been devoted to the use of the Huron Indians. The streets of Detroit are generally crowded

View of Detroit in 1796.

This engraving is from the original painting in Paris. The Brig General Gage *is at the wharf.*
Illustration courtesy of the Burton Historical Collection, Detroit Public Library.

with Indians of one tribe or other and amongst them, you see numberless old squaws leading about their daughters, ever ready to dispose of them, pro tempore, to the highest bidder. At night all the Indians, except such as get admittance into private houses and remain there quietly, are turned out of the town, and the gates shut upon them.

The American officers here have endeavored to their utmost to impress upon the minds of the Indians, an idea of their own superiority over the British; but as they are very tardy in giving these people any presents, they do not pay much attention to their words. General Wayne, from continually promising them presents, but at the same time always postponing the delivery when they come to ask for them, has significantly been nicknamed by them, General Wabang, that is, General To-morrow.

The country around Detroit is very much cleared, and so likewise is that on the British side of the river for a considerable way above the town. The settlements extend nearly as far as Lake Huron; but beyond the River La Trenche, which falls into Lake St. Clair, they are scattered very thinly along the shores. The banks of the River La Trenche, or Thames, as it is now called, are increasing very fast in population, as I before mentioned, owing to the great emigration thither of people from the neighbourhood of Niagara, and of Detroit also since it has been evacuated by the British. We made an excursion, one morning, in our

little boat, as far as Lake St. Clair, but met with nothing either amongst the inhabitants or in the face of the country, particularly deserving of mention. The country round Detroit is uncommonly flat, and in none of the rivers is there a fall sufficient to turn even a grist mill. The current of Detroit River itself is stronger than that of any others, and a floating mill was once invented by a Frenchman, which was chained in the middle of that river, where it was thought the stream would be sufficiently swift to turn the water wheel; the building of it was attended with considerable expense to the inhabitants, but after it was finished, it by no means answered their expectations. They grind their corn at present by wind mills, which I do not remember to have seen in any other part of North America.

The soil of the country bordering upon Detroit River is rich though light, and it produces good crops both of Indian corn and wheat. The climate is much more healthy than that of the country in the neighbourhood of Niagara River; intermittent fevers however are by no means uncommon disorders. The summers are intensively hot. Fahrenheit's thermometer often rising above 100; yet a winter seldom passes over but what snow remains on the ground for two or three months.

Whilst we remained at Detroit, we had to determine upon a point of some moment to us travellers, namely, upon the route by which to return back towards the Atlantic.

View of Detroit from the Canadian Shore.

This watercolor by Dr. Edward Walsh is dated June 22, 1804. The Huron church is in foreground. The site is today near the Canadian approach to the Ambassador Bridge. Illustration courtesy of the William L. Clements Library, University of Michigan.

We determined therefore to proceed by Presqu'Isle. But now another difficulty arose, namely, how we were to get there; a small vessel, a very unusual circumstance indeed was just about to sail, but it was so crowded with passengers, that there was not a single birth vacant, and moreover, if there had been, we did not wish to depart so abruptly from this part of the country. One of the principal traders, however, at Detroit, to whom we had carried letters, soon accommodated matters to our satisfaction, by promising to give orders to the master of one of the lake vessels, of which he was in part owner, to land us at that place. The vessel was to sail in a fortnight; we immediately therefore secured a passage in her; and having settled with the master that he should call for us at Malden, we set off once more for that place in our little boat, and in a few hours, from the time we quitted Detroit, arrived there.

❧

SOURCE: *Travels Through the States of North America: and the Provinces of Upper and Lower Canada During the Years 1795, 1796, and 1797, 4th ed. (London: Printed for J. Stockdale, 1807.)*

❧

British traveler Isaac Weld was born in Dublin, Ireland, on March 15, 1774. His journey to Canada and the new United States was prompted by the idea that the Irish people "would afterward be led to emigrate hither in great numbers." Arriving in Philadelphia in September 1795, he made his way, on horseback, on foot, and by canoe through dense forests and along rivers, trusting often to friendly Indians for safe conduct. In the cities he saw much of the best of society, and was introduced to George Washington and Thomas Jefferson. As a result of this trip he published his Travels through the States of North America and the Provinces of Upper and Lower Canada. *First printed in London in 1799, it went through several editions and was translated into French, 1800; and German, 1801-2. Weld also traveled extensively on the continent and for 56 years was a member of the Royal Society of Dublin of which he served as secretary and vice-president. Isaac Weld died near Bray, County Dublin, on August 4, 1856.*

A County Is Proclaimed:
The Founding of Wayne County
and Grosse Pointe Township

by Clarence M. Burton

On August 15, 1796, only a month after the arrival of the first American troops in Detroit, Winthrop Sargent, secretary and acting governor of the Northwest Territory, issued a proclamation formally establishing Wayne County. Named in honor of General Anthony Wayne, the county included most of Michigan, and parts of present-day Wisconsin, Illinois, Indiana, and Ohio. Two years later, on November 1, 1798, the county was divided into four townships, one of which was named Hamtramck. On April 1, 1848 Hamtramck Township was divided, and the Township of Grosse Pointe was formed.

Wayne County

THE FIRST MOVE to establish a county west of the Allegheny Mountains was made by the Virginia Legislature in October, 1778, when an act was passed creating Illinois County, which included all the region afterward embraced in the Northwest Territory. On June 16, 1792, four years before Detroit became an American possession, John Graves Simcoe, lieutenant-governor of Upper Canada, issued a proclamation establishing Kent County, which embraced all of the present State of Michigan and extended northward to the Hudson's Bay country. However, before the county was organized, that part of it west of Lake Huron became part of the United States and

Simcoe's proclamation was consequently ignored.

Wayne County was established August 15, 1796, by the following proclamation issued by Winthrop Sargent, secretary and acting governor of the Northwest Territory:

"To all persons to whom these presents shall come — Greeting:

"Whereas, by an ordinance of Congress of the thirteenth of July, one thousand seven hundred and eighty-seven, for the settlement of the Territory of the United States Northwest of the River Ohio, it is directed that for the due execution of process, civil and criminal, the Governors shall make proper Divisions of the said Territory and proceed from time to time, as circumstances may require, to lay out the same into Counties and Townships, and Whereas, it appearing to me expedient that a new county

should immediately be erected to include the settlements at Detroit, lying and being within the following Boundaries, viz.: beginning

"At the mouth of the Cuyahoga River upon Lake Erie, and with the said river to the portage between it and the Tuscarawa branch of the Muskingum, thence down the said branch to the forks, at the carrying place above Fort Lawrence (Fort Laurens, near the present City of Canton, Ohio), thence by a west line to the eastern boundary of Hamilton County (which is a due north line from the lower Shawonese Town upon the Sciota River), thence by a line west-northerly to the southern part of the portage between the Miamis of the Ohio and the St. Mary's River, thence by a line also west-northerly to the southwestern part of the portage between the Wabash and the Miamis of Lake Erie, where Fort Wayne now stands, thence by a line west-northerly to the most southern part of Lake Michigan, thence along the western shore of the same to the northwest part thereof (including the lands upon the streams emptying into the said Lake), thence by a due north line to the territorial Boundary in Lake Superior, and with the said Boundary through Lake Huron, St. Clair and Erie to the mouth of the Cuyahoga River, the place of beginning — which said county shall have and enjoy all and singular the Jurisdiction, Rights, Liberties, Privileges and Immunities whatsoever to a county appertaining, and which any other county that now is or hereafter may be erected and laid out shall or ought to enjoy, conformably to the ordinance of Congress before mentioned.

"In Testimony whereof I have hereunto set my hand and affixed the seal of the Territory, this fifteenth day of August, in the Twenty-first year of the Independence of the United States, A.D., one thousand seven hundred and ninety-six.

"Winthrop Sargent."

Figure 1

The boundaries of Wayne County, as named in the original proclamation, were indeed far-reaching (See Fig. 1). The county included a large tract of country in northwestern Ohio (about one-fifth of the state); a strip across the northern part of Indiana (all north of a line from Fort Wayne to the head of Lake Michigan); all the Lower Peninsula of Michigan; about three-fourths of the Upper Peninsula, and all that part of Wisconsin drained

into Lake Michigan — nearly seventy-five thousand square miles.

The consensus of opinion among the citizens of Wayne County was that the new civil division should be named in honor of Gen. Anthony Wayne. The general, having been officially informed of the tribute accorded him, replied as follows:

"To the Curé and Inhabitants of Detroit, and the Officers, Civil and Military, of the County of Wayne:
"Gentlemen—
"I have received with much pleasure your polite address of this date, which not only demands my grateful acknowledgment for the flattering testimonies it contains of your esteem, but affords me an opportunity to remark with what pleasure I have observed the general satisfaction which has appeared to reveal among the citizens of Detroit and its neighborhood upon the establishment of the Government of the United States, and the alacrity and laudable desire they have evinced to promote the due execution thereof; a conduct so wise, while it merits the warm regards of their fellow-citizens of the Union, must insure to themselves all the advantages which will flow from and be the natural effect of the administration of good laws, under so happy a government.

"I will with much pleasure communicate to the President the warm sentiments of zeal and attachment which you have expressed toward the Government of the United States; and I cannot permit myself to depart hence without assuring you that I shall always take a peculiar interest in whatever may contribute to promote the happiness and prosperity of this county, to which my name has the honor to be attached.

"I have the honor to be, gentlemen, with such esteem,
"Your most obedient and humble servant,
"Ant'y Wayne.
"Headquarters, Detroit, November 14, 1796."

On May 7, 1800, President Adams approved an act of Congress creating the Territory of Indiana, leaving the Northwest Territory composed only of the State of Ohio and that part of Michigan east of a line drawn due north from Fort Recovery, which line practically divided the state longitudinally into equal parts. By this act the boundaries of Wayne County were changed so as to include only that part of the original county which lay in Ohio, the eastern half of the Lower Peninsula and a very small section of the eastern part of the Upper Peninsula of Michigan.

A further reduction of the area of Wayne County was made July 10, 1800, when Trumbull County, Ohio, was

Portrait of General Anthony Wayne.

General Wayne, for whom Wayne County is named, was commander-in-chief of the Legion of the United States (as the American Army was known in 1796). He arrived in Detroit on August 13, 1796 and established his headquarters in a house on Jefferson Avenue just east of Washington Boulevard. Wayne remained in Detroit until November 15. He then left for Philadelphia but became seriously ill on the way and died at present day Erie on December 15, 1796. Illustration courtesy of the Burton Historical Collection, Detroit Public Library.

Figure 2   Figure 3

created by proclamation of Governor St. Clair. By this proclamation the eastern boundary of Wayne was fixed at a north and south line about five miles west of the City of Sandusky, Ohio, (*See Fig. 2*).

On November 23, 1801, the General Assembly of the Northwest Territory met at Chillicothe. This was the first session after the erection of Indiana Territory. Wayne County was represented by Charles F. Chabert Joncaire, George McDougall and Jonathan Schieffelin, the two last named having served as British soldiers under Henry Hamilton during the Revolution.

On April 30, 1802, President Jefferson approved the act of Congress providing for the admission of Ohio to statehood, but it was not formally admitted until February 19, 1803. Then that part of Wayne County lying west of Trumbull County, as erected by the proclamation of July 10, 1800, and south of the present boundary line of Michigan, was cut off and added to the new state (*See Fig. 3*).

The act of April 30, 1802, also increased the size of Indiana Territory to include the present states of Indiana, Illinois, Michigan, and Wisconsin, and that portion of Minnesota lying east of the Mississippi River and a line drawn due north from the source of that stream to the international boundary.

With the admission of Ohio into the Union and the large addition to the Territory of Indiana came the necessity for a revision of the boundaries of Wayne County. Consequently, on January 14, 1803, Gen. William H. Harrison, governor of Indiana Territory, whose capital was at Vincennes, issued a proclamation, the part of which pertaining to Wayne County follows:

"I, William Henry Harrison, governor of Indiana Territory, by the authority vested in me by the ordinance for the government of the Territory, do ordain and declare that a county shall be formed in the northeastern part of the Territory, to be known and designated by the name and style of the County of Wayne. And the boundaries of said

county shall be as follows, to wit:

"Beginning at a point where an east and west line, passing through the southern extreme of Lake Michigan, would intersect a north and south line, passing through the most westerly extreme of said lake and thence north along the last mentioned line to the territorial boundary of the United States; thence along the said boundary line to a point where an east and west line, passing through the southerly extreme of Lake Michigan, would intersect the same; thence west along the last mentioned line to the place of beginning."

As defined in the above, the boundaries of Wayne County included all the Lower Peninsula of Michigan, all of the Upper Peninsula, a strip about ten miles wide across the northern part of the present State of Indiana, a small tract in Northwestern Ohio and the peninsula lying between the Green Bay and Lake Michigan in Wisconsin (*See Fig. 4*).

On January 11, 1805, President Jefferson approved the act of Congress erecting the Territory of Michigan, the western boundary of which was a north and south line passing through the center of Lake Michigan, striking the Upper Peninsula about half way between the present cities of Escanaba and Manistique, which line also formed the western boundary of Wayne County — the only county in the new territory. As constituted at this time Wayne County embraced the Lower Peninsula, the eastern half of the Upper Peninsula and the islands about the Straits of Mackinaw (*See Fig. 5*).

After the formation of Michigan Territory no change was made in the area and boundaries of Wayne County for more than ten years. On November 21, 1815, Gen. Lewis Cass, then governor of the territory, issued a proclamation which materially reduced the size of the county. By this proclamation the western boundary was represented by a line running due north from the mouth of the Great Auglaize River to a point due west of the outlet of Lake

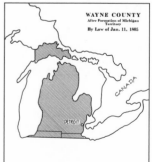

Figure 4   Figure 5

Figure 6   *Figure 7*   *Figure 8*   *Figure 9*

Huron. This point is almost on the northern boundary of the present County of Ingham, a short distance east of the City of Lansing. From there the boundary line of Wayne County ran in a northeasterly direction "to the White Rock in Lake Huron" *(See Fig 6)*.

The latter line and the one forming the western boundary of the county represented the limits of the tract ceded to the United States by the Indians at Greenville, Ohio, August 3, 1795. Under the proclamation of 1815 Wayne County included the present counties of Lapeer, Lenawee, Livingston, Macomb, Monroe, Oakland, St. Clair, Sanilac, Washtenaw, and Wayne; all of Genesee County except a small triangle in the northwest corner; and portions of Huron, Ingham, Jackson, Shiawassee, and Tuscola.

On October 18, 1816, Governor Cass issued another proclamation, adding to Wayne County the District of Mackinaw, which had been created on July 3, 1805, by proclamation of Gen. William Hull, the first territorial governor of Michigan, with the following boundaries:

"Beginning at the most western and southern point of the Bay of Saginaw; thence westwardly to the nearest part of the River Marquette; thence along the southern bank thereof to Lake Michigan; thence due west to the middle thereof; thence north, east and south with the lines of the Territory of Michigan and the United States to the center of Lake Huron; thence in a straight line to the place of beginning."

Wayne County was now composed of two separate and distance parts *(See Fig. 7)*. First, the county as established by Governor Cass' proclamation of November 21, 1815, and, second, the District of Mackinaw. The latter included the counties of Alcona, Alpena, Antrim, Arenac, Benzie, Charlevoix, Cheboygan, Clare, Crawford, Emmet, Gladwin, Grand Traverse, Iosco, Kalkaska, Leelanau, Manistee, Missaukee, Montmorency, Ogemaw, Osceola, Oscoda, Otsego, Roscommon, Wexford, and parts of Bay, Isabella, Lake, Mecosta, and Midland in the Lower Peninsula, and the counties of Chippewa, Luce, Mackinac, and Schoolcraft in the Upper Peninsula.

In 1817 the work of dismembering this imperial county was begun. By a proclamation issued on July 14th of that year, Governor Cass cut off Monroe County from the southern part of Wayne, the new county including the present counties of Monroe and Lenawee *(See Fig. 8)*.

On January 15, 1818, another proclamation of Governor Cass provided for the organization of Macomb County, in which proclamation the base line of the United States survey in Michigan was made the northern boundary of Wayne County, which then included the present counties of Wayne and Washtenaw, and a strip six miles wide across the eastern part of Jackson County *(See Fig. 9)*.

Washtenaw County was set off from Wayne by proclamation of Governor Cass September 10, 1822. As erected by this proclamation, Washtenaw included the present county of that name, the southern half of Livingston, the eastern tier of Congressional townships in Jackson, and the four townships in the southeast corner of Ingham. It was attached to Wayne for revenue, election, and judicial purposes until such time as its organization as a separate and independent country should be completed *(See Fig. 10)*. This complete organization occurred by legislative enactment November 20, 1826, since which time there have been no changes in the boundaries or area (626 square miles) of Wayne County *(See Fig. 11)*.

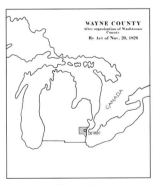

Figure 10   *Figure 11*

❦ ❦ ❦

Grosse Pointe Township

THE EARLY SETTLERS of New England adopted the township as the unit of local government, while in Virginia and some of the other southern colonies the county was made the unit. In the New England states the town meeting is still the popular medium for the expression of opinion on all matters touching the public welfare. Thomas Jefferson stated:

"Those wards, called townships in New England, are the vital principle of their governments and have proved themselves the wisest invention ever devised by the wit of man for the perfect exercise of self-government, and for its preservation."

A little later, when Mr. Jefferson was President of the United States, he learned the power of the New England township, when town meetings were held in all the New England states to protest against the enforcement of the Embargo Act of 1807, and by their concerted action defeated the purpose of Congress in the passage of that measure.

In the states erected out of the Northwest Territory — Ohio, Indiana, Illinois, Michigan, and Wisconsin — the county and township systems are combined in such a manner as to leave the latter free to exercise authority in all matters pertaining to local affairs, and yet remain tributary to the county in matters affecting the larger territory. In some of these states the affairs of the township are looked after by an official known as a trustee, and the county business is administered by a board of county commissioners, usually consisting of three members. In other states the most important officer in the township is the supervisor, the supervisors of the several townships constituting a board for the review of and final action on the county business, such as tax levies and appropriations.

Michigan followed the former plan until 1827, when the office of county commissioner was abolished by an act of the Legislature. It was revised by law in 1838 and was again abolished in 1842, when the board of supervisors was established.

An act of the Legislature of the Northwest Territory, approved by Governor St. Clair on November 6, 1790, authorized the Court of Quarter Sessions of the Peace to divide the counties into townships.

Wayne County was not established until August 15, 1796. On November 1, 1798, the Court of Quarter Sessions of the Peace divided the county into four townships, namely: Detroit, Hamtramck, Mackinaw and Sargent. At

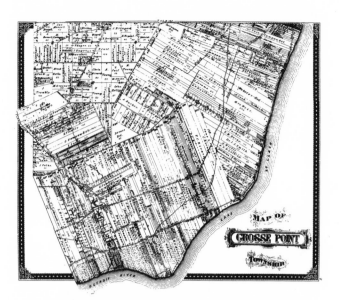

Map of Grosse Pointe Township – 1876.

that time the county embraced all the present State of Michigan except the western extremity of the Upper Peninsula, a strip across Northern Indiana and Northwestern Ohio, a little of Northeastern Illinois, including the site of the present City of Chicago, and the eastern part of Wisconsin. Hence, each of these first townships was considerably larger than any of the counties of today.

By the proclamation of January 15, 1818, Governor Cass erected the townships of Hamtramck, Huron, Monguagon, St. Clair and Springwells, within the present limits of Wayne County. The western boundary of these townships was the line of the private claims farthest from the Detroit River. No further change was made until after Wayne County was reduced to its present dimensions.

On April 12, 1827, the day Governor Cass approved the act abolishing the board of county commissioners, the county was divided into nine townships, to wit: Brownstown, Bucklin, Detroit, Ecorse, Hamtramck, Huron, Monguagon, Plymouth, and Springwells. Numerous changes have been made since 1827 by the erection of new townships and the alteration of boundary lines.

The territory comprising the Township of Grosse Pointe was originally included in Hamtramck Township. It was set off as a separate township on April 1, 1848, and was named Grosse Pointe from the point of land projecting into the water at the foot of Lake St. Clair. As then erected, Grosse Pointe was bounded "on the north by Macomb County; on the east and south by Lake St. Clair and the Detroit River; on the west by the section line two miles west of the line dividing ranges 11 and 12 east, the north line of Private Claim No. 394 and Connor's Creek, the line between sections 22 and 23, township No. 1 south, range 12 east, and the west line of Private Claim No. 725." It was divided in May, 1895, and the western and northern part were erected into the Township of Gratiot.

The first Settlers in this township were French, some of whom were descendants of those who came with Cadillac to Detroit in 1701. Here lived the Beaufaits, St. Aubins, Rivards, Gouins, the De Lorme family and others who were prominent in the early history of Wayne County. In 1764 Charles Chovin located near where the Detroit waterworks are now situated and built a rather unsubstantial cabin, in which he lived for about five years. He then bought the claim of Thomas Stewart and Jean Simare on the "Grand Marais," just west of Connor's Creek, and moved into the log house they had erected. In October, 1796, his son, Jean Baptiste Chovin, sold the property to William Park and George Meldrum, who a few years later conveyed it to William Macomb. Macomb died in April, 1796. Peter Van Avery purchased this place in 1816, remodeled and enlarged the house, which in 1875 was said to have been the oldest house in Michigan.

The Grand Marais, or big marsh, is laid down on the old maps as forming the larger portion of the present Grosse Pointe Township. This marsh was waste land covered by water and flags. Some years ago a large tract, covering several thousand acres, was reclaimed by Thomas W. Corby, who built a dyke along the lake and river front and pumped the water from the land.

At the head of the St. Clair River was a favorite crossing place for the Indians in their journeys to and from Canada. Frequently they came in large numbers and freely helped themselves to the property of the settlers, sometimes driving off whole herds of cattle.

Grosse Pointe is distinctly a district of pretentious and costly homes. The residential portion of the township is divided into Grosse Pointe Park, Grosse Pointe, Grosse Pointe Farms, and Grosse Pointe Shores. Upon entering Grosse Pointe Farms, at the terminus of city service of the Detroit Street Railways, Jefferson Avenue becomes Lake Shore Road, which winds its picturesque course along the shores of Lake St. Clair.

———————— ❧ ————————

EDITOR'S NOTE: In 1907, 1917, 1918, and 1926, portions of Grosse Pointe Township were annexed to the City of Detroit. In 1927 the Village of Lochmoor was incorporated, becoming the City of Grosse Pointe Woods in 1950. Today, all that remains of Grosse Pointe Township is the area comprised of the Village of Grosse Pointe Shores.

———————— ❧ ————————

SOURCE: *History of Wayne County and the City of Detroit, Michigan* (Chicago-Detroit: S.J. Clarke Publishing Co., 1930.

———————— ❧ ————————

Clarence Monroe Burton was born in 1853 in a log cabin near the mining town of Whiskey Diggings, California. His family later settled in Hastings, Michigan, where Burton grew up. After graduating from the University of Michigan in 1874 with a law degree, he moved to Detroit. Burton went to work at the law firm of Ward & Palmer where he stayed until 1891, when he started the Burton Abstract Company. Taking the advice of a college professor that every young man should have a hobby, Burton decided that his hobby would be the history of Detroit. By 1914 his private collection threatened to overtake both his home on Brainard Street, and his wife. He then agreed to give the house and the collection to the Detroit Public Library. When the new library building was completed in 1923, the collection was moved to the fourth floor and the house was returned to Burton in exchange for a substantial cash gift. Much of what Burton uncovered of Detroit's past, he published in an endless stream of books and pamphlets. Clarence M. Burton died in Detroit in 1932.

Grosse Pointe's First Settlers: From Whence Did They Come?

By Jean Dodenhoff

In the 1990 United States Census, only 6.8% of residents in the five Grosse Pointes claimed to have French ancestry. This small number reflects the changes which have occurred in the ethnic composition of these communities over the years. In the 1750s when the first Europeans settled this region, most Grosse Pointers were either French or French Canadian. Many of them had come west from the Quebec villages to which their French forefathers had emigrated 50 to 100 years before. The following is a survey of Grosse Pointe's pioneers from 1750 to 1770, where they settled along Lake St. Clair, their marital opportunities at Fort Pontchartrain, their settlement patterns in French Canada, and their family origins in Europe.

The Founders (1750)

DURING THE 1740s, France's King Louis XV became concerned about British incursions into the Great Lakes regions, which he considered to be French. He believed that increasing the number of his countrymen on the frontier would correct this situation. Thus, in May 1749, as ordered by the King, Quebec's Governor General posted the following proclamation in villages along the St. Lawrence River:

"Every man who will settle in Detroit shall receive gratuitously one spade, one axe, one ploughshare, one large and one small wagon. He will make an advance of other tools to be paid for in two years only. He will be given a cow of

which he will return the increase, also a sow; seed will be advanced the first year to be returned at the third harvest. The women and children will be supported one year. Those will be deprived of the liberality of the King who shall give themselves up to trade in place of agriculture."[1]

The Trombley brothers, Pierre, Augustin and Ambroise, were habitants, or citizen farmers, on the lower St. Lawrence River. In 1750, they accepted the King's "invitation" to settle near Detroit. With their families, they traveled aboard royal canoes to Fort Pontchartrain, the strategic fur trading post that later became the City of Detroit. Accompanying the Trombleys on this journey was Guillaume LaForest. He had married their niece, Marguerite

A view of the St. Lawrence River. *Photograph by Dr. Charles F. Dodenhoff.*

Trombley, in May 1746, just as several years earlier, in February 1741, Augustin Trombley had wed LaForest's older sister, Marie Judith. The other Trombley brothers had married cousins. Pierre took Magdeleine Simard as his wife in 1733 while Ambroise became the husband of Marguerite Simard in 1744.

According to the records of Robert Navarre, Fort Pontchartrain's Royal Notary, these four men received their authorized King's Rations in August 1750 and left the Fort for homesteads on the Grand Marais, or Great Marsh. Thus, the Trombleys and LaForests became the first permanent settlers of Grosse Pointe. Located near the junction of the Detroit River and Lake St. Clair, their farms, like most properties surrounding the Fort, belonged to the Crown. For use of the land, the Trombleys and LaForests, were required

to pay annual "Cens et Rentes." These usage fees were adapted from the Coutume de Paris, or French common law.

The Trombleys and LaForests came to Lake St. Clair from Baie St. Paul, a rural village on the north shore of the St. Lawrence River halfway between the City of Quebec and the Atlantic Ocean. Though a closely-knit group after arriving in North America, they had ancestors from very different parts of France. Before the mid-seventeenth century, the first Pierre Trombley had emigrated to Canada from the small northwestern town of Tourouvre, which was located inland on the border of Lower Normandy. About the same time, in southwestern France below Bordeaux, the first Pierre LaForest dit LaBranche[2] had departed from Agen on the Guyonne River. Perhaps, the two men met at Beaupre near the City of Quebec. Trombley signed an "engagement," or labor contract, in that village in 1647; LaForest appeared there in 1651.

The First Wave of Settlers (1751–1758)

The 1750s were a time of considerable uncertainty on the Lower Great Lakes. To the east, clashes between the French and British over the profitable fur trade had increased. In 1754, these escalated into a full-scale conflict known in North America as "The French and Indian War." Because of its prime location, Fort Pontchartrain became a major supply post for the French participants.

Founders (●) and 1st Wave of Settlers (●)

---

1 Paré, Father George, "The Cicotte Book." *Bulletin–Detroit Historical Society.* Vol. XIV, No. 5 p. 10.

2 French habitants were often given nicknames, or "dit" names, which were added to their surnames to distinguish them from other family members, to emphasize a predominate characteristic or to indicate their place of origin.

A view of the port city of Nantes. *Illustration from Henry James'* A Little Tour in France *(1900)*.

Neither the war, nor the disputes which proceeded it however, dissuaded other habitants from joining the Trombleys and LaForests in the wilderness known locally as "Grosse Pointe."[3] Among the earliest to arrive was Antoine Deshêtres, a gunsmith, who had previously lived on the St. Joseph River near the future site of Niles, Michigan. In 1751, he obtained a King's Ration and moved with his Montreal wife, Charlotte Chevalier dit Chesne, and their children to Lake St. Clair. Though his ancestral home in France is unknown, his birthplace in documented. He was born in New England. How this happened remains a mystery. Perhaps, prior to his birth, Deshêtres' mother had been captured during an Iroquois Indian raid into French Canada and taken south to the British Colonies.

Joseph Davignon dit Lafeuillade married a young Fort resident, Marie Anne Lemelin in April 1754, and joined the fledgling Grosse Pointe community. Using his King's Ration, the couple settled on land below present-day Moran Road.[4] Though from French Canada, only Lafeuillade's ancestry in the Old World is verifiable. He was a descendant of Louis Davignon dit Lafeuillade, a soldier from the diocese of Limoges. This city in west central France, was an early center for enamel work and porcelain.

Another early pioneer, Julien Freton dit Nantais, traveled to his new home directly from France. He arrived in Grosse Pointe in 1758 from Moisdon, a Brittany village above the port city of Nantes. Located some distance from other farms, Freton's homestead was on the wooded shore west of present-day Vernier Road. A year after arriving, he married a fifteen-year-old Grosse Pointer, Marie Joseph Gastignon dit Duchene. She was the daughter of François Gastignon dit Duchene.

---

3 Grosse Pointe means "Big Point." In the eighteenth century at the junction of the Detroit River and Lake St. Clair, there was a large point on the Grand Marais. It was this landmark from which the name of "Grosse Pointe" derived.

4 Approximate property locations were determined by plotting acreage noted in eighteenth century census and comparing the results with known private claims assigned by the United States government between 1808 and 1812.

5 The 1762 regional census shows a Dubois which some have considered to be Alexis Dubois. However, genealogical data concerning Lienard dit Durbois appears to fit the census entry more closely.

In 1759, according to the St. Anne Catholic Church Marriage Register, François Gastignon dit Duchene and his family had already established a farm in Grosse Pointe. Located to the east of present-day Cadieux Road, his fields were next to those of Michigan's first German residents, the Yaxs. Duchene was born in Montreal, the city to which his father, Leonard, had immigrated by 1697. The elder Duchene had come from the diocese of Tours, a famous university center in north central France. By 1738, his son was at Fort Pontchartrain for there, in January 1739, he married Marie Joseph David. She, too, was born in Montreal.

A final pioneer, Jean Baptiste Lienard dit Durbois, had marital ties to Grosse Pointe. At Fort Pontchartrain in May 1754, he married Anne Deshêtres, the daughter of Antoine Deshêtres. Baptismal certificates of the Durbois children suggest that the family lived on Lake St. Clair as early as 1755. A 1762 regional census indicates that their farm was on land near present-day Kerby Road. Durbois came west from the village of St. Foy near the City of Quebec. His grandfather, Sebastian, immigrated to Canada before 1655 leaving behind a home at St. Michel in Lorraine on France's northeastern border.[5]

The Second Wave of Settlers (By 1762)

By 1759 the tide of "The French and Indian War" had turned in favor of the English. They captured the City of Quebec on September 13 and took Montreal the following year on September 6. Two months later, on November 29, 1760, Major Robert Rogers and his famous Rangers arrived at Fort Pontchartrain and placed it under British control. Despite a formal treaty between England and France in 1763, the frontier remained subject to a military government. Fortunately, the habitants in

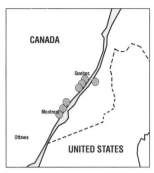

2nd Wave of Settlers (●)

Grosse Pointe retained the right to occupy and cultivate lands assigned under the French regime. The fees which they paid for this privilege were used to support the British garrison at Fort Pontchartrain.

The Fort's first British Commandant, Captain Donald Campbell, was generally respected by Fort residents. But, he was required by his superiors to restrict participation in the fur trade. While some habitants left the Fort in protest, most, due to the stability which came with peace, took up agriculture as an alternative to the fur trade.

By the early 1760s, much of the shore east from the Grand Marais to present-day Kerby Road was in the hands of habitants. A 1762 regional census listed at least ten new individuals with grants along the lake. Of those who actually occupied this land, the majority — Nicholas Patenaude, Jean Baptiste Aide dit Créqui, Jean Baptist Prudhomme dit Nantais and Pierre Estève dit Lajeunesse, Jr. — settled on the shore between present-day Fisher and Kerby Roads. Some, including Charles Moran dit Grimand and Luke Antoine Rivard, selected plots further west close to present-day Cadieux Road. Though not listed in the 1762 census, Jean Baptiste Rivard, a cousin of Luke Antoine, obtained a farm next to that of the Yaxs. There, in January 1763, he became a proud father for the first time.

Three of the more affluent grantees, Guillaume St. Bernard, Claude Jean Gouin and André Charles Barthe, had homesteads closer to Fort Pontchartrain. Aware of land values, they, like Luke Antoine Rivard, acquired extra property in Grosse Pointe. They chose their sites carefully. St. Bernard preferred the Grand Marais next to fields belonging to Pierre Trombley, Gouin selected acreage between the farms of Pierre Sr. and his two sons, Pierre Jr. and Louis Michel. To the east, Rivard and Barthe chose properties near present-day Fisher and Moran Roads.

These men, Grosse Pointe's first "real estate developers", had a typical French Canadian approach to improving the land. They selected one plot as a primary farm. Since there were few nearby markets for extra wheat and corn, they treated their other properties as "summer farms" to be

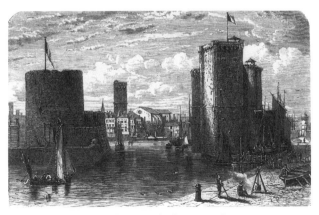

The port of La Rochelle, Bay of Biscay.
Illustration from George Musgrave's Nooks and Corners in Old France *(1867).*

A typical French-Canadian village. *Illustration from Beckles Willson's* Quebec: The Laurentian Province *(1913).*

cleared whenever they had the time. Once suitable for cultivation, the use of the property and its buildings could be sold at a profit or bequeathed to a family member.

If land was of primary importance to the habitants, so too were families. While Prudhomme and Luke Antoine Rivard married in French Canada, their compatriots preferred to seek wives from established households on the frontier. Gouin was the first of the group to marry. At the Fort's St. Anne Catholic Church, he became the husband of Marie Joseph Cuillerier dit Beaubien in 1742. Five years later, Barthe succeeded in winning the hand of Marie Theresa Campau. In 1754, her cousin, Marie Josephe Campau, became the wife of St. Bernard. The year 1762 was an important one for Grosse Pointe marriages. Neighbors, Créqui and Patenaude, wed two of Grosse Pointe's Duchene sisters, Magdeleine and Catherine, while Jean Baptiste Rivard took Michael Yax's daughter, Marie Catherine, as his wife. Moran dit Grimand, a confirmed bachelor, waited until 1767 to marry. His wife, Marguerite Simard was the widow of Grosse Pointe pioneer Ambroise Trombley. Except for the last two women, each of these brides had family from the Montreal area.

Habitant wives had much to do with the development of Grosse Pointe. They worked beside their husbands clearing the land, cultivating the fields and planting the orchards which later became so famous. Though restricted by the British, habitant men continued to prefer trading and trapping. They were frequently away for extended periods, leaving their wives to tend the fields and care for the children. Lacking a local church, women had the added responsibility of teaching their families the tenets of Catholicism, the official religion under the previous French regime.[6]

Most Grosse Pointe habitants came from Catholic settlements along the St. Lawrence River. Several of the pioneers had connections to the Montreal area. Patenaude was originally a resident at Longueuil while Barthe and Prudhomme came from the city proper. The latter married Marguerite Bigeot dit Dumouchel there in 1758. Some habitants came from villages between Trois Rivieres and the City of Quebec. Créqui was born at Pointe aux Tremblés near Montreal, but his family had its origins downriver at Lotbinière on the South side of the St. Lawrence River. Jean Baptiste Rivard grew up on the opposite bank at Les Grondines while Luke Antoine Rivard spent his childhood further west at Bastican. Between these two villages was Ste. Anne de la Perade where Gouin and Moran dit Grimard originally lived. This hamlet was also the site of Luke Antoine Rivard's marriage to Genevieve Brisson in 1746. Only Lajeunesse, who was born at Fort Pontchartrain, and St. Bernard, who arrived there directly from Europe, were exceptions to this pattern.

Many of these early Grosse Pointe residents were descended from men whose forefathers dwelt in west central France. Until some time before 1663, Gouin's grandfather, Mathurin, lived in Angeliers, a village northeast of Poitiers. Capital for the former Duchy of Aquitaine, Poitiers was the site of considerable strife during the seventeenth century Wars of Religion. Only one progenitor from west central France lived near the Atlantic Ocean. The first Jean Aide dit Créqui was a native of St. Sornin, south of Rochefort. He left France by 1689 probably from nearby LaRochelle, the port used by so many to embark for the New World. Northeast of Limoges, near the southern border of Acquitaine, St. Bernard bid good-bye to family and friends at Ambazac in the early 1750s.

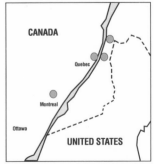

3rd Wave of Settlers (●)

─────────────────────── ⚓ ───────────────────────

6   To participate in Catholic rituals and holiday celebrations, Grosse Pointe families had to travel to St. Anne Catholic Church at Fort Pontchartrain.

The City of Quebec. *Illustration from* Picturesque America, *edited by William C. Bryant (1874).*

Other Grosse Pointe habitants traced their families to northern France. Nicholas Rivard dit Lavigne, the ancestor of Luke Antoine and Jean Baptiste, left the inland village of Tourouvre in 1653. To the northeast, Patenaude's great grandfather, Nicholas, set forth from the Normandy hamlet of Barville on the English Channel about 1650. Pierre Mauran, the grandfather of Moran dit Grimard, was a resident of Paris until he took leave of the capital city some time before 1679. Some 78 years later, Grosse Pointe's Prudhomme embarked from his native city of Nantes, a port on Brittany's Atlantic coast.

Only two in this Grosse Pointe group had family in southwestern France, and both were late arrivals in North America. A resident of Toulouse, Pierre Estéve dit Lajeunesse, Sr. left for New France near the end of the seventeenth century. Barthe's father, Theophile, waited until shortly before 1721 to leave the Pyrennes town of Tarbes.

The Third Wave of Settlers (1763-1769)

In July 1762, Major Henry Gladwin became Commandant at Fort Pontchartrain. His rigid control of the fur trade quickly brought objections from both Indians and habitants. The Ottawa chief, Pontiac, rallied midwestern tribes in the hope of forcing the return of Indian hunting grounds. His conspiracy to capture Fort Pontchartrain in 1763 was thwarted by an informer, but the Indian siege which followed lasted all summer. During the standoff,

Pontiac's village was on a farm across from Belle Isle. Indian activity must have frightened the habitants in nearby Grosse Pointe. They likely took refuge at Fort Pontchartrain, further straining its meager resources. With autumn, Pontiac's warriors grew restless, and the chief was compelled to seek peace. Rebuffed by the British, he capitulated and with his followers finally departed in late October. His attempts to marshall new forces proved fruitless, and in 1764, he signed an unofficial peace treaty before returning briefly to Fort Pontchartrain. The next year, he formally accepted British authority.

Perhaps concerned for their safety, few settlers came to Grosse Pointe between 1762 and 1769. Among those who ignored the possible danger was Louis Greffard. Yet, even he waited until 1765 to bring his new wife, Marguerite, to a homestead beyond present-day Vernier Road. The daughter of Pierre Casse dit St. Aubin, she probably would have selected a location closer to other Grosse Pointers. However, Greffard apparently preferred the untrodden forest. He came to the frontier from St. François de la Riviere du Sud on the south shore of the St. Lawrence River below the City of Quebec. His great grandfather, Louis Greffard dit LeCocq, had emigrated there by 1634 from the village of Chaille sous les Ormeaux in west central France north of La Rochelle.

The next arrival in Grosse Pointe was Joseph Marie Saucier. About 1767, he settled east of the LaForest farm on property formerly developed by Luke Antoine Rivard.

Grosse Pointe's Earliest Settlers: From 1750-1769

	Location in Canada	Location in France
FOUNDERS		
Pierre Trombley	Baie St. Paul	Tourouvre
Augustin Trombley	Baie St. Paul	Tourouvre
Amboise Trombley	Baie St. Paul	Tourouvre
Guillaume LaForest	Baie St. Paul	Agen
FIRST WAVE OF SETTLERS 1751–1758		
Antoine Deshêtres	(New England)	?
Joseph Davignon dit Lafeuillade	?	Limoges
Julien Freton	- - - -	Moisdon
Francois Gastignon dit Duchene	Montreal	Tours
Jean Baptist Lienard dit Durbois	St. Foy	St. Michel (Lorraine)
SECOND WAVE OF SETTLERS BY 1762		
Nicholas Patenaude	Longueuil	Barville
Jean Baptiste Aide dit Créqui	Point aux Tremblés (Lotbiniere)	St. Sornin (Rochefort)
Jean Baptiste Prudhomme dit Nantais	Montreal	Nantes
Pierre Estève dit Lajeunesse, Jr.	(Ft. Pontchartrain)	Toulouse
Charles Moran dit Grimard	Ste. Anne de la Perade	Paris
Luke Antoine Rivard	Bastican	Tourouvre
Jean Baptiste Rivard	Les Grondines	Tourouvre
Guillaume St. Bernard	- - - -	Ambazac
Claude Jean Gouin	Ste Anne de la Perade	Angeliers
Andre Charles Barthe	Montreal	Tarbes
THIRD WAVE OF SETTLERS 1763–1769		
Louis Greffard	St. François de la Riviere du Sud	Chaille sous les Ormieux
Joseph Marie Saucier	Riviere Ouelle	Paris
Alexandre Blondin dit Ellair	Terrebonne	Nouville
Ignatius Thibault	Chateau Richer	Rouen

In August of that year, he joined the Trombley family when he wed Marie Genevieve, the third child of Ambroise Trombley. Saucier was a native of Riviere Ouelle across the St. Lawrence River from Baie St. Paul. His great grandfather, Louis Saucier, had traveled to the New World from Paris by 1671.

Alexander Blondin dit Ellair was the next to appear along Lake St. Clair. About 1768, he took over the land developed by Prudhomme. In January of that year, he married Duchene's daughter, Marie Josephe. She had lost her first husband, Julien Freton, in July of the previous year and needed a father for her three young children. Before settling in Grosse Pointe, Ellair had been a resident of Terrebonne near Montreal. His paternal grandfather, Hilaire Sureau had immigrated to Quebec by 1691 from Nouville, a small town northeast of Poitiers.

Ignatius Thibault also settled in Grosse Pointe about 1768. That same year, he married Marie Catherine St. Aubin, a cousin of Greffard's wife and the daughter of Jacques Casse dit St. Aubin. The couple's farm was on the edge of the Grand Marais near the present Detroit city limits. Thibault's childhood home had been at Chateau Richer downriver from the City of Quebec. His ancestors had come from the Normandy cathedral town of Rouen where his great grandfather, Guillaume, lived until some time before 1655.

Conclusions

In the years between 1750 and 1770, at least 23 pioneers acquired the right to develop farms in the wilderness along Lake St. Clair. While a few, like Barthe and Gouin, could be called "land speculators" since their homes were elsewhere in the region, most of Grosse

The cathedral at Poitiers. *Illustration from Henry James'* A Little Tour in France (*1900*).

The Hotel de Ville, Paris, 17th century.
Illustration from Maria Lansdale's The World's Famous Places and Peoples: Paris *(1898).*

Pointe's founders lived on their lands year round. In the 1750s, only a few families occupied scattered farms along the lake. The Trombleys and LaForests, as the first to arrive there, likely promoted the region, and by the 1760s homesteads lined much of the shore between the Grand Marais and present-day Kerby Road. In the later 1760s, the farms of Prudhomme and Luke Antoine Rivard changed hands, and a few isolated clearings, like that of Greffard, could be found east of the primary settlement.

Despite being some distance from Fort Pontchartrain, Grosse Pointers were affected by political events of the time. King Louis XV provided the initial impetus for settlement with his gifts of equipment and stock in 1750 just as, ten years later, the shift from French to British rule caused some at Fort Pontchartrain to seek less regimented opportunities in Grosse Pointe. During the 1760s, in contrast, Chief Pontiac's tribal alliances and hostile attitude had the opposite effect. Grosse Pointe experienced a slow rate of expansion for several years following Pontiac's 1763 siege of the Fort.

Out of necessity, Grosse Pointe's pioneers were quick to marry. Most selected their spouses from either Fort Pontchartrain residents or Grosse Pointe settlers. Of the 23 granted land, only six married while in French Canada. None who came directly to the frontier from France brought wives with them. Frequently, the new arrivals selected daughters from the region's most affluent households. In addition to members of the Campau and St. Aubin families, Grosse Pointe's Duchene sisters apparently were highly esteemed since four Grosse Pointers married into that family. Often habitant couples had ancestral ties to a specific locale on the St. Lawrence River. Patenaude and his wife, Catherine, for example, had connections to the Montreal area. Indeed, the families of many habitant brides came from that region.

Most of Grosse Pointe's early residents emanated from small communities along both sides of the St. Lawrence River in French Canada. While some lived for a time at Fort Pontchartrain before moving out along Lake St. Clair, only one pioneer, Lajeunesse, was actually born at the fur trading settlement. There were other exceptions as well. Deshêtres came to his new home from Michigan's St. Joseph River. Freton and St. Bernard, Grosse Pointe's only true Frenchmen, arrived on the frontier directly from Europe.

Of those living in Quebec communities, a significant number were second or third generation French Canadians. Those arriving in Grosse Pointe during the 1750s or later 1760s had their origins in villages near or downriver from the City of Quebec. The village of Baie St. Paul was particularly well represented because of the Trombleys and LaForests, who became the founders of Grosse Pointe. Settlers who appeared by the early 1760s were often from hamlets between Trois Rivieres and the city of Quebec. Given the close proximity of villages between Bastican and Les Grondines, it seems likely that families from this region were acquainted before coming to Grosse Pointe. Certainly, both Gouin and Moran dit Grimard were originally residents of Ste. Anne de la Perade. Further upriver, Montreal and its surrounding territory were also a source of habitants such as Duchene in the late 1750s and Ellair in the 1760s.

Rue de l'Epicerie, city of Rouen. *Illustration from Ernest Peixotto's* Through the French Provinces *(1909).*

The European ancestors of most early Grosse Pointers, except the Yaxs who were German, had their beginnings in western France with equal numbers inhabiting its northern and central regions. Most came from small villages. A few, including Thibault and Duchene, had their origins in large cities or provincial towns. In the north, the capital of Paris and the rural village of Tourouvre each were home to two Grosse Pointe forebears. Freton and Saucier had connections to the former while the Trombleys and the Rivards had family ties to the latter. Further south, the region around Poitiers and Limoges provided the ancestral source for men like Gouin and Lafeuillade. Only four, Patenaude, Prudhomme, Créqui and Greffard, had forebears who lived near the sea. A few such as LaForest and Estève had ancestors in France's southwestern provinces, but only one, Durbois, had antecedents from its eastern border.

Descendants of pioneers, like the Trombleys and the Rivards, continue to live in Grosse Pointe today. Though all that is left of their ancestors' farms are subdivisions which follow the original property lines or streets which bear their early owners' names, the community's French tradition remains strong. New residents of Grosse Pointe, regardless of their nationality, quickly learn of the areas French origins. The tradition of French and French Canadian pioneers, who arrived between 1750 to 1770, is likely to remain a significant part of Grosse Pointe's heritage for many years to come.

BIBLIOGRAPHY

Sources for Historical Information

Burton, Clarence, *The City of Detroit*. Vol. I & II Detroit, Clark, 1922.

Catlin, Bruce, *The Story of Detroit*. Detroit, Detroit News, 1936.

Eccles, W.J., *France in America*. Rev. Ed. East Lansing, Michigan State University Press, 1990.

Keating, Sylvia L., "The French Farmers of Grosse Pointe." *Detroit in Perspective: A Journal of Regional History* Vol. 5, No. 3 Spring, 1981, pp. 72-84.

Paré, Father George, "The Cicotte Book". *Bulletin– Detroit Historical Society* Vol. XIV, February, 1958.

Ross, Robert and Catlin, Bruce, *Landmarks of Detroit*. Detroit, Detroit Evening News, 1898.

Sources for Genealogical Information

Charbonneau, Hubert and Legare, Jacques, Ed., *Repetoire des actes de baptisme, mariage, sepulture et des recensements du Quebec ancien/Programme de recherche en demographie historique*. Montreal, Presses de l'Universite de Montreal, 1980.

Cicotte, Edward V. Papers, *The Cicotte Book*. Burton Historical Collection, Detroit Public Library.

Dennison, The Rev. Father Christian, *Genealogy of the French Families of the Detroit River Region*. Vol. I & II Ed. by Harold F. Powell; Rev. Ed. by Robert Pilon. Detroit, Detroit Society for Genealogical Research, 1987.

Detroit Notary Records. Vol. A & B. Burton Historical Collection, Detroit Public Library.

Jette, René, *Dictionaire Genealogique des Familles du Quebec*. With the collaboration of the Program of Research in Historic Demography of the University of Montreal. Montreal, Presses de l'Université de Montreal, 1983.

Russell, Donna Valley, Ed., *Michigan Censuses 1710-1830*. Detroit, Detroit Society for Genealogical Research, 1982.

St. Anne Catholic Church Marriage Register. Burton Historical Collection, Detroit Public Library.

Since 1980, Jean Dodenhoff has held the position of Curator at the Grosse Pointe Historical Society. The skills learned at Smith College and at Wayne State University, combined with an interest in genealogy and local history, led Ms. Dodenhoff to the research and writing of this article.

Grosse Pointe and le Grande Marais

By Mina Humphrey Varnum

In this article, first published in Detroit Saturday Night, *February 26, 1916,*
Mina Humphrey Varnum tells her story of "Grosse Pointe and le Grand Marais."

Oh, de Frenchman, he no like-a die in de fall
When de mash ees full of game.
An' de beeg musk-rat, she's sleek an fat.
An' de bull-frog, jus' de same,
Bob-a-le, bob-a-lo
Bob-a-le, bob-a-lo
An' de bull-frog jus de same.

❧ ❧ ❧

LE GRANDE MARAIS (the big marsh) situated a few miles above the old French town, *La Ville Detroit*, must have been a veritable land of plenty to the early French habitants that lived on its borders, for the "beeg musk-rat" and the bull-frog were in undisturbed possession, then.

The words, *le grande marais*, are meaningless to the army of people who pass along the "river road" from Detroit to Grosse Pointe and beyond, as is also *la cote du Nord*, the name the French gave to all that section of waterfront lying east of what is now Woodward Avenue.

No one ever considers calling the point on which the lighthouse is situated "Presque Isle" and yet that was its every-day name when the French people bumped over the old corduroy and soft sand of the river road nearly two centuries ago. Later it became Windmill Point.

Le Grande Marais was indeed a "big marsh." It is said to have extended over the vast tract of land lying between the Grosse Pointe lighthouse and Conner's Creek, and to have reached as far inland as the Clinton road. The old river road took a turn around this, because roads could not be laid across it, and the Jefferson avenue that we now know does not follow the route of this old road. In some places it ran much nearer the river; at Water Works Park, where the Van Avery roadhouse flourished, it ran nearly to the water's edge.

Beginning with Windmill Point the *grosse* or larger *pointe* extended into Lake St. Clair beyond what is now the line between Wayne and Macomb counties, past Milk River, or *River au Lait*, to the small bay known for many years, and on all old land descriptions of that section, as *L'Anse Creuse*.

Following the coming of Cadillac in 1701, all of the land from the boundaries of the small village of Detroit to beyond L'Anse Creuse were, from time to time, given out to French settlers by grants from the Commandant of Detroit and the Governor of New France and confirmed by the French king. These farms were long strips of land with frontage on the Detroit River and Lake St. Clair, so narrow that the families in the little white-washed log dwelling could call across to each other and so pass the news of any important event or choice bit of gossip all along the water front.

The houses were built close to the water's edge and usually were surrounded by cedar pickets for protection. In the rear were orchards of apples and pear trees, the seeds for which it is said were brought originally from France. A little farther back corn and wheat were planted, sufficient for current needs; and beyond that the wilderness remained unbroken until the coming of the American settlers after the Revolutionary War.

The Grande Marais was low, flat, marshy country covered with a most luxuriant growth of wild grass, and this was public property to be cut by any one who would take the trouble. What was not cut was usually set on fire in the winter and would burn for days. As there were similar marsh fires along the mouth of the River Rouge at the same time, the people of Detroit were given free displays of fire works for the flames would leap through the dry grass illuminating the sky above the marsh so that it could be seen for many miles. Anyone can gain a vivid realization of the stillness and weirdness of this section of the water front when it was the home only of the French habitants and wild animals by taking a canoe and paddling at sunset along the shore line of the Canadian "Flats." The song of the bull-frog can still be heard, the noiseless slipping and sliding of water creatures among the rushes, the call of the birds and wild-fowls among the waving rice while the intenseness of the great quiet that exaggerates the mystery of the little noises, still thrills and excites the imagination.

But the water front along the Grande Marais and Grosse Pointe was not always quiet. During the day the many windmills that made prominent landmarks to the voyageurs on the river were busy grinding the corn of the farmers and Indians. The long arms turned and groaned as the wind pressed against the tattered sails so that the sound could be heard for miles. Bands of Indians—Hurons,

"The Grande Marais was low, flat, marshy country covered with a most luxuriant growth of wild grass."

Ottawas, Foxes, Pottawattomies—were coming and going both on the river in their canoes and on the shore road on their ponies. Voyageurs setting forth for Mackinac and the hunting grounds of the Mississippi and Wisconsin invariably passed along the river and usually camped at the farther end of Grosse Pointe their first night out.

As late as 1820, when Governor Cass and Henry Rowe Schoolcraft, with a company of distinguished gentlemen started for Sault Ste. Marie to treat with the northern Indians, the first camp was made at Grosse Pointe and the next day a large party of gay people, the aristocracy of the city, drove out on the river road to bid them God-speed and to wish them a safe return.

For many years in the months of June the orchards along the river front held thousands of Indians, their squaws and papooses, who were on their way to Malden to receive their annual presents from the British government. The beach for many miles would be lined with their canoes, while their tents and bright camp-fires dotted the landscape.

On still calm evenings the Indian war drums and hammers could be heard up and down the river; during the years from the coming of the earliest explorer until only a century ago, their blood-curdling war cries echoed across river and lake, and brought terror to the farmers of the region.

In the spring of 1712, at the time of the attack on Fort Pontchartrain by the Fox Indians, the final battle was fought at Windmill Point, between the Foxes and the allied Indians who were helping the French. There all of the braves of the Fox nation were massacred by the allied Indians and their squaws and papooses taken into captivity. The river road must have witnessed many heart breaking and tragic scenes at this time as the captive women and children were driven to Detroit.

There were other Indian wars in this vicinity, different nations attacking the Fort at Detroit in 1703, in 1707 and in 1746. At the time of this last siege the great Pontiac, chief of the Ottawas, defended the Fort as an ally of the French. Later in 1763 he entered into conspiracy with other Indian nations and attacked the fort at Detroit, then in the possession of the English.

At the time of this Indian war the river road, the Grande Marais and Grosse Pointe were the scenes of Indian councils, thrilling escapes of English prisoners from the savages,

"Milk River Bay — Grosse Pointe."
Illustration from Picturesque Detroit and Environs, 1893, *courtesy of the St. Clair Shores Public Library.*

raids, massacres, the flights of frightened cattle, war dances, intrigues, wholesale murders and other events which present day imaginations almost fail to grasp.

It was at Grosse Pointe that Pontiac assembled his allied forces of Hurons, Ottawas and Pottawattomies, after the massacre of the Fisher family, on Hog Island. (Belle Isle); and it was at Grosse Pointe that his camp was established during the seige of Detroit, although an advance guard was stationed at the Meloche farm nearer the town.

It has been variously estimated that Pontiac had from 600 to 3,000 Indians in his army. Probably the number was about 1,000. There were enough of them, however, to make the whole of Grosse Pointe and the road along the beach a panorama of moving savages, their naked bodies daubed with bright colored paint in fearful pictures and symbols; their heads covered with feathered war-bonnets; and tomahawks, guns, knives and other arms at their sides or in their hands ready for instant use. The moonlight must have fallen on weird moving pictures at Grosse Pointe and the entire cote du Nord during this summer of 1763.

In 1761 Sir William Johnson, Superintendent of the Indian tribes for the English visited Detroit and made the following entry in his dairy:

"Monday (September) 14th . . . I took a ride before dinner up toward Lake St. Clair. The road runs along the river side, which is all settled thickly nine miles. A very pleasant place in summer but at other seasons, too low and marshy."

The battles of the War of 1812 in the region of Detroit were mostly fought below the town, at Brownstown, Frenchtown, and the River Raisin. Grosse Pointe and the Grande Marais were comparatively quiet, except as they were traversed by various war parties, and expeditions.

The troops for an expedition under General McArthur were camped at Grosse Pointe in October of 1814. They went from there to Swan Creek where they crossed the St. Clair River to the old town of Baldoon and then marched to the Thames River.

A year later, in September, a band of marines under Lieut. Alexander T. E. Vidal from the British schooner, *Confiance,* anchored "at the rapids of the St. Clair River" landed at Grosse Pointe and, according to the oath of John Miller, Henry Tucker, Charles Rivard, Charles Nowlett Green, (the latter a lieutenant in the First regiment of Michigan militia) and other residents of the Pointe, did forcibly "seize the said Thomas Raynor and hustle him towards the canoe. The said Thomas Raynor strove to get from them as much as he could but being intoxicated could not make any effectual resistance and he was taken by force on board the canoe."

As the right of the English to search American vessels for British sailors was a large issue in the War of 1812, the landing of a party of British sailors on American territory and the seizing of a sailor must have created great excitement along the shore. One of the "deponents" swore that the said Thomas Raynor was a member of a party of men who were coming from a camp a mile or so along the shore. When they saw the canoe with the British officers and sailors coming toward Grosse Pointe "the party all scattered. Deponent went towards the woods and while lying in ambush," witnessed the abduction. The case was tried and Lieut. Vidal was fined $612.48, on October 13. But an entry of October 14 in the records of the Supreme Court states that Lieut. Vidal was acquitted.

On Grosse Pointe, so far along the shore that his Private Claim, No. 231, had its frontage along Lake St. Clair in what is now Wayne County, with its rear across the line in Macomb County, dwelt Commodore Grant with ten lovely daughters. His house was called "The Castle," and was so popular with the naval officers in the ships stationed in the Detroit River, and with the army officers at the Fort in Detroit, that every day was a gala day and every evening a "social function." It was at the castle of Commodore Grant that the one and only harpsichord owned in Detroit at that time was placed. Its being there was rather a joke, for it was so dilapidated that it was useless, and Commodore Grant complained to its owner, his friend Dr. Harpfy, of Detroit, and Dr. Harpfy had Mr. John Askin come and take it to his store house in the village. Mr. Grant's private claim was occupied before 1796, and was confirmed in July, 1808.

By the time Michigan was ready to be admitted into the union, and become a state, the country of the Grande Marais, Grosse Pointe, L'Anse Creuse, and as far along the shore line as Swan Creek, was well settled, and but few Indians were to be found. A census taken in 1836 gave 180 Chippewas residing at Swan Creek, and but 230 at Black River, near Port Huron, as the only Indians in the vicinity.

New roads were being built; some had been built even earlier than this; the old Moravian road which "runs in a line straight through the bush" from a temporary Moravian settlement near Mount Clemens to Detroit, was built in 1785. This avoided the Grande Marais and the undulations of the shore line.

Some time soon after the conclusion of the War in 1812 a stage line was established between Detroit and Mount Clemens, which ran through the Grande Marais along the shore of the lake and the banks of the rivers. Capt. Benjamin Woodworth, the genial proprietor of the Steamboat Hotel, who owned the stage line, was one of the prominent citizens of Detroit.

When it was decided, in 1874, to place the Water Works for the city of Detroit on the Van Avery farm, on the Grosse Pointe Road, the tide of emigration towards Hamtramck and Grosse Point began. Before many years the intervening country was laid out into city lots, the lines of the old private claims of the French period became entirely obliterated, the Grande Marais was filled in with rubbish from the city and dirt dredged from the river; the river road became Jefferson avenue, graded, straightened, leveled and paved with asphalt, and neat lawns now cover the old time hunting grounds of the French habitant, the bull-frog and the "beeg musk-rat."

Mina Humphrey Varnum was born in 1874. She married Thad S. Varnum, a prominent newspaperman. Mrs. Varnum worked as a beat reporter for the papers, covering every type of story from fashion to crime. She was assistant editor for the Michigan Historical Commission and was a regular contributor to Detroit Saturday Night. Mrs. Varnum was appointed assistant publicity manager of the Michigan State Telephone Company in 1921, the first woman in the country to hold so high a position. Mina Humphrey Varnum died in 1954.

ILLUSTRATION CREDIT: Page 29 illustration from *Picturesque Detroit and Environs, 1893*, courtesy of the St. Clair Shores Public Library.

French-Canadian Verse

Part II

One of the most entertaining pieces of literature of the early Detroit River region

is this collection of poems written in the French-Canadian dialect of the period.

These three delightful poems, selected from the writings of William E. Baubie,

help to tell the story of the French settlers of old Grosse Pointe.

T HE THREE POEMS which follow here were selected from William A. Baubie's small book of poetry entitled *French-Canadian Verse*, published in 1917. In the preface to his book Baubie wrote:

Many years of the writer's life were spent in old Quebec and Montreal, where he was thrown in personal contact with the "habitants," young and old; and his close association with them ripened from mere acquaintance into friendship, and, later, into affectionate regard. It was, however, in the rural districts and upon the lakes, rivers, and marshes of Canada and the bordering territories, where the writer has fished and hunted, that he has heard the real Canadian "patois" spoken, as only one may hear it, and these humble efforts are mainly the result of such travel.

Ole Cheneau

Ah'll Nevaire Go Hunt For De Mush-Rat No More

OLE CHENEAU go hunt for de mush-rat wan day;
He tak hees dog Ponteau, to show heem de way,
He got soaken wet, in de wataire he fall,
Ah he don faine no game or no mush-rat at-all.
Hees feeling deesgust, for hees not satisfy;
Hees wet an hees getting so mad bye and bye
Dat he say to hessef, as he cussed an he swore:
"Ah'll nevaire go hunt for de mush-rat no more!"

He wade tru de mash an he wade tru de hay
Till he get purtay close where de mush-rat he lay;
Hees dog's hon de point for dey all smell de game,
So he up wid hees muskette an tak a good aim.
As he pull hon de trig den he maike a beeg sneeze,
An down in de wataire he go to hees knees.
Den he say it out loud as he jaump hon de shore:
"Ah'll nevaire go hunt for de mush-rat no more!"

A beeg mallarde dock shes was sitting close by.
Dat's luckay, for Cheneau's no good hon de fly,
So he tak a good aim, but de gaun she don't go:
De bullette she's wet an de pauder also.
He ript an he cussed at de gaun an de pauder,
Hees voice she go higher — an den she go lowder,
Den he sai it all ovaire, more loud as before:
"Ah'll nevaire go hunt for de mush-rat no more!"

But de ole mallarde dock she sits hon de creek,
So he sai, "Mistaire mallarde Ah'll show you de trick.
Ah'll pass a few salt hon your fedder behaind—
Ah'll fix you so easay dees tam, you will faind."
But de dock smell de salt in Cheneau's tin pail,
She hawl off her main sheet, an den she maike sail.
De ole man he yelled, an he ript, and he swore:
"Ah'll nevaire go hunt for de mush-rat no more!"

Den he jaump in hees boat, hees mad an hees wet,
Hees using som vere strong langage, you bet.
He sai to ole Ponteau, "Ah want you to know
Ah'm de boss of dees mash, an mah name is Cheneau!"
Wile he paddle so lively hees baump hon a log
An ovaire goes Cheneau, de gaun, an de dog.
Den he holler lackell an he holler encore:
"Ah'll nevaire go hunt for de mush-rat no more!"

He climb hon de bottome, for help he was call,
He sai, "Ah go drown wid mah muskette an all."
Som habitant hear all de noise an de splash
An Batteece, hees son, he com down to de mash.
He pull out de dog an he pull out Cheneau,
But he loos hees ole gaun in de channel below.
Batteece sai, "pawpaw, your so safe hon de shore—
Don't hunt hon de mash for dose mush-rat no more!"

He spread hon de grass hees shirt and hees pants—
Dey dry in de sun if you geev it de chance,
But a beeg hurricane she was passing close by:
She pick up dose pants an she blow it sky high.
Wen Cheneau he notice hees pants in de air,
He sai, "We'll go home while de wind she be fair.
Au diable wid de mash! Ah'll keep hon de shore!
Ah'll nevaire go hunt for de mush-rat no more!"

Hees waife grab de hole man an put heem to bed
Wid two-tree flat iron hon top of hees head,
She pass hon de shin bone som muster plastaire,
She rub heem wid kerosine oil everywhere,
She geev heem som sassaperell wid de spoon,
Den he sai as he open hees eye purtay soon:
"Such luck hon de mash, Ah don't hav it before
To hell wid de mush-rat! Ah'll hunt heem no more!"

The Old-Time Fishing
On Detroit River

DE hole tam fisherman hees gone,
  We ain't see it no more;
We loose dem slowly wan by wan,
  Dere passing from our shore.

Doun below from Sandweech toun,
  Way doun to Petit Cote,
So many you could see aroun
  De hole tam shaintay an de boat.

Up to de fall of seexty-hate
  De feeshing it was all O.K.
Along de Reever of de Strait,
  Dere feeshing all de naight and day.

Dey catch de tourgeon and dore
  An de whitefeesh all de tam
An wat you spose datcost you, eh!
  Wan poisson blanc for haf a dime.

An dere's de hole tam shaintay.
  An de man wat set de float,
De capstaine an de ponay,
  An de man wat pulls de boat.

An dere dey go at sunset;
  Dere's four man at de oar:
Dere's Covion and Joe Payette,
  Dere's Nadeau and Bedore.

Pete Valliquette hees at de stern,
  Hees passing out de net,

The Return

Drouilliard hees at de capstaine
  Wid hees French ponay, you bet.

So softly up de stream dey row
  Tree hunderd yard or more,
Dey make de turn an roun dey go
  Raight past de shaintay hon de shore.

De seine is set, you see de float,
  De trip for shore it won't take long.
An den dose Frenchman in dat boat
  Dey sing dees hole French song:

Count de stroke as you hear de song,
  Keep up de tam, hole man;
You'll like de tune, it won't take long.
  Now sing wid me, Ah'm sure you can.

Wan, two, tree, and wan, two tree,
  An den agan and den some more.
Den wan, two, tree, de song's finis—
  Dere landing at de shore.

Agan dere at de shaintay,
  Dere jaumping from de yawl;
Dere sure to faind it plaentay
  Of whitefeesh in dat hawl.

An den you see de chaudiere,
  In de shaintay always hot;
All dose fisherman was dere
  To eat de bouillon from de pot.

Dey light de pipe, an taike a drop,
  Den Covion was geeve de call.
We ain't gat tam for long to stop—
  Look sharp, mah boy, for nodder hawl!

Helas! dose tam she com no more,
  For dose good man she's pass away.
Ah hope dere hon som odder shore
  Where de feeshing's good to-day.

If fisherman wat's in de ciel
  Can hear our voices down below,
No musique dey would love so well
  As dees ole song of long ago.

The Finish

The Race At Petit Cote

DID you ever saw mah ponay—
    De wan wat win de race?
She's hon de cutter every day,
    She maike de rack an pace.

She's only fair French ponay,
    She hav no padda-gree;
Her color was de ches-not bay
    But shee's good nuff for me.

"Catin" was mah ponay's name
    (De saime as ba-bee doll);
Across de Grande Marais she came,
    She's five year hole las fall.

Gouleau's got a pacing horse,
    Ban Butlaire was hees name;
He bring it over from Ecorse,
    From Meechegane he came.

Gouleau he always maike de blow
    About hees gait an paddagree;
Dat felleure try it hard to show
    Hees plog could maike de two-tortee.

He say hees modder was a dam,
    De fadere was a sire
Wat win de race mos every-tam,
    Was full of blood an fire.

He hav a ceefecate to show
    Hees fadere it was de Pilot R.
An also dat hees dam could go,
    For dat was Floray Temp de star.

We ain't see Floray for long tam,
    An Pilot long ago was die.
Ba gosh! An tink dat dam an sire
    Was Gouleau's dam beeg lie.

Mah fren Cicotte from Wyandotte
    Was tole me hon de sly
De record wat dat plog hees got—
    You'll hear de finish by an by.

He say dat some wan was a liar;
    For he see hees racker long ago—
He pull de hengine to de fire
    In de good ole citay of Munroe.

Hees gallop for de fire brigade,
    De force was like heem well;
Hees hon de job, so Cicotte said,
    Til some-wan rings de bell.

An den he say de dev's to pay,
    Dat bell was change hees mind;
He'll turn an go sum odder way—
    An leave de fire brigade behind.

For he was hongrey all de day,
    Hees hongrey all de naight—
De corn, de bean, de bran, de hay,
    Hees gobble everting in sight.

Hees appetite she can't be beat,
    For hees always feel so well.
Hees sure dat was de tam to eat
    Wen some wan rings de bell.

Gouleau was start again to holler
    Dat Ban, hees pacing horse,
Would beat mah ponay for tree dollar—
    Ah cover up de bet, of course.

Dat was to be de two-mile race
　　At Petit-Cote, along de shore.
No trot, no gallop, joust de pace,
　　Tree dollar cash, an notting more.

You know de road by Jeem MacKee?
　　At de bank shee's turning round.
Dat's de plaice, we was agree,
　　Would be de starting ground.

Den doun de reever we must go
　　For two mile straight, no more,
To Louie Youngeblod's plaice below—
　　De poplaire tree was hon de shore.

De week behind las Saturday
　　We fix it for de go.
De wedder she was frostay
　　De hice was cover wid de snow.

We bring de ponays to de scratch,
　　All de habitant was dere.
Dey put dere monay hon de match;
　　Dere betting freelay hon mah mare.

"Dees be de race for pace an rack,"
　　Joe Covion, de judge, hees say.
"So clar de way! Gott off de trak!
　　We start de ponays raight away."

Den neck an neck we start to go,
　　But de judge say, "Start wance more!"
We off agan, hees calling "Whoa!
　　Start off agan, same as before."

We're off at last, an hon de speed.
　　L'enfant! dat was som pace!
Ah'm trying hard to take de lead,
　　But ole Ban still was in de race.

De snow she fly as we pass by,
　　Mah ponay try to show de way,
But to see dat ole Ban Butlaire fly
　　You'd tink dere was a fire dat day.

Neck an neck we're pacing fast,
　　We're hon de plaice of Tom MeLoche;
Ah do mah best, Ah can't get past
　　Dat ole-tam hengine horse.

De habitant call from de shore
　　An geeve de cheer, as we pass bye.
"Avance, Catin!" "Avance, encore!"
　　"Wake up! wake up, ole Ban! dey cry.

Ba gosh! Ah never see such race—
　　Raight togedder side by side
Dey go two-toree hon de pace;
　　For taike de lead each ponay tried.

De Taverne Rouge we're going past,
　　Neck an nec, an all was well;
Ban Butlaire he was going fast
　　Wen de cook she ring de bell.

Den Ban he break, he break some more,
　　"Whoa donc!" hees driver yel.
He turn an gallop for de shore
　　An still de cook she ring de bell.

Wid me, Ah finish hon de pace;
　　Dey cheer as Ah pass by.
De judge decide Ah win de race
　　For ole Ban was deesqualify.

"Dat's put op job," Gouleau he say,
　　"Cicotte's de wan can tell—
Dat's heem wat pay de cook dat day
　　To ring dat dinner bell."

———————— ❦ ————————

William A. Baubie was born in Chatham, Ontario, and educated in Montreal and Quebec. As a young man he moved to Detroit, where he practiced law for nearly 60 years. In addition to his book of poetry, Baubie also wrote The Man Condemned, *a novel of French-Canadian life published in 1936. Mr. Baubie died in Detroit at the home of his son in December 1938.*

The Cursed Village:
A LEGEND OF L'ANSE CREUSE

Retold by Marie Caroline Watson Hamlin

Rediscovered by Arthur M. Woodford

Some of the most interesting literature of the Lake St. Clair region is the folk lore of the

early French habitants. Many of these stories were gathered together and first published in

1883 by Marie Caroline Watson Hamlin in her delightful book, "Legends of le Détroit."

Here is one of those tales in which there is more than a little "grain of truth."

IT WAS NOT long after the settlement of Detroit in July of 1701, that the French habitants began to establish their farms up and down the river from Fort Pontchartrain. They spread south along the river to Springwells, the Rouge River, Ecorse, Brownstown, and on past Frenchtown, the site of present day Monroe. To the east and north the settlements spread through Grosse Pointe, along the shores of Lake St. Clair up to the Clinton River (site of present-day Mount Clemens), past the Flats, and on up to St. Clair River.

While Detroit grew from a French outpost, to a British village, and finally an American town, the settlements up and down the river remained largely rural and largely French. Nowhere was this more true than in that area stretching northward along the shores of Lake St. Clair from the Milk River, the northern boundary of Grosse Pointe at Gaukler Point (the present site of the Edsel and Eleanor Ford Estate), to the Clinton River. Well into the 19th century this region, known as L'Anse Creuse, re-

tained its French heritage. Today this region encompasses the city of St. Clair Shores and the township of Harrison.

The words L'Anse Creuse will be found on maps from the 18th century well into the 20th. Noted by the slight curve of the shoreline from Gaukler Point to the mouth of the Clinton River, the term L'Anse Creuse has a variety of meanings: little crescent, small bay, shallow saucer, and little dipper. The phrase L'Anse Creuse was never anglicized, and through it had a variety of meanings, it has always retained its original French name.

Today the region is home to more than 100,000 people, and the shores of the lake are lined with year-round homes, summer cottages, marinas, canals, parks and beaches. The region is also rich in folklore. One of the earliest folktales is entitled "The Cursed Village" and dates from the early 1800s. This version of the story comes from the book *Legend of le Détroit* by Marie Caroline Watson Hamlin and was first published in 1883.

The farmhouse of the Navarre family much as it would have looked in 1797, and similar in style to those of the French-Canadian habitants of L'Anse Creuse. Photo courtesy of the Monroe County Historical Commission.

❦ ❦ ❦

Ms. Hamlin's Tale

It was on a glorious September morning that our carriage rolled along the picturesque shore of Grosse Pointe. The soft, misty waves of fog which trailed over the smooth cut lawn and over the broad lake were gradually curling themselves into graceful, spiral wreaths, to dissolve in the sunlight. If there is a touch of sadness in Autumn, an indescribable yearning after something indefinable, there is a strength to resist the depression in the fresh, bracing atmosphere which lends roses to the cheek and buoyancy to the step. Nature, as if conscious of this tinge of melancholy, dons her brightest colors, throws around her that mystic, mellow light which rounds the sharpest outline and softens the roughest landscapes, and whilst we are enchanted by her gorgeous devices we forget the sad reflections of this season of decay.

We passed the fashionable drive, bordered by its handsome villas with their evidences of culture and refinement, crossed the tottering bridge over the Milk River, into a strange country and a past age. Occasionally signs of a well-to-do farmer greeted us, but these were rare. Silence, monotony and dilapidation were written everywhere. The lake here swept majestically into the shore forming a graceful curve. This was the Bay of L'Anse Creuse from which the village on its banks derived its name, we were told. Dim, shadowy memories of a legend connected with this place drifted confusedly through my brain, and asking the driver about it, he told us that there lived not far an old habitant who was well versed in all such lore, and who would be but too happy to have a listener. Ten minutes later we entered a humble cottage, stated our errand, and were received with that genuine courtesy, the peculiar heritage of the French, which caused Sydney Smith to envy the manners of his cobbler in Paris.

The old raconteur introduced us to his children and grandchildren, who eyed us politely, but with curious, speculative eyes, unused to a sudden inroad of strangers. The habitant evidently relished telling a story, and smacking his lips after the manner of an epicure, told us the legend of L'Anse Creuse.

It was the feast of Corpus Christi in June, and the whole neighborhood of L'Anse Creuse was in a whirl of excite-

An interior view of "salle a manger" (dining room) of the Navarre house ca. 1797.
Photo courtesy of the Monroe County Historical Commission.

ment. For today the Bishop was coming from the fort at Detroit accompanied by the new pastor, to consecrate the little chapel. The young men on horseback with their guns to fire a salute, had gone to meet them, whilst the children, dressed in white, bearing flowers and looking like so many butter-flies, were flitting to and fro, and the habitants in their Sunday attire were gaily chatting. All of a sudden a discharge of guns announced the near approach of the clerical party, and in a few moments all were formed in a procession. Banners were unfurled, voices were raised chanting the Te Deum, clouds of incense rose to perfume the air and the pathway was strewn with flowers.

Thus were they escorted to the church, and amidst that grand silence so appealing in its solemnity, the imposing ceremonies took place. They were followed by a short but eloquent address from their new pastor, Father Gabriel. He thanked them for their welcome and hoped that God would bless his efforts; he would endeavor to prove a true shepherd, but his flock must aid him to keep in the narrow path. He alluded lightly to that greatest of all temptations,

excessive drinking, which brought so many evils in its train, and which was so difficult to overcome.

Perhaps the eagle eye of the priest had noted the recess on the banks, where old Francois Fontenoy, the celebrated Indian trader (who had buried a brass kettle of gold at Presque Isle and which has caused as many explanations and conjunctures as Kidds treasure), had tapped a barrel of genuine eau de vie.

After the blessing, all dispersed to give themselves up to the enjoyment of the day. The young men amused themselves by shooting in the air, which caused a stranger, who seemed by his manner and dress to take no part in the day's rejoicing, to say, "They are shooting the devil out of the neighborhood." One near him jestingly replied, "Perhaps he was never here until you came; you must have brought him." An angry flush crept over the swarthy face of the stranger, who with a muttered something, turned on his heels and joined old Fontenoy and his flowing glass.

This man, Lizon by name, had recently settled at L'Anse Creuse. Being reserved in his manner, he merely stated that he came from Montreal. He formed a contrast to the light-hearted villagers, who lived as one family, shared each others joys and sorrows, and who were closely bound by the ties of early associations and relationship. Lizon rejected in a morose manner their friendly overtures, and was soon left to the solitude he seemed to covet. He possessed means, for he had purchased land, and built an auberge where liquor was the chief inducement.

One day it was announced that Lizon had asked Julienne, the daughter of a respected habitant, to marry him. The amazement of the good people was intense, as Julienne was a sweet, pious girl, and had rejected half of the youths of L'Anse Creuse, whilst this Lizon was ugly, cross-eyed and had a halt in his walk, and beside had never been known to enter the church.

How he won the damsel was a sort of mystery to all, a constant theme of conjecture. Some boldly said it was sorcery. The parents of the girl were opposed to the marriage, but seeing how headstrong she was, left her to her own devices.

Lizon refused to be married in church, as he would then be obliged to attend to his religious duties. Julienne besought him, but to no avail. What argument he used, what witchcraft he employed, is not known, but Julienne deserted her home and came to live with Lizon. Father Gabriel, who had been absent, returned a few days after and found his community excited over the scandal. He immediately sent for both culprits. Neither obeyed his command. The following Sunday he hurled against them the fearful ban of excommunication, and stated that Lizon had a wife and children whom he had deserted, living in Montreal. From that date on no one crossed the threshold of Lizon's door, — the grass grew rank, and seldom was Julienne seen. Lizon's rage knew no bounds; he repaired a dilapidated barn and there kept liquor for all who desired to procure it. Those who had feared to go to the auberge flocked to this new place and soon the evil influence of this drinking was felt. The peace which reigned in this Arcadia of Lake Ste. Claire was broken; dissensions, quarrels and scandals arose. The voice of the priest seemed powerless and his efforts paralyzed by the demon of liquor.

Julienne, who was seldom seen, startled the congregation on Sunday morning by standing in front of the altar and

"How he won the damsel was a sort of mystery to all."

asking public pardon, through the priest, for the great scandal she had caused. All in the church were melted into tears, and the voice of the pastor was tremulous with emotion as he welcomed back the erring sheep into the fold.

When Lizon discovered the flight of Julienne, that she had returned to her God and to her parents, his anger was fearful. He swore that he would have her back, that he would spurn anything that stood in his way. The bay would sooner break its bonds than he forego his design.

It was New Year's Eve, and every household was making preparations, for each expected a visit from the d'Ignolee. This is an old custom, traced to France, and by fragmentary history and tradition way back to the Druids[1] and is still kept up at Grosse Pointe and in Lower Canada. A number of young men gather, masked and armed with stout sticks, and visit each house successively, in the village. They halt at the door and sing their song. They are bidden in, and after greeting the host and hostess, continue their song in which they state that they come in accordance with their promise to visit annually. "We ask but little," they say, "a little piece of chignee, nothing more. Will you give it? If not, say so, and we will take your eldest daughter." The chignee to which allusion is here made is a piece cut from a newly slaughtered hog, with the tail depending therefrom. It is invariably put aside, with clothing and provisions, for the singers, who place the offerings of all in their cart, and afterward distribute them among the poor.

The d'Ignolee knocked for admittance at the door of Julienne's father; they were welcomed and received their offerings. Whilst the party was singing a sudden cry of distress caused all to rush to the door. Nothing was seen and the d'Ignolee immediately departed. The father called Julienne for the evening rosary and received no answer, went to her room; she was not there. Immediately they suspected that Lizon was among the d'Ignolee. The cry they heard was hers and a warning of the d'Ignolee to leave. Messengers flew to stop the d'Ignolee and others ran to Lizon's, but they did not find Julienne. Father Gabriel was sent for, and he went to demand Julienne of Lizon who laughed at him, saying he did not recognize his authority and did not understand why he, Father Gabriel, should interfere with what did not concern him. The priest an-

---

[1] Freya, the wife of Odin, the Saxon god, made all things swear not to harm Balder, the Sun, except the mistletoe, a plant so diminutive that she did not think it worth noticing. Lake, god of evil, found out his weak point however, and tearing up the mistletoe gave it to Odin, the blind god, who with it fatally pierced Balder. That was the fable, and it was to prevent Lake from slaying Balder that the Druids solemnly sought the oak trees and gathered the mistletoe from the boughs with the joyous cry, "Au gui l'an neuf," of which La d'Ignolle is a corruption, meaning the mistletoe—the new year.

swered that Julienne was one of his flock, she had willingly left Lizon and he had stolen her. A scream for help from the house was heard and Julienne's father and others rushing in, found her and brought her back. The night of horrors was too much for her; she became a maniac. Lizon, maddened by liquor and the defeat of his plans, in his rage struck the priest in the face and blasphemed everything sacred. A few sprang forward to seize Lizon, but the majority looked on.

Father Gabriel raised his hands and said that Lizon had brought a curse on the place, and caused others, by his bad example, to follow in his footsteps; and he again pronounced the awful edict of excommunication against him. That unless he repented, even in the grave he should have no rest; and all who aided or abetted him in his evil deeds would suffer. Their church would be swept away by the rising waters.

Father Gabriel left for Fort Pontchartrain, and Lizon took every occasion to distribute his vile liquor and to malign the good character of the priest. But somehow nothing seemed to prosper. The season set in wet and stormy, the fruit failed to ripen and was blasted on the trees. The crops were all destroyed and clouds of locusts devoured the young grass. The people murmured among

"Lizon had brought a curse on the place . . . Their church would be swept away by the rising waters."

themselves and looked for the return of the good priest, whose interest in their behalf they had rewarded with ingratitude, and on whose departure disaster had come. One day the old auberge was closed, and it was said that Lizon had died unexpectedly. He was hurriedly placed in a coffin and a grave dug in unconsecrated ground. As the bearers were about to place the coffin in its final resting place, they suddenly felt it grow lighter, whilst out of the grave issued loathsome serpents without number. For many days these occurrences were common gossip. Phantom forms in white could be seen moving about, and those who looked towards Lizon's grave saw it roll and heave, whilst the few follet skipped about in all directions.

A fearful storm set in, lashing the waves into foamy billows mountain high and dashing them against the shore with such force as to sweep over the road. Higher and higher the waters crept, climbing up towards the orchards of fine apples and the stately pears, survivors of the days of "le grand monarch." Closer and closer the angry surf came to the little church; the water had undermined the quicksand beneath it, and with a groan and deafening crash it sank into the mighty element. The people, frightened by the fearful disaster fled in terror to the woods, where they

Artist's conceptual sketch of the home, barn, and cookhouse of the Navarre farm, ca. 1797.
Artwork by Gerry Wykes, courtesy of the Monroe County Historical Commission.

remained through the night. Day dawned peaceably; the habitants returned to their deserted homes, rebuilt their church, and by their prayers and the faithful observance of their duties, removed the curse which rested on L'Anse Creuse.

❦ ❦ ❦

This, then, is one of the early folktales, and there actually appears to be some truth to the legend. As early as 1798, Father Gabriel Richard ministered to the families living up and down the river from Detroit, including those at L'Anse Creuse. In 1808 he recorded a census of his parish as follows:

Ecorse River . . . . 20 families
Rouge River . . . . 30 families
Southwest Detroit. 35 families
Northeast Shores (Grosse Pointe). . . . . . . 100 families
L'Anse Creuse. . . . . 22 families
Clinton River . . . . 22 families
St. Clair River. . . . . 28 families

It was sometime in 1826 (we are not certain of the exact date) that French missionary Father Pierre Dejean erected a small log mission church on the banks of Lake St. Clair in the region known as L'Anse Creuse. The church measured 30 feet by 40 feet and was located at the end of the Rattell farm, property that is now just north of Fourteen Mile Road; the site is today under water some distance from the shore. The little church was named Saint Felicity. Ten years after the church was built the level of the lake rose to an unprecedented height and the building, situated on low ground, was nearly destroyed. The *Michigan Pioneer and Historical Collections* record that:

Although the spring of 1836 was very dry, about the 10th of June the rain commenced falling, and in such abundance that the whole county was flooded . . . This and the succeeding year, 1837, were known as the years when the water in the rivers and great lakes was higher than it had ever been known. Many of the farms bordering on Lake St. Clair were underwater from six inches to two feet.

Although the building was severely damaged, the lake level receded and the local habitants were able to rebuild their little church. In 1851 and 1852 the area experienced another period of heavy rain and high water. Again the church was damaged and again it was rebuilt. Then, in the summer of 1855, the region experienced a rainfall of catastrophic proportions. In June and July of that year nearly two and a half feet of rain fell. Noted historian Silas Farmer recorded in his *History of Detroit* that six feet of rain fell in 1855 (three and a half feet was the normal annual average of the decade). The little church was damaged beyond repair and the adjoining cemetery was completely covered by water. This time the level of the lake did not recede and the habitants were forced to abandon their church and move to higher ground.

Thus, in 1856, the Reverend Francis DeBroux purchased land for the building of a new territorial mission on the west side of the old Lake Shore Road (present-day Jefferson Avenue) near Martin Road in St. Clair Shores, and the church was rebuilt there. Today this is the site of the parish church of St. Gertrude which traces its origin to Saint Felicity, that first mission church of old L'Anse Creuse.

———————— ❦ ————————

EDITOR'S NOTE: Over the years, the exact location of the original mission church and its cemetery was lost and became the subject of much speculation. Various parish priests and parishioners tried to locate the original site but with little success. Then, in the fall of 1995, St. Gertrude associate pastor Reverend Michael B. Ruthenberg located the site some 2,000 feet off shore and with the help of scuba divers from the Dossin Great Lakes Museum pinpointed the location. Further dives were undertaken in the spring of 1996 when a formal archaeological survey and mapping of the site was begun and the exact location of the little mission church and cemetery of old L'Anse Creuse was finally known, and the legend of "The Cursed Village" finally told.

———————— ❦ ————————

SOURCE: Originally published as "The Cursed Village," in *Legends of le Détroit*, Throndike Nourse, 1883.

———————— ❦ ————————

Marie Caroline Watson Hamlin was born in Detroit on February 22, 1850, the daughter of John Watson and Elisabeth Virginia Godfroy. She was married to William Yates Hamlin at SS. Peter and Paul Church on June 13, 1878. Mrs. Hamlin was a regular visitor to Tonnancour and it was here that she "listened to many a tale of the mystic past,"—the legends and folklore of the early French settlers of the Detroit River region. The first edition of her now famous "Legends of le Détroit" was published in 1883.

Theodore Parsons Hall, 1859

Alexandrine Louise Godfroy Hall

Theodore Parsons Hall, 1892

Marianne Navarre Goudet Marantette Godfroy

The Hall Family of "Tonnancour"

by Thomas W. Brunk

"Tonnancour" was the name of the summer estate of Theodore P. Hall and his wife

Alexandrine. Built on the shore of Lake St. Clair in 1880, the home soon became a local

cultural center with visitors like Silas Farmer and Marie Caroline Watson Hamlin.

It is this literary connection that led us to select Tonnancour as the title for this publication.

The story of the Hall family is here told by historian Thomas W. Brunk.

THEODORE PARSONS AND his wife Alexandrine Louise (Godfroy) Hall began building their elaborate sixty-three acre estate called "Tonnancour," on Private Claim 617 facing Lake St. Clair in Grosse Pointe Farms in 1880.[1] This summer home was an elegant wooden Victorian Swiss-chalet style mansion designed by Detroit architect Mortimer L. Smith.[2] Hall's brother Charles S. Hall described the estate in 1896.

Here he [Hall] has laid out a beautiful park filled with fruits and flowers and every imaginable variety of shrubs and trees. In the midst of this paradise of his own creation stands his summer home, from which stretch vistas in every direction through the foliage, and before which is the broad

expanse of the lake, with the tonnage of a continent passing in steady procession, the view intercepted only by the boathouse bedecked with streamers, and the grotto in which stands Ste. Claire gazing out over the waters.[3]

The name "Tonnancour" was taken from the 18th century stone mansion of the same name built by René Godefroy de Tonnancour (1669-1738) on the St. Lawrence River at Trois Rivières, Québec. The exact family relationship between Alexandrine Louise (Godfroy) Hall (1838-1918) and René Godefroy de Tonnancour remains to be explored in a future *Tonnancour* article.

Theodore Parsons Hall, fourth child of Samuel Holden Parsons and Emeline Mehetable (Bulkeley) Hall, was born at Rock Hill, near Hartford, Connecticut on December 15,

---

1   The location is between Moross Road and Provencal Street, at present-day Tonnancour Place.

2   For additional information on Mortimer L. Smith (1840-1896) and his architectural practice see: *Smith, Hinchman & Grylls: 125 Years of Architecture and Engineering 1853-1978* by Thomas J. Holleman and James P. Gallagher. Wayne State University Press for Smith, Hinchman & Grylls Associates, Inc., Detroit, 1978.

3   Charles S. Hall. *Hall Ancestry* (New York and London: G. P. Putnam's Sons. The Kinckerbocker Press, 1896). 432-33.

*Hall Children in 1879: Nathalie Heloise (top center),
Alexandrine Eugenie, Marie Archange Navarre,
and Godfroy Navarre (lower left).*

sity where he was graduated in 1856. He studied law for a year in his brother's law office in Binghamton and worked as an assistant manager of a newspaper for a short time before taking a job with the Central Bank of Brooklyn, New York. Following the bank's suspension in 1857, Hall entered the Wall Street brokerage firm of Thompson Brothers.

Desiring to establish a system of banks in Michigan, Thompson Brothers sent L. E. Clark, son of New York Governor Myron H. Clark, and the twenty-four-year-old Hall to Detroit in the fall of 1858. They organized the State Bank of Michigan on February 1, 1859, with $50,000 capital and Clark as president and Hall as cashier. The Civil War and growing concern over the future of banking, led Hall to resign on August 1, 1861.[4]

Hall received a life appointment as a Commissioner for United States Courts on August 4, 1862. These appointments were made by US Circuit Judges and the commissioners were paid from fees levied.[5] About the same time, he took a position with the Detroit commission house of Voorhees & Company and in 1863 entered the grain commission business on the Detroit Board of Trade.[6] In 1868 he and Rufus W. Gillett established Gillett & Hall, a grain-shipping partnership with an office at 5 Chamber of Commerce Building.[7] Hall retired from active business in 1888 to pursue his interests in literature, publishing, agriculture, his summer home "Tonnancour," and to travel.[8]

He was a member of the Detroit Young Men's Society and served as its president in 1877–78. A member of the Detroit Club, Hall was affectionately called the "Sage of Tonnancour." Hall was Democrat, "but very independent in his political action."[9]

Theodore Parsons Hall was married in the Jefferson Avenue home of Reverend Bishop Lefevre at Detroit on 11 January 1860 to Alexandrine Louise Godfroy. Alexandrine, a daughter of the Honorable Pierre and Marianne Navarre (Goudet Marantette) Godfroy[10], was born on the

1835. Two years later the family settled at Binghamton, New York where Theodore attended the Binghamton Academy and, later, the private school of Dr. T. Romeyn Beck in Albany. In 1852 Theodore attended Yale Univer-

---

4 Farmer, Silas. *History of Detroit and Wayne County and Early Michigan.* (Detroit: Silas Farmer & Co., 1890; reprint, Detroit: Gale Research Company, 1969), 176 (page references are to reprint edition). The bank was located on the southwest corner of Jefferson Avenue and Griswold Street.

5 Farmer, 176

6 The Board of Trade was organized in 1856 and incorporated in 1863. It was comprised of all branches of business, but with the enormous harvests of 1877 and 1878, grain and produce assumed dominance. Richard Edwards, ed., *Industries of Michigan, City of Detroit* (New York and Chicago: Historical Publishing Co., 1880), 63-71.

7 R. W. Gillett served as vice president of the Board of Trade in 1867 and president in 1870. Hall served as vice president in 1872. *Industries of Michigan.* 63.

8 *Hall Ancestry.* 432 and Albert Nelson Marquis, ed., *Book of Detroiters* Chicago: (A. N. Marquis & Company, 1908), 204.

9 *Hall Ancestry.* 434

10 Pierre Godfroy (15 June 1797 – 21 May 1848) was the son of Jacques Gabriel and Thérèse Douaire de Bondy Godfroy. Mac Cabe's 1837 Detroit Directory lists "Godefroy Peter, agriculturalist, Springwells," on page 56, and on page 95 he is listed among the wardens of St. Ann's Cathedral on Larned Street. He married Marianne Navarre Goudet Marantette (8 April 1800 – 19 November 1878), daughter of Dominique Goudet and Marie Louise Archange Navarre Marantette, in 1821. According to Silas Farmer, Godefroy Avenue was named for Peter Godfroy (sic) in 1864 (941) and Marantette Street was named for Mrs. Peter Godfroy (sic) in 1868 (943).

Godfroy Navarre Hall

Nathalie Heloise Hall

Marie Stella Holden Hall (left) and Josephine Emeline Hall.

Marie Archange Navarre Hall

Madeleine Macomb Hall

Jesuit College where their first child was born. The following year they moved to Elizabeth Street West where they remained until 1869 when they moved to 170 East Congress. In 1880, Hall purchased the property fronting on Lake St. Clair and began building their summer home "Tonnancour." Here they spent subsequent summers developing the estate. During the winter months, the family occupied various quarters in the city, sometimes at the Hotel Cadillac or a home on Jefferson Avenue. In their later years, the Halls wintered in Florida or on the Pacific coast.

The Hall children were educated in private Catholic schools. Their formal education was enhanced with Hall's literary interests and extensive family travels. Hall took his children to visit the homes of their Revolutionary War ancestors in Connecticut and Massachusetts, as well as those of their French ancestors at Trois Rivières, Québec. They visited the Centennial Exposition of 1876 at Philadelphia and in 1879 Hall, his wife and two eldest daughters, Marie and Josephine, traveled in Europe for six months. Josephine remained in Paris at Miss Mason's Pension to complete her formal education.

Their union produced ten children, one of which died at birth.

Marie Stella Holden Hall
(26 December 1860, Detroit–13 April 1907, Grosse Pointe Farms)married William Toone St. Auburn (25 March 1852, London, England–15 April 1905, Detroit) on 2 January 1880.

Josephine Emeline Hall
(5 June 1862, Detroit – 9 December 1941) married Lieutenant Robert J. Crombie Irvine (17 July 1851, St. Johns, NB–7 May 1910) on 10 February 1886 in her parents' Jefferson Avenue home.

Samuel Holden Parsons Hall
(30 June 1864, Detroit–15 December 1864, Detroit).

Nathalie Heloise Hall
(1 June 1866, Detroit–6 November 1945, New York) married James Lee Scott (9 January 1856. Ballston Spa, New York) on 27 October 1886 at the rectory adjoining Church of St. Paul, Grosse Pointe Farms.

Corinne Alexandrine Hall
(11 February 1868, Detroit–2 February 1869, Detroit).

Alexandrine Eugenie Hall
(4 December 1869, Detroit–17 February 1892, Detroit).

Pierre Godfroy Farm at the foot of 14th street in Springwells Township, near Detroit on 11 May 1838.[11] Pierre Godfroy served as Springwells Township supervisor 1827–1830 and 1837–40, a Wayne County commissioner in 1842, and in the state legislature in 1843.[12]

Alexandrine attended a private school near her home until age 12 when she was sent to Miss Scott's school in Detroit. Two years later attended the newly opened boarding school of the Ladies of the Sacred Heart on Jefferson Avenue where she was the first boarder. Her studies at Sacred Heart were conducted mostly in French. In 1854, sixteen-year-old Alexandrine was sent to the Academy of the Visitation at Georgetown, DC where she remained for one year. Due to "failing health," she spent the following year at Mt. Sales near Baltimore, a school operated by the same religious order.

The Halls boarded the winter of 1860 at the Russell House Hotel and in the spring moved into Mrs. Cole's furnished house on Larned Street. In the fall of 1860, they rented the Lyons' house on Jefferson Avenue opposite the

---

[11] Her tombstone in Mt. Elliott Cemetery, Detroit has the birthdate of May 4, 1836. The cemetery's burial plot ledger indicates that she was 82 years old when buried on November 8, 1918 which would make her birth year 1836. However, the 1892 and 1896 genealogies cite her birthdate as May 11, 1838. The Pierre Godfroy Farm is Private Claim 726, formerly the Angelique Cicot Farm.

[12] I am indebted to Peter W. Buchanan, Director of Mt. Elliott Cemetery, who kindly showed me the Hall-Godfroy burial plot, cemetery records, and *The History of Mt. Elliott Cemetery*, an unpublished manuscript written by Fern Freeman, with information on Pierre Godfroy on pages 28-29.

"Tonnancour." *Courtesy of the Burton Historical Collections, Detroit Public Library.*

"Marie's Room."
Courtesy of the Grosse Pointe Historical Society

"An Interesting Book."
Courtesy of the Grosse Pointe Historical Society.

Hallway. *Courtesy of the Grosse Pointe Historical Society.*

Dining room.
Courtesy of the Grosse Pointe Historical Society.

A Protest from the Camera Victims to the Camera Fiend

by Theodore Parsons Hall

The Kodak's come to Tonnancour, and with it days of woe.
We do our best to stand it, we've nowhere else to go.
And so we try to bear it, and pray it's but a phase,
For Marie – little Marie Hall – has caught the camera craze.

We've acid in our finger nails, and acid everywhere,
We find it in our tooth mugs, I tell you it is rare.
We try to stand this state of things, and pray it's but a phase,
For Marie – little Marie Hall – has caught the camera craze.

We see ourselves in attitudes no moral ever struck,
With leer distorted features, having our pictures took.
We try to take this sweetly, we hope it is a phase,
For Marie – little Marie Hall – has caught the camera craze.

Swearing is the fashion since Kodaks entered in,
Sunlight's at a premium, a rainy day's a sin,
For then she can't print pictures, oh, may this be a phase,
For Marie – little Marie Hall – has caught the camera craze.

We cannot take our morning bath, for photos in the tub,
Our talk is all of focussing and lens, and now, the rub is
Should this last? But no, it can't, oh, may this be a phase,
For Marie – little Marie Hall – has caught the camera craze.

Marie Archange Navarre Hall

(7 September 1872, Detroit – 30 November 1961, Detroit); 1st marriage to Lieutenant Frederick William Füger (21 February 1869, David's Island, New York – 26 November 1915, at Tonnancour, Grosse Pointe Farms) on 28 June 1899 by Reverend Bishop Foley at the Church of St. Paul, Grosse Pointe Farms; 2nd marriage to Claude Edmund Delbos (?– 27 January 1949) on 15 November 1924.

Godfroy Navarre Hall

(31 May 1877, Detroit – 16 February 1885, Detroit).

Madeleine Macomb Hall

(21 July 1881 at Tonnancour, Grosse Pointe Farms – 2 January 1902, Washington, D.C.).

Theodore Parsons Hall died of heart failure on January 3, 1909, about an hour after Father Nacey received him into the Catholic church.[13] Alexandrine Hall continued to live at "Tonnancour" until it was severely damaged by fire and demolished in 1914. Following the fire, she moved to 162 Joseph Campau, Detroit until the residence at 383 Lake Shore Road was completed. This house was later the home of Nathalie Hall Scott. Marie Hall Füger and her husband erected a house 395 Lake Shore Road in 1914 designed by Washington, DC, architect Edward W. Donn, now 55 Tonnancour Place. Josephine Hall Irvine built her house at 403 Lake Shore Road in 1915. Alexandrine Louise Godfroy Hall died on 20 August 1918 and was laid to rest with her husband, family and ancestors in Mt. Elliott Cemetery.[14]

I am grateful to several individuals who have assisted my research for this essay. Mrs. Alexander Ingersoll Lewis, Jr., of Lutherville, Maryland and Mrs. Pierre G. Füger of Grosse Pointe Farms, Michigan kindly provided family background and generously shared their family photographs for this publication; Marie Phelan Füger of Grand Rapids, Michigan made available her extensive genealogical research, photograph of Madeleine Macomb Hall, and a copy of the poem by Theodore Parsons Hall; and Peter W. Buchanan, Director of Mt. Elliott Cemetery, Detroit, showed me the Godfroy-Hall cemetery monuments and shared historical data from cemetery records. The Burton Historical Collections, Detroit Public Library, has provided the exterior view of "Tonnancour." The Grosse Pointe Historical Society graciously provided interior images of "Tonnancour " taken by little Marie Hall.

SELECTED BIBLIOGRAPHY

Farmer, Silas. *History of Detroit and Wayne County and Early Michigan.* Detroit: Silas Farmer & Co., 1890; reprint, Detroit: Gale Research Company, 1969.

Freeman, Fern. *A History of Mt. Elliott Cemetery.* Detroit: 1981, TMs.

Hall, Theodore P. *Family Records of Theodore Parsons Hall and Alexandrine Louise Godfroy of "Tonnancour," Grosse Pointe near Detroit.* Detroit: privately printed by Wm. C. Heath, 1892.

Hall, Theodore P. *Genealogical Notes Relating to the Families of Hon. Lyman Hall of Georgia, Hon. Samuel Holden Parsons Hall of Binghamton, NY, Hon. Nathan Kelsey Hall of Buffalo, NY.* Albany, NY: privately printed by Joel Munsell's Sons, 1886.

Hall, Charles S. *Hall Ancestry.* New York and London: G. P. Putnam's Sons, The Knickerbocker Press, 1896.

Marquis, Albert Nelson, ed. *The Book of Detroiters.* Chicago: A. N. Marquis & Company, 1908.

Thomas W. Brunk, an art historian and architectural historian, is completing his doctoral dissertation, The Ceramic Connoisseurship of Charles Lang Freer, *at The Union Institute in Cincinnati. Mr. Brunk has lectured and published extensively on Detroit history and architecture. He received a Master of Arts degree in art history and architectural history from Norwich University. His undergraduate work was in archival administration and art history at the University of Paris and Wayne State University.*

---

[13] Fern Freeman. A History of Mt. Elliott Cemetery. (Detroit, 1981), TMs 29.

[14] Section B, lots 15, 16, 17 and 18. These four lots were purchased on April 2, 1866 for $500 (purchase #76) by Marianne Navarre Goudet Marantette Godfroy. Interestingly, she is listed as "Mary Ann Godfroy" and her signature reads the same. Each lot measures 15 x 20 feet. Mrs. Godfroy arranged to have other family members reinterred in these lots from the older section of Mt. Elliott Cemetery or other cemeteries. It seems that she was the first family member to be directly buried in the plot. Her burial was November 22, 1878.

Early Days in Grosse Pointe

by Friend Palmer

Friend Palmer was one of the city's most prominent citizens in late-nineteenth-century Detroit. The General, as he was called by his family and friends, kept a diary and at the urging of his cousin Senator Thomas W. Palmer wrote out his reminiscences as articles for the Detroit Free Press. *These articles were later gathered together in book form and published after his death in 1897. Included in this book are Palmer's reminiscences of people and places in early Grosse Pointe.*

THE "GRAND MARAIS," what a garden it has become! A few years yet, and it will be hard to realize (and even now it is), that the present broad fields of corn and waving grain, and the splendid grounds and buildings of the Blue Ribbon race track were in the early days, and not so very remote either, one vast swamp or quagmire, covered with a most luxuriant growth of marsh grass and bull-rushes, the home of the muskrat and all kinds of horrid snakes.

> "The bullfrog with his croaking harsh,
> And the fat muskrat, haunt the marsh;
> The wild duck floats among the reeds."

I have often been through it in its wildest state, have many times skirted its borders on the river to Windmill Point, and when a little more than a year ago, I gazed over the same country from my seat in the electric car, it was hard to believe the evidence of my senses. I have been up along the Grosse Pointe road often while this change has been going on, but it never struck me so forcibly as it did the time of which I speak.

In those days Windmill Point, with its roofless stone tower slowly falling to decay, was always an object of great interest to me. The Point, as now, was quite a high piece of ground, and had the same stunted apple orchard. Why the mill was abandoned I never knew, nor who was the builder of it. I think it has now entirely disappeared.

Just this side of the Country Club, on the river bank, lived Henry Hudson — "Old Hudson" everyone called him. He and his family were considered for some reason an unsavory lot, and were known far and wide through this section of the country. Besides Hudson and wife there were three or four boys. They were stalwarts all, parents and the boys, and when the sheriff or any of his deputies had occasion to visit their premises in their line of duty, they went prepared, for they were fully aware that they might meet with trouble. On one occasion Sheriff Wilson had a warrant for Hudson for some alleged misdeed. He went up to the house to serve it. Mrs. Hudson saw him coming, and divining his mission, she at once provided herself with a large basin of scalding water and stationed herself behind the open front door, so she could give it to him good and plenty. The sheriff fortunately discovered the enemy and her means of defense through the crack of the door, and struck the basin from her hands with the heavy but of his riding whip, spilling its scalding contents over her bare feet. The outcome tickled the officer immensely. Mrs. Hudson was a masculine looking woman, marked with smallpox. She wore a broad-brimmed straw hat, winter and summer, and out of doors when the weather demanded it, a sailor's heavy sea jacket.

At the French dances the boys were most always on hand, and almost sure to get into a muss of some kind before the party was over. One occasion I call to mind. The dance was given at a house on Jefferson Avenue, just above the present water works. About the usual number and quality of people were on hand, as were two of the Hudson boys, also some five or six youngsters from the city, myself among the number. The dance proceeded merrily for quite a while, and everything bid fair for an enjoyable, peaceable party. But along in the small hours it became apparent that some of the party had partaken quite liberally of liquid refreshments, so much so that it made them inclined to be ugly, particularly the two Hudson boys, and they appeared to be spoiling for a muss of some kind. The opportunity soon came. John Demas, whom very many will remember, was present on this occasion, and as usual was very busy enjoying himself. He was quite a favorite among the French girls, and his attentions were eagerly sought. It seems that John had been during the evening more than polite to the elder Hudson's "fancies," a young Grosse Pointe beauty. This angered Hudson to that degree that he determined to put a stop to it, and he did. A dance was called, the couples including Demas and his partner (Hudson's girl), and were in their places on the floor; the music and everything was ready and waiting for the "caller," when in rushed Hudson, nothing on but pants and shirt (it was in summer), a short iron bar in his hand and crazed with drink. He at once proceeded to stampede the party; pell mell, dancers, music and spectators hustled for

Friend Palmer

the doors and windows, any way to get out. Hudson, after they were all out, proceeded with his bar of iron to smash the furniture in the room, knock all the plastering off the walls and put out the lights, and broke up the party completely. I never learned the outcome of the matter. I presume, though, that John Demas, being the better man, came out first best.

What finally became of the Hudson family I never knew. I have, however, one pleasant remembrance of them. Adjoining their homestead was a fine cherry orchard, and I have often visited it during the season. Visitors for cherries were always welcome, whether they brought the price or not, showing that they were not so bad as they were painted. A Mr. Fisher succeeded them. I think he bought the Hudson property. He opened a roadhouse there, and "Fisher's" was known as a house of entertainment for years and years. Who have not danced at "Fisher's," dined and otherwise enjoyed themselves under the hospitable roof?

Fisher in the early thirties was a grocery merchant on lower Woodward Avenue. He married a daughter of Coon Ten Eyck, of Dearborn, then sheriff of Wayne County. Directly after his marriage he disposed of his grocery business in the city and moved to Grosse Pointe. Mrs. Fisher carried on the business quite successfully at the Pointe for many years after her husband's death.

I knew George Moran very well and who did not know George Moran? His place on the bank of Lake St. Clair, a mile or so above Fisher's, was a welcome spot to all journeying in that direction, besides those that made it their special business to call on George. He was full of reminiscences of the early days, and took special delight in relating them. He married a daughter of the adopted son of Commodore Grant, who commanded the British government vessels on the lakes before the surrender of the country to the United States in 1796 under the Jay treaty, and he once owned the farm where George lived. The commodore died there about 1813. The homestead is there yet, or was a few years ago. It stood directly opposite Moran's place, a short distance back from the road and had a large pine or evergreen tree in front of it. The late Judge Witherell has this to say of the adopted son:

The first distinct recollection that he (Grant) has of his childhood is that he was a captive boy about three years old among a wandering band of Chippewa warriors. Whence he came, his name or lineage he never knew. The Indians had brought him to Detroit and while roaming about the street, the little captive attracted the attention of the lady of the late Commodore Grant. He was a kind-hearted old sailor, and his wife was one of the excellent of the earth. As they were riding out one day, she discovered the little blue-eyed prisoner among the savages, and his condition aroused all the sympathies of a mother's heart. She pointed him out to her husband, and asked him to buy the boy. The old tar was ever ready when a good deed was to be done. So, dismounting from his carriage, he went among the Indians, and finding the owner, he gave him $100 for the little Che-mo-ka-mun, and carried him home, giving him his own name, John Grant. The little captive was a great favorite of the commodore, who raised him to manhood, and he well repaid the kindness shown him by his unremitting care and attention to the interests of his benefactor. Captain Grant, as he grew up to manhood, understood that he was a native of the United States, and never for a moment wavered in his allegiance, though as the adopted son of a British officer, it might have been supposed that he would have acted differently.

The captain was alive in 1854.

❦ ❦ ❦

Reynard Creek (Fox Run, a short distance above Connor's Creek, and where the Grosse Pointe Road crosses), about five miles from the city, was the turning point in the supremacy of some of the Indian tribes. Great numbers were slain in the battle, and it is believed the vast number of human bones found in the fields of George Moran, of Grosse Pointe, are the remains of some who fell in the fight. They are evidently of great age and some have the mark of the spike of the war club in their skulls. Mr. Moran had quite a collection of these relics, also rusty knives and tomahawks, as well as quite a number of small tomahawks measuring about four inches, wrought out of native copper. They give quite conclusive evidence that the Aborigines had a knowledge of the copper deposits in the Lake Superior regions, and the skill to mine the mineral and to fashion it into various articles of use.

❦ ❦ ❦

Commander Alexander Grant married, in 1774, Thérèse, daughter of Chas. Barthe and Marie Thérèse Campau. He was of the clan of Grants, of Glenmoriston, Scotland. He entered the navy at an early age, but resigned in 1757 to join a Highland regiment raised for the army of General Amherst in America. In 1759 he reached Lake Champlain. General Amherst, desiring able officers for his fleet on the lake, commissioned Lieutenant Grant to the command of a sloop of sixteen guns. After the conquest of Canada, Grant was ordered to Lakes Erie and Ontario. Detroit was then an English garrison, and it was here that he met his fate in Thérèse Barthe. He built his castle, as it was called at Grosse Pointe (its site is at present occupied by T. P. Hall's summer residence, "Tonnancour.") It was a place noted for the courtesy of its host, and his open, generous hospitality. Tecumseh and his warriors were frequent guests at the Grant castle. In 1805 the commodore belonged to the executive council of Upper Canada. In a letter to his brother "Alpine," dated from York (Toronto), July 5, 1811, he says:

My duty where my naval command requires me is such a distance from here that I cannot travel in the winter when the legislature meets, but I come down at my ease in the summer and take some sittings in the council. A gentleman who has served his country upwards of fifty-five years requires some indulgence and my superiors allow it to me.

He was a man of commanding presence, a great favorite and a good officer. He had ten daughters who are represented by the English-Canadian families of Wrights, Robinsons, Dickinsons, Woods, Duffs, Gilkersons, Millers, Jacobs and Richardsons. Mr. Jasper Gilkerson, of Brantford, has been in charge of the Indians in Canada for many years. So faithful has he been to his charge that any promise made to the Indians by him has always been kept by the government. A worthy representative of his grandfather, Commodore Grant, who, when administrator, with the power of giving free grants of land, never granted any to his family or their connections.

❦ ❦ ❦

Mr. Provencal, a French gentleman, owned a farm a short distance above George Moran's. He was one of the old school, and of commanding presence. Presume many will remember him.

❦ ❦ ❦

I have omitted thus far the "Church farm," so-called, this side of the Cook farm. I think Beller's garden is a portion of it. I do not call to mind the name of the original owner (I think the Chenes claimed some ownership), but I well remember the small Catholic church that stood on the bank of the river above Beller's and just this side of the late Levi Dolson's tannery. It was called St. Phillippe's. "When the rays of morning creep down the gray spire of St. Phillippe's and cast its shadow o'er the way, just at the foot of Grand Marias, the wooden cock that at its peak stood opening wide his gilded beak." Also the St. Phillippe's college for boys, adjoining the church. This school was quite

Residence of George Sunderland, Grosse Point Tp., Wayne Co., Michigan.

celebrated in its day, and many scions of our first families used to attend it. There were some fine French pear trees on this farm, and they were included in the Beller property. They remained of vigorous, sturdy growth until quite recently, but their constant use as hitching posts gradually killed them and they went the way nearly all their kind have gone in the past few years.

Next this side of the residence of Abraham Cook (Cook farm), between it and St. Phillippe's, lived one of the Chapoton families. There were sons and daughters, but their personalities have faded from my memory. The only thing in relation to them that I remember is that they kept tavern, as did Peter Van Avery.

Somewhere between Connor's Creek and Hudson's (Fisher's) lived the McQueens. Along in the early thirties, our hired man and myself used every fall to make excursions in a two-horse wagon to Grosse Pointe, and Milk River points, exchanging Jackson ware, that my uncle turned out at his pottery, where is now West park, for apples, cider, potatoes, and other farm products. These trips usually occupied two or three days' time. We were welcome guests, wherever night overtook us. One night, I remember, caught us at McQueen's. It is the only all night stopping place that I do recall, and the reason that it remains in memory, arises, I presume, from the fact that during the night there was quite a fall of snow, the first of the season, and in the morning the ground was covered to the depth of nearly two inches. That night we had bargained for a quantity of apples,

which we were to gather ourselves. The orchard was located in front of the house, between it, the road, and the river, and it is the gathering of those apples I never can forget, nor the McQueen's.

———————— ❦ ————————

SOURCE: *Early Days in Detroit*. Detroit: Hunt and June, 1906.

———————— ❦ ————————

Friend Palmer was born in New York in 1820 and came to Detroit at an early age. His father was a soldier in Detroit and an 1812 veteran. Palmer derived his local history knowledge from the eyewitnesses that gathered around the Palmer hearth. He graduated from the University of Michigan when it was located in Detroit at Larned and Bates streets and went into the bookbinding business. During the Civil War he was Assistant and finally Quartermaster General of the State of Michigan, a post he held until 1871. Palmer then went into the real estate business before finally retiring to live with his cousin, Senator Thomas W. Palmer. Friend Palmer kept a log, or diary, for many years of the comings and goings in the Palmer household. These logs make up the story of Detroit society at the turn of the century and served as the basis for his book Early Days in Detroit.

The Wardwell House:
A LEGACY OF OLD GROSSE POINTE

by Henry Heatley

The oldest brick structure in Grosse Pointe is the Wardwell House. Located on Jefferson

Avenue between Audubon Road and Three Mile Drive, this building's story has long been

shrouded in folklore. Following extensive research, Henry Heatley wrote and published this

article. Mr. Heatley's research also provided the necessary documentation for the house to be

listed on the state register of historic sites, and for the erection of a Michigan historical marker.

THE WARDWELL HOUSE is an exceptional cultural resource worthy of preservation for the benefit of future generations. It is the oldest extant brick house and the third oldest house in the Grosse Pointes.[1] The Wardwell House is one of the few structures that reflects the political, economic, and social forces that transformed Grosse Pointe from a sleepy farming community to a bustling suburb of industrial Detroit. Despite its importance, the house has been the subject of at least forty-five years of often totally erroneous speculation about its age and builders.

The Wardwell House, located at 16109 East Jefferson, Grosse Pointe Park, was named after Mrs. Helen Wardwell, nee Russel, who in 1912 moved into it as the bride of Mr. Harold Wardwell.[2] She resided there until her death in 1976. Mr. Wardwell had died in 1962. It is the only early structure on the French ribbon farm originally known as Private Claim 391 (P.C. 391).[3]

---

1 The two older houses, both built of clapboard, are the Cadieux House located at 16939 E. Jefferson, City of Grosse Pointe, and the Provençal House at 376 Kercheval, Grosse Pointe Farms.

2 The earliest recorded number, which antedated the 1920/21 city-wide number change was 3931. Address Directory (cross-reference) Listing. Burton Historical Collection, Detroit Public Library (hereafter cited BHC).

3 *Belden Atlas of Wayne County, Michigan.* Gale (Detroit, 1967), p. 7.

Interest in the house began in 1936 with its examination by a commission from the Historic American Buildings Survey. The Survey concluded that it was built "prior to 1860," and this dating was registered with the Library of Congress.[4] Dr. Milo Quaife, then head of the Burton Historical Collection, became involved in 1936, but he concluded that the necessary documentary records were unavailable to permit more exact dating. Henry Ford, however, had sufficient confidence in the Survey's dating that he offered to buy the house and rebuild it in Greenfield Village as a showplace. Harold Wardwell refused to sell.[5]

The confusion in dating resulted from three sources. First, a French coin, dated 1789, was found in a wall cavity; thus, it has been assumed that the wall must have been built about the same period. Second, several major alterations, which, among other things, tripled the size and floor space of the house, suggest that the original structure was quite old. Third, misinterpretation and failure to consult the extant land records have abetted confusion.[6]

A persistent and incorrect folklore has also misled investigators.[7] One belief is that the house was built in the late 1700s or very early 1800s. Another view holds that the house was formerly a log cabin that was subsequently bricked over. The most popular view is that the bricks to build the house were brought from France in about 1780, as ballast for sailing ships.

Such notions are mere myth. The dating is far too early, as the remainder of this essay will demonstrate. Moreover, the bricks used in the Wardwell House were typical of those purchased in mid-nineteenth century Detroit and

Wardwell House reflects the political, economic, and social forces that transformed Grosse Pointe from a sleepy farming community to a bustling suburb of industrial Detroit.

available in brick clay deposits near the house.[8] The same type and dimension of brick appears in the Moross House which was built between 1845-1850 and is also located on East Jefferson Avenue. These bricks were taken from kilns located at Chene and Canfield Streets. There was a local clay deposit and kiln at the foot of Fisher Road on the Rose Terrace or the Grosse Pointe Memorial Church grounds by about 1835.[9] It was from this source that Merritt Fisher, a merchant, built his three-story brick hotel on that site about 1850. Moreover, the enormous physical problems and costs associated with portaging bricks from France make it unlikely that the Wardwell House bricks were shipped to Detroit.[10]

In order to date the Wardwell House it is essential to understand the geology of the area. The geological make-up of the region effected land reclamation schemes which, in turn, effected the location and timing of home building. The land surface undulates along the Emmet Moraine which follows the Lake St. Clair shoreline. The crest of the Moraine rises 620 feet, near the center of the township, or about 45 feet above lake level. Drainage flows naturally to the southwest by Fox Creek and to the northeast by the Milk River which empties into Lake St. Clair in the vicinity of Gaulker Pointe. Much of the land close by the site of the Wardwell House was marsh in the last century. Later, however, this area was reclaimed.[11]

The ribbon farm system planned by the early settlers for the Detroit vicinity is peculiar to southeastern Michigan. This system of land parcelling nicely fitted the geology of the area. It provided ease of approach from the lake and

---

4 Photocopies of correspondence and miscellaneous articles and clippings were kindly provided by Mr. John Wardwell of Midland, Michigan, son of the late senior Wardwells.

5 *Detroit Free Press*, 1 September 1963.

6 Deed registry and tract index is land history only in the legal sense; neither directly reflects building construction or other cultural uses of land.

7 *Detroit Free Press*, 27 May, 1978, p. 1B; *Grosse Pointe News*, 11 Oct. 1979, p. 1, 1 Jan. 1948; *The Grosse Pointer*, ca. 1965.

8 Silas Farmer, *History of Detroit and Wayne County and Early Michigan*. (Detroit, 1890), 2:4, 802.

9 *Hubbard Atlas of Wayne County, Michigan, 1818-1841*, BHC. A date as early as 1818 might be questionable, but records at the Burton Historical Collection state that Bela Hubbard copied this map from Land Office records between 1838 and 1841.

10 From an unpublished paper by Mrs. Charlotte Giltner of Renaud Rd., Grosse Pointe Shores, Michigan, dated 18 Feb. 1978. Mrs. Giltner has been involved with genealogical work and local history. Written from a systematic approach utilizing genealogical and other data, the paper tries to show how unrealistic a late eighteenth or early nineteenth century date for the house is. While it was not her intent to actually document the house, if the author had had access to the extant land records she could have more fully developed and proven her position.

11 W. H. Sherzer, *Geological Report on Wayne County*. (Lansing, 1913), pp. 295-297.

river, easy access to water for transportation, and equitable distribution of the better (and poorer) land, and relative ease of defense. The course of the later roads, private lanes, and other access routes were determined in large part by the long axial lines which constituted the borders of the private claims.[12]

In the early eighteenth century, a windmill was reportedly erected on a parcel of land extending into Lake St. Clair at the foot of what is now Lakepointe Avenue. This particular land configuration constituted a pronounced peninsula, and during an early period was often called Presque Isle.[13] The names Grosse Pointe and Windmill Pointe derived their origins from this land form. The windmill was in operation until about 1800, but at this early date it served a grist mill function only. Since it appears on some of the late maps, it must have been replaced or rebuilt and may well have served a drainage function. By 1870 clay dykes were built and a drainage canal constructed 100 feet from, and parallel to, the lake front. A pumping station was erected to drain the marsh. The station was located at the foot of what is now Audubon Road.[14]

In about 1880, William Moran, descendant of the old Detroit Moran lineage, formed a partnership with his cousin, Charles, to promote a real estate venture.[15] The Morans, acting under the name Windmill Pointe Development Company, filled in the Grand Marais with rubbish from Detroit and with dirt dredged from the river.[16] As a result, the once distinct peninsula was virtually obliterated. Obviously, a two-story "triple brick" house, with a full basement, could not have been built in the 1830s or before on land this close to Lake St. Clair. It was too swampy; the weight of the house would have caused foundation problems and excessive settling.

Wayne County was organized in August of 1796,[17] but Grosse Point Township, comprised of the Old Grosse Pointe and Grand Marais, did not become a legal entity until March of 1848. Formerly the area was part of the District of Hamtramck, which accounted for most of the land east of Detroit and north to the Base Line.

Grosse Pointe during the first-half of the nineteenth century was remote from Detroit. Some areas were not long removed from a true frontier condition, and the dwellings therein were of either round or squared logs, or of studded walls with planked or clapboard siding. They were usually of one level, with a field stone fireplace and chimney at one or both ends, and a subterranean cellar. At that time, no dwelling, except in Detroit, could have been of the magnitude of the Wardwell House. The Detroit hinterlands of this period have been described as being an unbroken series of swamps, bogs, and sand barrens unfit for cultivation. Further, Detroit residents seldom, if ever, penetrated more than five miles into the interior.[18] Aside from the old river road, later to become known as the Grosse Pointe Road before being renamed Jefferson Avenue, the only other routes heading in an easterly or northeasterly direction were the Ft. Gratiot Road and the Moravian Road, which was reputedly in use since about 1782.[19] The route of the Moravian Road is not known, but it began at the Conner's Creek settlement and apparently traversed the northern parts of Grosse Pointe Township on its route to the Moravian Village at the settlement on the River Huron, today known as the Clinton River, outside Mt. Clemens.[20] Most travel, therefore, was by water. Only gradually did the evolving street network within Detroit extend to other settlements.[21] The Plank Road Act in 1848 permitted the Grosse Pointe Road to extend eastward by nine miles from Detroit. It frequently washed out during the spring run-off when the drainage ditches discharged their great volumes of water into the then overflowing Conner's and Fox creeks. Nonetheless, the road was a distinct improvement; prior to the 1848 Act a round trip from Detroit to the Milk River took a full day to complete. The stage line, which began at the Steamboat Hotel in Detroit and skirted around the Grand Marais, took at least two days to reach the settlement that is now Mt. Clemens. Only with the creation of a township political structure and a direct and improved travel link with Detroit would a building like the Wardwell House be likely to be built.

The property abstract accounts of the land on which the Wardwell House sits casts further doubts on the early dates assigned to its construction.[22] The earliest surviving entry for the land upon which the Wardwell House sits reveals that Isidore Moran was the owner.

1. NICHOLAS PATENAUDE, and MARIE JOSETTE, his wife, with ISIDORE MORIN, for himself and PIERRE MORIN CHARLES MORIN and LOUIS MORIN his brothers, and GENEVIEVE, his sister, authorized by her husband IGNACE PARRE.
Volume 2 Deeds, page 68.
Agreement
Dated October 22nd, 1803

Consideration 20 bushel of grain per year during the life of Marie Josette Patenaude, except the 1st year.

Conveys a farm or plantation in the District of Hamtramck, County of Wayne, and Territory of Indiana, consisting of 3 arpents in front, and 40 in depth, bounded on the upper end by Petit Marsac, and on the lower end by Joseph Tremble, which farm or plantation formerly belonged to J. Bte. Bodin dit Benoit, first husband of said Marie Josette, and said Marie Josette by her marriage contract with the late Isidore Morin, her second husband, dated January 11th, 1772, by mutual consent, gave him said land if he outlived her without living children, or to the children then living, if any after his decease, and in pursuance of said contract the said Isidore Morin, his brother and sister, are now heirs to 1/2 of said land on account of the death of their father, said Marie

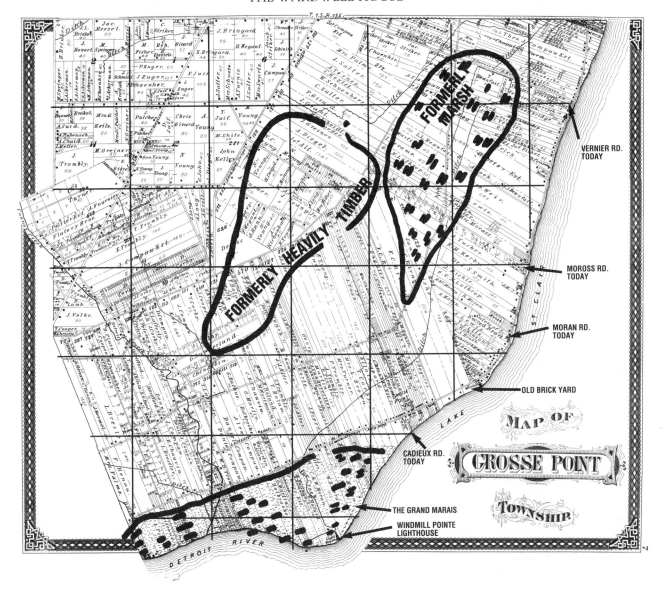

An 1876 map of Grosse Pointe Township. *The hatched areas indicate former marsh or swamp.*

12 *Belden Atlas*, pp. 7, 50-51.

13 Ibid. P. McNiff, *Plan of the Settlement at Detroit, 1796; Hubbard Atlas*, BHC; *Hancock Atlas of Wayne County, Michigan* (Detroit, 1854).

14 *Grosse Pointe Guide* (n.p., n.d.) This work is a more or less informal profile of the Grosse Pointe of some years ago. It consists of a compilation from several sources and authors, and outlines some of the social, political, and economic structures and mechanisms which were extant in the area. It also contains some historical data, some of which is very informative, some of these data consist of oral histories from informants who have since died. It is especially useful for historical data on roads, road houses, and transport.

The *Guide* is not especially well indexed, some of the page number are in error as they relate to the index, and many of the pages have more than one number inscribed on them, indicating the material was taken from another source, which is not always cited. The *Guide* is reposited in the Grosse Pointe Library, 10 Kercheval, Grosse Pointe Farms.

15 Ibid, p. 284.

16 *Detroit Saturday Night*, n.d.

17 Farmer, *History of Detroit*, 2: chp. 20.

18 *Michigan Pioneer and Historical Collections*, 5:533.

19 McNiff map, BHC.

20 Farmer, *History of Detroit*, 2:550-51.

21 Ibid, Chp. 87.

22 Abstract of title to the described premises situated in the City of Detroit, County of Wayne, State of Michigan to wit; Lot 766 of Henry Russel's Three Mile Drive Subdivision #1. In possession of the author.

Josette was married a third time to Nicholas Patenaude without having made any inventory and without accounting to said Isidore Morin, his brothers and sister, for the real and personal property in existence at the time of decease of said Isidore Morin, their father. These presents are made to avoid any and all difficulties in regard to said estate.

Said grantees to protect grantors against all claims.

Acknowledged October 22nd, 1803.
Recorded October 29th, 1803.

The seemingly unusual system of property transfer, whereby a married couple owned all property in common, was in fact quite common under old French custom. At the death of one, therefore, the surviving spouse automatically acquired full control of any and all assets.[23] In this instance, there were four children, including a junior Isidore, presumably the first born, who were heirs to half of the property. It is unclear, subsequent to their mother's third marriage, what the "without accounting" clause means and what other understandings were agreed upon.

When the property was sold in 1808, Isidore apparently acquired all other interests to the land. There was no reference to Bodin, Benoit, Morin, or Patenaude as possessing property in the vicinity of P.C. 391; nor is there a "Bodin dit Benoit" listed in Detroit French genealogies.[24] Apparently, under French law registration of a change in land ownership was not necessary.[25] It was not uncommon for property to remain in the hands of several generations with no official record of the transfer rights and will provisions. In the last third of the eighteenth century Joseph Lionard Tremble owned a parcel of land in which P.C. 391 was situated.[26] Isidore Morin's later purchase of the property is handwritten in French, displaying the legal terminology of the period, but it is nearly illegible and therefore difficult to translate. The agreement, however, was signed as follows:

Peter Audrain   Nicholas X Patenaude (L.S.)
J.P.D.D.   Marie Josette X Patenaude (L.S.)
                       Isidore X Moran (L.S.)[27]

Peter (Pierre) Audrain, as the letters under his name signify, was a Judge of Probate in the District of Detroit. As a notary public he played a prominent part in the later re-registration of lands after the great fire of 1805. He was a judge by 1797 and died in 1820. The "X" in the names of the parties concerned do not necessarily signify that they were illiterate (although they might well have been), as the entry "his (her) mark" usually accompanies the X if the person is illiterate. The X can also mean the surname by which the person is known. This would make the mark somewhat akin to the French "dit," meaning "also known as." The spelling of Moran in the earlier entry was "Morin." It is unusual that Audrain, who was French-born, would have put an Anglicized, or even "Irish-ized," spelling to a French name. Genealogists assert that "Moran" and "Morin" are two distinct lineages, both French, which can be contrasted with the Irish "Moran" line of a slightly later Detroit period. Nevertheless, the connected letters "in" are pronounced in French as "an;" therefore, "Moran" could be the French pronunciation of "Morin." The "L.S." after the "surnames" probably stands for "legal signature."

In 1807 these lands were transferred to Charles Gouin who proceeded to seek a verification for the title to P.C. 391 from the United States government. Aaron Greeley, the surveyor for Wayne County was a prominent figure in affairs involving private claims.[28] Gouin went to great pains to prove title to the land, undoubtedly because of the chaos produced in land records as a result of complications and ambiguities created by the fire of 1805, which destroyed most of Detroit and extant land records, and the French custom of not always registering land transfers. The system by which lands began to emerge as distinct entities consisted of land court hearings to establish clear title for legal possession. Greeley played an important role in these proceedings. All claimants were to have actually possessed and improved their properties by July 1, 1796, the official date on which the Michigan Territory passed from British to American control. By an act of 1807, all lands were to be surveyed under direction of the surveyor-general, and the certificates issued were to be entered at the land office at Detroit.

P.C. 391 was the second farm owned by Charles Gouin. His other holdings were P.C.s 12 and 13 located in Detroit, which measured 1½ x 80 arpents (an arpent is roughly equivalent to an English acre) upon which was situated one house, and presumably out-buildings. His other personal property included 2 slaves, 2 oxen, 2 cows, and 1 horse.[29]

---

23 Giltner, unpublished manuscript.

24 McNiff map; Bouquet Chart, 1796; Rev. Fr. Christian Denissen, *Genealogy of the French Families of the Detroit River Region, 1701-1911*, BHC.

25 Giltner, unpublished manuscript.

26 Land Office Records, Liber 2 p. 68. Wayne County Archives microfilm. BHC.

27 *American State Papers, Documents. Legislative and Executive of the Congress of the United States commencing 3 March, 1789, and ending 3 March, 1815.* (Washington, D.C., 1832), 1:427. These papers are especially useful for research because they contain abstracts of the hearings to validate the Private Claims.

28 Aaron Greeley's map of the land claims can be seen in the *American State Papers*, 5:428.

29 Farmer, *History of Detroit*, 2: chp. 4; *Michigan Pioneer and Historical Society*, 8:535. VIII: 535, 347.

It was not uncommon for the French to maintain summer farms outside Detroit. Because of the amount of time involved in travelling between the two locations, the "out farm" was usually worked on a limited scale. Land clearance was a problem anywhere, so this endeavor was always undertaken on the basis of a few acres each year with settlement achieved only after enough land had been cleared to enable the production of an adequate food supply. The census report of 1810 shows a Charles Gouin as residing in the Grand Marais, which at that period was distinct from "Grosse Pointe."[30] In all probability the census takers made their rounds of the rural areas during the warmer seasons; hence the person recording the population for Grosse Pointe would most likely have found M. Gouin working his second farm, upon which most likely stood a dwelling place of some sort.

Charles Gouin sold P.C. 391 to a Henry Hudson in February of 1815, with the mortgage being satisfied in June 1816. The mortgage, or consideration, consisted of $200 and two notes totalling $500.[31]

Hudson was a colorful character. He apparently built the wharf at the foot of Bates Street, but most of his exploits seem to have fallen somewhat short of social acceptability.[32] In a biographical sketch, C. M. Burton writes:

Henry Hudson married Mary Watson; and their son, Alexander, was born September 23, 1806 and was buried May 2, 1808. No record has been found of Hudson's birth or the date of his arrival in Detroit. It is probable that he was not a property owner in the old town at the time of the fire of 1805, because his name does not appear among those eligible for a donation lot. In September of that year he was indicted for stealing 212 lbs. of coffee from Charles Curry on June 11.

Hopelessly light fingered, Hudson at one time faced 10 indictments. He owned property in Grosse Pointe, which he sold to Merrit Fisher, after whom Fisher Road was named. Hudson died in 1852.[33]

What Burton said about the property was not entirely accurate. Hudson did in fact own the property, and Judge James May in 1823 stated that Hudson House was standing in 1778, but the eventual outcome was different than Burton states.[34]

Just this side of the country club lived Henry Hudson, "Old Hudson" everyone called him. He and his family were considered an unsavory lot for some reason and were known far and wide through this section of the country. Besides Hudon there was his wife and three or four boys who were stalwarts all, and when the sheriff or any of his deputies had occasion to visit their premises in their line of duty, they went prepared, for they were fully aware they might meet with trouble. On one occasion, Sheriff Wilson had a warrant for Hudson for some alleged misdeed. He went up to the house to serve it. Mrs. Hudson saw him coming and divining his mission, she at once provided herself with a large basin of scalding water and stationed herself behind the open front door so she could give it to him good and plenty. The sheriff fortunately discovered the enemy and her means of defense through the crack of the door and struck the basin from her hands with the heavy butt of his riding whip, spilling its scalding contents over her bare feet. Mrs. Hudson was a masculine looking woman, marked with smallpox. She wore a broad brimmed straw hat, winter and summer and out of doors, when the weather demanded it, a sailor's heavy sea jacket. . . . A Mr. Fisher succeeded them. I think he bought the Hudson property. He opened a road house there.[35]

If the Hudson property was "just this side of the country club," the site was on what is now known as Rose Terrace, (the former Dodge Estate) where Fisher discovered the brick clay deposit. Fisher was, in the 1830s, a grocery merchant on lower Woodward Avenue.[36] He married a daughter of Conrad Ten Eyck, then sheriff of Wayne County. After his marriage, he disposed of his grocery business in the city and moved to Grosse Pointe, where he built the hotel. Fisher purchased the old Hudson property, then known as the Ten Eyck Farm. Conrad Ten Eyck was subsequently owner of the Wardwell property. In a letter dated January 26, 1821, Henry Hudson stated (aside from being a tavern keeper in Detroit prior to moving to Grosse Pointe) that he owned four farms in Grosse Pointe.[37] These farms either had a lien against them or were simply lost to pay a debt. Money was lent to Hudson by Oliver Miller in 1819, which he apparently could not repay. A sum of $820 was also involved with Robert Smart, and Conrad Ten Eyck.

---

30 Joseph Watson's Census Report for Grosse Pointe and the Grand Marais, of 1810, Witherell Papers, BHC.

31 Burton Abstract and Title Co., BHC. All of the following land transactions in the text were taken from this abstract.

32 *Michigan Pioneer and Historical Society*, 8:237, *The Grosse Pointe Guide* p. 214.

33 Clarence M. Burton, "Hudson Henry." Biographical Index, BHC.

34 *Belden Atlas*, p. 66.

35 Friend Palmer, *Early Days in Detroit*, (Detroit, 1906) p. 657; *Grosse Pointe Guide*, p. 217.

36 Ibid.

37 Henry Hudson to William, January 26, 1821, Woodbridge Papers, BHC.

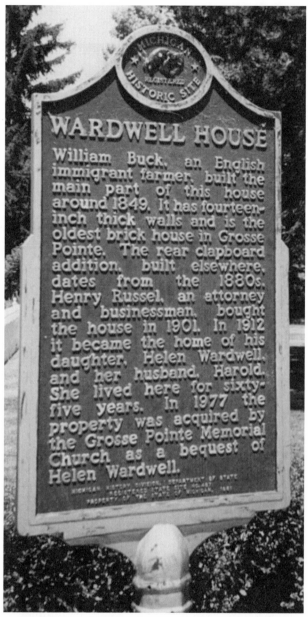

WARDWELL HOUSE

William Buck, an English immigrant farmer, built the main part of this house around 1849. It has fourteen-inch thick walls and is the oldest brick house in Grosse Pointe. The rear clapboard addition, built elsewhere, dates from the 1880s. Henry Russel, an attorney and businessman, bought the house in 1901. In 1912 it became the home of his daughter, Helen Wardwell, and her husband, Harold. She lived here for sixty-five years. In 1977 the property was acquired by the Grosse Pointe Memorial Church as a bequest of Helen Wardwell.

The Michigan historical marker on the grounds of the Wardwell House. Mrs. Helen Wardwell lived there for 65 years, bequeathing it to Grosse Pointe Memorial Church on her death in 1976. The house was subsequently sold, most recently to Dr. and Mrs. Douglas L. Ross, who still live there.

---

38 "Michigan Territorial Census for Wayne County, Witherell Report of Census of 1820," Witherell Papers, BHC.

39 *Michigan Pioneer and Historical Society Collections*, 1:258, 441; 10:85.

40 Ibid, 2:13. Farmer, *History of Detroit*, p. 457.

41 *Michigan Pioneer and Historical Society Collections*, 2:178.

42 ibid. 2:178, 574; 4:106; 8:574.

43 ibid, 13:319-20.

44 *Belden Atlas*, BHC.

In sum, Hudson signed off his four farms, one of which must have been P.C. 391. Thus, it seems likely Hudson did not sell to Fisher. Rather, Fisher bought the farm from his father-in-law, Conrad Ten Eyck, who acquired P.C. 241, probably with P.C. 391 and two other farms, by a default on the part of Henry Hudson. A hand written letter exists in a quasi-legal style that described and transferred the Hudson farms on September 30, 1820.

Thus Messrs. Oliver Miller, Robert Smart, and Conrad Ten Eyck became owners of P.C. 391 by a warranty deed dated March 1817. The consideration was $6,000, which surely reflected other interest or transactions between the parties. Of course the 1817 date is totally inconsistent with the foregoing; there is always the possibility of error in transcription. Hudson might have had to sign the later letter for some other reason. It is doubtful that the actual land record is in error. Since all the other pieces of the puzzle fit together, it is unlikely that the transfer of P.C. 391 was a fifth and earlier land transaction.

Little is known of the new owners, except that none of them resided in Grosse Pointe.[38] Oliver Miller was active in Detroit government and civic affairs. Conrad Ten Eyck, aside from holding the position of sheriff, was a goods merchant, county commissioner, and Treasurer of Detroit at various times.[39] Robert Smart was a Scottish immigrant who was in Detroit by 1806. He was involved in real estate dealings, had a sawmill on the Black River, and built Smart's Block of stores on the northeast corner of Jefferson and Woodward Avenues.[40]

In 1818, the property was sold to Edward Brooks, a former colonel in the American army. He was a resident of Detroit from 1822 to 1852, when he moved to Washington, D.C. [41] Prior to his departure, he was a salesman and land agent, an auctioneer for Wayne County and commander of Brady's Guards, a volunteer militia unit that served in the Blackhawk War.[42]

Late in 1818, Edward Brooks sold the farm to a David Gwynne and John Biddle as joint owners. By 1823, Biddle had purchased Gwynne's half of the property. A retired major of the American army, John Biddle was a well known person in Detroit. He was a prominent hotelier (he operated the Biddle House, located at Jefferson and Randolph), and was active in real estate and other business and civic functions. Also in 1818, Biddle purchased 2,200 acres in the area of what is now Wyandotte, after Indian title had been "extinguished" by the federal government. He built a homestead on this property in 1835, and moved his family from Detroit.[43] The consideration to Gwynne and Biddle was $1,400. John Biddle expanded the size of the farm to 210 acres by acquiring a back concession of 90 acres. The inclusion of the back concession brought the northern boundary of P.C. 391 to its final line.[44] The road that was later cut through, which was built on a line of farm boundaries, was called the DeRasse Road, and later renamed Harper Avenue.

In 1834, John Biddle sold P.C. 391 to a Loan Hills, and his wife, Esther. They did not reside in Wayne County as of 1840.[45]

In 1835, and almost concurrent with the discharge of their own mortgage, the Hills sold the property to Michael Cadieux, who at the time had his own farm, P.C. 506, in the vicinity of what later became Cadieux Road. With this purchase, Cadieux tripled his acreage for farming. He might also have wanted the property for the lumber it contained on the north end or simply for speculation. In 1837, 28 acres of the back concession were sold to a George LaForge.

In 1845, Cadieux, and his wife, Archange, sold the farm (excepting LaForge's 28 acres) to a Philip Martz. Martz does not seem to have been a farmer either. In a later period, he was a Water Commissioner in Detroit and probably owned the Martz Brewery.[46] In 1850 no Philip Martz was residing in Wayne County.[47]

In October of the same year, Martz sold the farm to a Charles Moran. This was Charles Moran Junior (who died in 1876, aged 79 years), whose father's name appeared earlier but with the French spelling "Morin." The junior Moran was apparently the father of William Moran who reclaimed part of the Grand Marais. The consideration was only $200; obviously, this transaction involved other commitments. Moran's mortgage apparently fell through, since in October 1845 Martz also sold P.C. 391 to a William Buck. In 1847, William Buck acquired from George LaForge, for a consideration of $160, the 28 acres LaForge bought in 1837; thus, Buck had all 210 acres of P.C. 391.

Up to this point only two of the owners were known to be farmers. They were Charles Gouin and Michael Cadieux. All of the other owners had other livelihoods, and all but Gouin and Cadieux had their residences, at locations other than Grosse Pointe. These early purchases and

Wardwell House has fourteen-inch thick walls and is the oldest brick house in Grosse Pointe.

sales of the property point to the incipient land speculation schemes which peaked in the Detroit area during 1834-1841. It is most likely that the other previous owners of P.C. 391 were involved in land and homestead promotion schemes. They would hire someone to homestead for them, while paying all their expenses, and then sell (they sometimes advanced an initial down payment to the homesteaders) the improved property, as the price escalated. Their most likely prospects for this exploitable labor would naturally have been the landless laborers, especially immigrants. The first buildings were normally the land clearer's cabins, and were usually not the clear title holder's dwellings. Most likely P.C. 391 was a working tenant farm. There was little probability that any one of the property owners would have erected a brick dwelling of the proportions of the Wardwell House.[48]

The evidence is conclusive that the Wardwell House was a mid-nineteenth century structure. It was standing by 1854. The architecture displays strong elements of Greek Revival with returning boxed cornices which wrap around the sides of the house at the eave line, and which follow the gabled roof configuration. The fireplace mantle is also indicative of the same period, as is the corbelled brick form of support beneath the fireplace. The Greek Revival style is usually associated with the decade of the 1850s, but was present beginning during the late 1830s or 1840s in midwestern America and Canada. Thus, architectural style alone cannot be used to date the house.

Other observed features in the Wardwell House fit with the 1850s although some of these features appeared in buildings erected in subsequent decades. The windows of the house are of wood, in the Colonial double-hung style, with the crossbars thinner than were used in later periods. The mitered joints of the windows are secured with wooden pegs, rather than with nails. The transoms are original and are pegged at their corners. The window panes that have not been replaced are somewhat bubbled. More sig-

45 U.S. Bureau of Census, *Index to the Sixth Census of the United States, Michigan.* BHC.

46 Farmer, *History of Detroit,* 2:499.

47 U.S. Bureau of Census, *Seventh Census of the United States, Michigan.* Microfilm No. 189, Reel No. 21, visit/entry no. 54, BHC.

48 Documentation of the house is on two levels, that of architectural analysis and research into the written record. To be able to provide architectural data, a note of thanks must go to the Grosse Pointe Memorial Church, and to Mr. Gust Jahnke, Administrator, for providing access to the house and grounds. A second note of thanks is due Mr. James Conway of the Detroit Historical Museum for providing information regarding architecture, construction techniques, and building materials.

nificantly, some window casings contain a segmental arch capped by keystone brick, which came into use during the 1840s. The exterior window sills are fashioned from solid pieces of wood. The brick is typical of the period for Detroit. The lime mortar is of the same consistency back to the rear portions of the brick, thus indicating a durable grade to which some natural cement was added during construction. This cement occurred in downriver areas. The basement walls and presumably foundation are constructed of what is commonly called Trenton limestone, which was readily available from downriver commercially-operated quarries.[49]

The columned and enclosed porch attached to the front of the house, and the two-storied porch seen on the west side are early twentieth century additions and consequently of no particular historic value. The lower west-end porch houses a sitting room window upon which is mounted what seems to be an original shutter, with original hinges and latching assembly. The original floor beneath the overlying hardwood floor is of ship-lap construction that pre-dated the familiar tongue-and-groove hardwood flooring.

Across the short axis of the house from front to rear through the center, traverses the main supporting beam. It is of a hand-hewn hard wood, probably oak. The floor joists were sawed, and not hand-hewn. The vertical saw marks on the attic ceiling joists indicated they were pit-sawed. Attachment to the lateral oak beam is by a mortice and tenon joint. These features were typical of mid-nineteenth century.

At mid-century William Buck owned the property. He held it from 1845 until his death in 1873. In the 1850 census Buck appeared as a resident and owner of P.C. 391. The complete entry follows.

Name	Age	Race/Sex	Occupation	Birthplace
William Buck	45	White male	Farmer	England
Elizabeth Buck	38	White female		England
John Buck	12	White male		Michigan
Helen Spavin	16	White female		Michigan
William Thorndyke	17	White male		New York

If William and Elizabeth Buck had a son who was born in Michigan, the couple must have lived somewhere else in the state before buying P.C. 391, although no William Buck appears in the earlier censuses. Probably John Buck was a nephew whose surname was Gott. The fact that the Bucks were English immigrants would explain the difficulty in locating them; they simply were not here before buying

the farm in 1845. Helen Spavin and William Thorndyke were most likely a servant-housekeeper and farmhand, respectively. The census taken in 1850 valued Buck's real property at $2,000.

The value of the property as assessed by the Township tax collector for 1853 was $1,700, which is almost triple the 1852 assessment of $685.[50] An increase of this magnitude usually implies a major property improvement, often in the form of a building. While this indication was by no means conclusive, it seemed that 1852-53 was the date of construction of the house. However, it appears that all farms experienced a significant assessment rise; some doubled, some tripled, and at least one of the largest holdings actually quadrupled in assessed valuation. Obviously, there was a Township-wide re-evaluation of all properties, which would mask an 1852 date of construction for the house. The 1850 census data includes the property value estimate of $2,000, which is almost double the 1850 township assessment of $1,121. The township property assessment for 1849 was just $719; in other words, the assessment increased in 1850 by a full one-third over that of 1849. The 1848 assessment totalled $634, just $85 less than the amount in 1849.

These data suggest the Wardwell House was constructed between 1847 and 1850, probably in 1849. William Buck bought the property in 1845 and probably discharged the mortgage in 1846. If he had recently emigrated to America, he was one of the relative few to have done so with sufficient assets to purchase a farm with clear title within a year. He apparently also had enough money to finance the construction of a brick dwelling. There was an essentially nominal assessment rise of $85 between 1848 and 1849 to a total of $719. The rate for 1850 increased by $402 to $1,121. This amount becomes significant when placed in the light of the census estimate for 1850 of $2,000. The usual practice was to assess property at one-half of the market value. Therefore, the market value of P.C. 391 actually increased by some $900 in 1850. This increase undoubtedly reflected the construction of a brick dwelling. The cost of the brick portion of the house would have been approximately $1,000. The projected date of 1849 is therefore based on the increase in the market value of approximately $900, which, when added to the consideration of $1,225 (which was a reasonably accurate entry, though probably not exact) gives a total of $2,125 for the real property. This amount is consistent with the presumably unbiased estimate of $2,000 placed on the property by the census taker.

---

49 Farmer, *History of Detroit*, 2:802.

50 Township of Grosse Pointe, Wayne County Tax Assessment, 1848-1873, BHC.

51 U.S. Bureau of Census, *Eighth Census of the United States, Michigan*. National Archives Series No. M-653, Roll No. 564, p. 16, BHC.

The Wardwell House, 1996.

The assessment rise reflected in 1853 continued throughout the extant tax rolls on an incremental basis. This trend likely reflected the effects of the political restructuring of Grosse Pointe on the Township level, and of the increased social, political, and economic ties which resulted from the improved road networks connecting Grosse Pointe with Detroit and adjacent areas.

The 1860 census reveals no John Buck.[51]

Name	Age	Race/Sex	Occupation	Birthplace
William Buck	55	White male	Farmer	England
Elizabeth Buck	50	White female	Housewife	England
Augustus Jacques	23	White male	Farmhand	Belgium
George Cordy	21	White male	Farmhand	Canada
Sarah Cordy	23	White female	Housewife	Michigan
Charles Cordy	2	White male		Michigan

Two farmhands, one with family, indicates an expanded farming operation requiring additional help. The 1876 Belden Atlas shows a structure situated on the Buck Farm,

further north on the Mack Road. If this was extant in the 1850s, it was probably a dwelling for the hired help. The census taker placed a real estate value of $8,400 on the property, plus a $1,000 personal estate. The assessed values for 1854–1860, in contrast ranged between $1,870 and $2,640 inclusive. When these values were doubled for an approximate market value, the maximum was just $5,280, which is significantly less than $8,400. If the census person was totally objective in his estimations, the Buck Farm was intentionally or unintentionally undervalued on the assessment rolls by the tax assessors throughout at least this decade. On the tax roles, Buck's personal estate averages $200 each year for the decade, while the census person in 1860 estimated it at $1,000. Given the size of Buck's inventory, the latter figure seems more accurate.

William Buck died in December 1873, supposedly intestate, leaving no children or lineal descendants. However, a nephew by the name of John Gott did present himself. While hard evidence is lacking, John Gott just might be the John Buck listed in the 1850 census record, since Gott seems to have come from out of nowhere.

In 1874, Elizabeth Buck was appointed administratrix of the estate of William Buck by direction of the Probate Court. In 1875, Mrs. Buck married another farmer, Charles Turner, who at the time owned P.C. 394, a 337 acre tract in Conner's Creek. Elizabeth Turner inherited her first husband's estate just prior to her marriage to Turner. A will dated November 1878 and admitted to probate in April 1880 named Charles Turner the heir to his wife's estate, which included P.C. 391. Elizabeth Turner had died in March 1880, aged 80 years, and Charles was appointed executor of her estate.

Shortly after William Buck's death, John Gott initiated what turned out to be a 12-year legal battle over ownership of P.C. 391. Gott may well have been a nephew (although no proof is present in the abstract). He might have gone by the surname Buck for some reason; for example, protection afforded him by William Buck if John was an orphan. Possibly William Buck had intentions of legal adoption.

In 1875, John Gott claimed that he was the sole heir of William Buck, and was therefore entitled to any real estate. He claimed to be the sole surviving child of Mary Buck, formerly Mary Gott, who died about 1845, and was the only sister of William Buck. Thus, it seems plausible that John Gott as a nephew might well have been listed on the 1850 census as John Buck, a son of William and Elizabeth Buck. In October of the same year, an order was entered in the Probate Records stating the John Gott, or the sole heir of William Buck, was entitled to inherit his real estate.

The legal difficulties begin in 1880, when Sarah Buck Rickabus filed for a probate of will, stating that when she was eight years of age in 1843 she came to live with the Buck family for seventeen years. She indicated that William Buck had stated that she would inherit a share of his estate when he died. This petition was denied and later in the same year appealed. The data in the censuses of 1850 and 1860 suggest Sarah fabricated this claim in an attempt to gain control of part or all of P.C. 391. In April 1881, a trial jury found that William Buck made a last will and testament about the year 1862 that devised all his property to his wife excepting 40 acres, which he devised to Sarah Buck Rickabus. After another appeal, a jury concluded in 1882 that William Buck did not leave a last will and testament, but died intestate. A verdict in 1885 reversed this decision and reaffirmed the 1881 decision. Motions for a new trial were denied.

Following Elizabeth's death in 1880 Charles Turner became executor and heir (excepting the above-mentioned 40 acres) of the Buck Farm. Also in 1880, John Gott coerced Turner, under threat of commencement of proceedings to dispossess him, into signing an agreement that gave Gott possession of the remainder of the farm. Gott's claim of title was challenged in the Circuit Court for Wayne County by Turner and Sarah Rickabus. In 1888 the bill of complaint was dismissed. The matter was referred to the Michigan Supreme Court, but before that court rendered a decision on the validity of William Buck's will, the parties reached a compromise. John Gott received as his share of the property $10,000 in cash, and his attorneys received $2,000. Costs against the complainants were dismissed in favor of the defendant Gott. For a consideration of $1 and "other valuable considerations," Charles Turner conveyed the Buck Farm to Sarah Rickabus by a quit claim deed in 1880.

Following the death of Elizabeth Turner the house was not regularly occupied until 1901 when the farm was acquired by Henry Russel and Henry Potter. The occupants of the house were tenants paying rent or tenant farmers on the land who lived elsewhere. For at least a brief period in the 1890s the house was used for grain storage. Even after Henry Russel purchased the property, he and his wife, Helen, never lived on it; instead, they resided in Detroit. Henry's daughter, Helen Russel Wardwell, moved into the home in 1912 following her marriage.

The Wardwell House was built much later than has been supposed by either residents or by previous investigators. It was erected in 1849 by a prosperous English emigrant who had included in its construction most of the building features typical of mid-nineteenth century architecture in Michigan. The evidence strongly suggests that the folklore surrounding the house has mislead several generations of residents about the history of this oldest of brick houses in Grosse Pointe.

———————————— ❧ ————————————

SOURCE: Originally published as, "The Wardwell House: A Legacy of Old Grosse Pointe," *Detroit in Perspective: A Journal of Regional History*, Vol. 5, No. 2, Winter 1981, pp. 22-44.

———————————— ❧ ————————————

Henry Heatley, a native eastside Detroiter, was born on Cadillac Boulevard near Kercheval Avenue. He has been employed at Michigan Bell, now Ameritech, for over 40 years. With an interest in archaeology and local history, he wrote this paper on the Wardwell House while a graduate student in the Department of Anthropology, Wayne State University.

The Civil War Letters of George Frederick Neff

by Gwen Balance

George Frederick Neff, an original member of the 24th Michigan Regiment of the Iron Brigade, loved to write, both keeping a diary and sending frequent letters home. From his diary we have this account of his experiences during the Battle of Gettysburg, July 1-3, 1863.

GEORGE FREDERICK NEFF, a farmer of German ancestry, was born in 1839. His father, Christopher, had homesteaded their land in Grosse Pointe in 1837. The 1860 census indicates that Fred, as he was known by his family, was married and had four children: Helena, Rosa, Gilbert, and Sylvester. From his letters to his wife, Mary Ann, we know that there also was another son, Julius.

Neff was an original member of the 24th Michigan of the Iron Brigade, having volunteered for the infantry when the regiment was formed. During his leisure time, Neff loved to write, both keeping a diary and sending frequent letters home. He was wounded at Gettysburg and killed at

Writing Home.

the Battle of Laurel Hill, Virginia, May 12, 1864, in one of the bloodiest battles of the war. His body was found within thirty feet of the Confederate breastworks. Neff Road in the City of Grosse Pointe was named to honor him.

From his diary, which is now part of the "George Frederick Neff Papers, 1862-1864," Burton Historical Collection, Detroit Public Library, we have this account of his experiences during the Battle of Gettysburg. It is a different picture from the one we most often have of the war. This passage from Neffs diary is reprinted here verbatim, with the original spelling and punctuation (in most cases, lack of punctuation) as originally written by Neff.

❦ ❦ ❦

July 1, 1863

after a hard fight and taken a lot of prisoners we changed our posision where I Received a slight wound on my thigh I was taken to hospital where I staid about half an hour when we Received orders to go in the city I was taken in by george krumbach of our company we were directed to a meeting house. We staid a very little while when we got our orders to go in the court house a large substantial building all the rooms was crowded except the court room there was no other way of getting in that room except through the window all the doors were locked I made out to get in through the window and was safe the cannonading was very fearful that afternoon our troops retreated through the town and took possession of the hill and held it and darkness set in and that ended the first days fighting

2nd day: the Rebels had possession of the town I got out and had quite a talk with them there was no fighting that morning I amused myself with the Johnnies I found some of my own country men and prussians one gave me a drink of whiskey the Rebel officers were busy in taken the names of our men and marching them of those that could walk I went and got in my Room nobody came to look for me when they got through and I heard no more noise I came out again but in the afternoon the fight commenced again and lasted until late at night

3rd day: I again spent my time in talking with the Rebs we had some great arguments about the war and when they found that we would talk to them they would leave us and you darn yanks we can't get ahead of you nohow you beat us in talking and in fighting too, in the afternoon someone got a lot of firecrackers and set them all afire at once a whole brigade of Rebels were laying in a street and had their guns stacked when the firecrackers started it sounds like muskets you ought to see them Rebs jump some took their guns some hid behind barns and houses til they found out the Joke then they had quite a laugh over it but then the battle commenced again and fearful was the cannonading and every now and then we would see a Rebel officer come through town and his men would ask him how it was going and he would say if we cannot drive the yankees of that hill we will fall back towards night an officer came through town and they all gathered around him he told them that all hell could not drive the yankees off that hill there was quite a dishardtent look among them there was a Rebel captain and some staff he was riding around and blowing away and that he had the best war horse but the next morning he was a prisoner our Boys when they saw him they said hollo captain how is your war horse this morning he hung his head down as he went along he was so ashamed the day before he was so brave in Riding around and swinging his sword we will give the yankees hell but he happened to sleep a little to long in the city and our sharpshooters grabbed him and marched him to the Rear our Boys plagued him well cap you was goin to give the yanks hell but we Rather think the yankees are givin you hell he dare not look up when our sharpshooters came through town you could see the Rebs hide wherever they could find a place and the people gathered in the streets and waved their handkerchiefs and shouted for the glorious fourth of July and for the union victory and a glorious fourth it was I crossed the street and went in to the house where most all our Boys were that was wounded and I came to the Back yard and drawed water to wash myself the lady of the house told me that I must stay for breakfast that it would be Ready in a few minutes she had a large table sot and that table was filled three times with men every man that came in she invited it made no difference wounded or not captain Richardson on general meredith staff also came in and had his meal he politely offered to pay before going but no pay she took she said all the pay asks is to clean the Rebels out I saw an old lady in that same house and very old she was I saw her break bread into a cup of coffee and go in another Room and feed a man that was wounded in both arms their front room was full of our wounded men Iying on their carpets and on their lounges and the children of the house would fan and keep the flies of the men and that aint all this lady would bake bread and make coffee for a great number of men that was in the court house besides feeding fifty or sixty that was in her own house every man that came in got something eat it was a sight to see the people carrying sheets pillows quilts bandages all to make our soldiers comfortable men and women with baskets full of eatables so good and charitable was the people of gettysburg. I had been in the courtroom on the third day I took my coffee bag and pail and went across the street to this house I had never been in before I was somewhat surprised to find so many of our men I asked the lady if she would be so kind as to make me a cup of coffee she told me yes with the greatest pleasure I handed her my coffee sack and pail she kept all my coffee and she told me as long as I staid in the village I could have my meals and she gave me my pail full of coffee and some pies and bread after breakfast on the fourth we got orders to leave town there was a hospital established about four miles from the village I went to the Court room and pack up my traps and sat out as well as I could the Rumor was that the Rebs would shell the town but it did not come to pass I finally Reached the Regiment captain edwards was the first man I saw with the colonel I asked the captain where the Boys was he told me right ahead of me then he went on and told me who was killed of my co. I then went to the co. and found but 12 men went into battle with 35 active men some were killed, some wounded, some taken prisoner I regretted the loss of our orderly sargeant very much he was such a good fellow the Rivard boys I miss very much to I sat down and had a talk with all of the Boys they wanted to know how I got clear from the Johnnies I told them the whole story and they said it was well done the capt said he thought I would be gobbled up in the village by the Rebs he asked how I done it I told him he said that was smart so he told me I must go and stay in the hospital til I could walk well so I left the Boys and started out to get there when I arrived at the hospital it was filled with wounded men they were putting up large hospital tents but only for those that were badly wounded I put up a tent with James ford of company G he was slightly wounded in the ankle it Rained very hard that afternoon we had our tent near the hospital tents in the first place I thought of taking a place in the hospital but I was forced to get out the bad smell of the wounded men drove me out I couldn't endure it it should have made me sick I was comfortable in my little tent but we were Rather short on grub I had nothing only what I got by chance I inquired of the nurses how it was about our grub that they would have plenty in a few days but that did not

satisfy my appetite . . . I told several of the Boys that I was going to the Regiment they all said that if I went they would go . . . .

SOURCE: "George Frederick Neff Papers, 1862-1864," Burton Historical Collection, Detroit Public Library.

REFERENCES

Curtis, O. B. *History of the Twenty-Fourth Michigan of the Iron Brigade*. Published by O. B. Curtis, 1891.

George F. Neff, Private Company F 24 Michigan Inf. Pension Records Date of Filing 1865, Feb. 13 Application #82818 Certificate #71077 by his widow Mary A. Neff.

Grosse Pointe News, February 15, 1982. "Pointer of Interest: Harold Neff."

Neff, George Frederick *1862-1864 Letters to his wife, Mary Ann, and his Diary*. Burton Historical Collection. Detroit Public Library.

Smith, Donald L. *The Twenty-Fourth Michigan — Of the Iron Brigade*. The Stockpole Company: Harrisburg, Penn., 1962.

United States Census, 1860. Wayne County, Michigan, Grosse Pointe Township. Neff, Frederick G. 211.

Gwen Balance, a long-time resident of Grosse Pointe Park, retired after 25 years as an English teacher with the Detroit Public Schools. She has an avid interest in local history and is an active volunteer with the Grosse Pointe Historical Society.

The Michigan 24th at Gettysburg

Painting by Robert Thom

Text by F. Clever Bald

In all at the Battle of Gettysburg, seven Michigan regiments of infantry and five of cavalry were in the hottest of the fighting. When the first day of the battle ended, the Michigan 24th Regiment had suffered some of the most severe casualties of the war. By nightfall seven color bearers had been struck down. Of its 496 men, 399 were killed, wounded or missing for a causality rate of 80 percent. Of the four hundred Union regiments participating in the three days at Gettysburg none surpassed the causality rate of the 24th Michigan of the Iron Brigade.

OF THE MANY brave actions of the Civil War in which Michigan men participated, the one shown in this painting is the first day at Gettysburg, July 1, 1863. Fighting had erupted prematurely at eight in the morning west of town in a wooded area bordering a shallow creek named Willoughby Run. Two Confederate brigades advancing east toward Gettysburg were held by Buford's Union cavalry which, though outnumbered, had an advantage in rapid fire, breech-loading carbines.

The gunfire soon attracted more troops to the scene. When Archer's Confederates advanced, Union troops of Meridith's Iron Brigade maneuvered in a wide flanking action to the left.

The Michigan 24th Regiment from Wayne County, commanded by Colonel Henry A. Morrow of Detroit, was a part of the Iron Brigade. Charging across Willoughby Run behind Archer's unit, they routed the southerners, cap-

turing close to 100, including Brigadier General Archer.

The Iron Brigade's trademark was a black hat with a black feather. The regulation "Jeff Davis," as it was called, was looped up on the right side for officers and cavalrymen, on the left for infantry. One in the collection of Alan Nolan, Indianapolis attorney and author of the *Iron Brigade* was used as a model. Some hats display the red dot, some the brass "A," both denoting 1st Corps, 1st Division. This lack of uniformity was typical of many aspects of equipment, especially with the Confederates, whose uniforms ranged from elegant to ragged.

In the early days of the war, every kind of firearm available was pressed into action. Many troops were armed with flintlocks, although these obsolete weapons were replaced or converted to percussion arms as soon as possible. However, as late as 1863, the North still listed as official 100 models of rifles, muskets, musketoons, and carbines. The musket we show in detail in the lower left foreground

Detail from a painting "The Michigan 24th at Gettysburg" by Robert Thom.

is a converted flintlock from the collection of the Chicago Historical Museum. The Model of 1861 became the standard infantry arm. These were generally known as "Springfields" although many were made at other armories. They were very accurate at 200 yards and still effective at 1000 yards. Using black powder ignited by percussion caps, they fired "Minie Balls." Muzzle loading was slow; three shots a minute was fast shooting.

To load, a paper cartridge was taken from the case, and the powder end torn open with the teeth. Faces were soon black with powder. (Note figures in the left foreground.) The powder was emptied down the barrel and the bullet pressed down with the thumb. The ramrod was then withdrawn from under the barrel and used to ram the bullet firmly against the powder. The ramrod was returned, the hammer pulled back to halfcock and a percussion cap pressed over the nipple.

Colonel Morrow brandishes a regulation sword, on exhibit in the Museum of the Gettysburg National Military Park. In his left hand is a Colt Army Revolver Model 1860.

Reference photography for the painting was done at the actual site in Gettysburg under the direction of James Flack,

member of the Civil War Round Table, Birmingham, Michigan, and with advice by Dr. Harry W. Pfanz, Chief Historian, Gettysburg National Military Park, Gettysburg, Pennsylvania. Grateful thanks is also given to Glenn Stille, curator, Ft. Wayne Military Museum, Detroit, Michigan, and Alan Nolan, Indianapolis, Indiana.

———————— ❦ ————————

SOURCE: *A History of Michigan in Paintings,* 1967.

———————— ❦ ————————

Frederick Clever Bald (1897-1970) received his BA degree from the University of Michigan in 1920 and his Master's degree from Wayne State University in 1937, where he studied under Milo M. Quaife. He received his PhD from U of M. A major figure in the promotion of state and local history, Bald wrote Michigan in Four Centuries, *(1954, rev. ed. 1962), which became the standard text in its field. He taught at the U of M and served as director of the University's Michigan Historical Collections from 1960 until his retirement in 1967.*

John S. Newberry and James H. McMillan:
Leaders of Industry and Commerce

by Thomas A. Arbaugh

During the last half of the nineteenth century no two men had a greater impact on the

industrial growth of Detroit and the residential growth of Grosse Pointe than did

John S. Newberry and James H. McMillan. Here the story of these two remarkable men, and

their many accomplishments, is told by Thomas A. Arbaugh.

THIS STORY IS about change. How two men, above all others, change nineteenth century Detroit from a small town on a strategically located river that is primarily a railroad and Great Lakes transit point, into a mighty industrial city that by 1900 manufactures essential goods, shipping them on railroad cars and steam-powered boats made in Detroit factories and ship yards, factories and ship yards owned and operated by John S. Newberry and James H. McMillan. In so doing, these two men also change Grosse Pointe from an isolated, French speaking, agrarian community on Lake St. Clair into an exclusive suburb for the principal beneficiaries of Detroit's industrial growth.

Into Detroit's industrial genesis comes John Stoughton Newberry in 1832 when just five years old, and James McMillan in 1855 when 17 years of age. Upon Newberry's arrival there are no railroads, many sailing vessels but only several steam boats, no Upper Peninsula mines, no blast furnaces or stove works, scarcely any industry and only a

couple of untrustworthy, wildcat banks. By the time of Newberry's 1887 death, he and his partner, James McMillan, had taken Detroit's industrial development from a cool, spring daybreak, transforming it into a blazing midsummer's afternoon sun. Quickening Detroit's modest industrial beginnings, they built scores of their own companies that stimulated the creation of hundreds of others. They led Detroit's surge into the world's foremost producer of every kind of railroad car, every imaginable type of cast iron stove, every variety —both passenger and freight— of Great Lakes steam ship and were in the nation's forefront for implementing Edison's new electrical generating equipment and Bell's telephone.

The dawn of it all really begins with Newberry's uncle Oliver taking a hike in 1819 to Detroit from Buffalo, New York, walking the shortcut trail across the Canadian province of Ontario. Once before, just after the War of 1812, Oliver Newberry ventured to Detroit, that time traveling by cumbersome sailboat, battling the erratic Lake Erie winds. Detroit was a mess, wharves falling into the

river, the fort's stockade logs rotting and toppled, many houses burned and the people looking starved. The ravages of the War of 1812 still were in strong evidence and he hastily returned to Buffalo.

After the digging of the Erie Canal started on July 4, 1817, promising freighting rate reductions across New York state from $32.00 a ton per hundred miles to just one dollar a ton, Uncle Oliver comes back, first starting a wholesale commission business, then locating a ship building yard where Cobo Hall is today. Just two years after the Erie Canal begins funneling thousands of people west, the steam ship *Argo* is built in Detroit. Picking up Erie Canal passengers at Buffalo, it takes them to Detroit, returning to Buffalo with produce for the East. By 1837 Detroit's waterfront is very busy, and among the hundreds of boats using its wharves are steamers built and registered in Detroit by Oliver Newberry.

Elihu Newberry (John's father) at the urging of his brother, Oliver, visits Detroit in 1829, evaluating its prospects. Liking what he sees, Elihu returns to New York, sells his farm, and comes back to Detroit. But instead of staying in bustling Detroit, feeling more comfortable in a rural setting, and using the proceeds from the farm sale, he buys a wagon and sundry goods to sell. Then setting out to establish a business, he settles in Romeo, Michigan, about 30 miles north of Detroit.

There the family thrives (there is a Newberry street in Romeo) allowing them to build a substantial home and enlarge his store. Romeo prospers so much at the time — in addition to being a farming center, there also is a small foundry and farm-wagon factory — the new University of Michigan establishes a branch campus. Taking advantage of the local educational opportunity, in 1844 young John Newberry starts his freshman year studying literature. After completing his first year in Romeo, his father sends him on to Ann Arbor for his last three years.

Upon graduating in 1848, and at the head of his class, he disregards his literary degree, which primarily qualifies him for teaching. Instead, under the influence of his Uncle Oliver, seeing a better future in business, he hires on with the Michigan Central Railroad. Working for two years in their engineering department, he learns engineering management and architecture while laboring to complete the

line from its landlocked old terminus in the middle of the state at Kalamazoo, to the new more economically logical terminus for midwest transportation at New Buffalo on Lake Michigan. Once the railroad is completed across Michigan to the lake, it then is profitable to build a railroad across Ontario, Canada, connecting Detroit by rail directly to both Boston and New York City, thereby strengthening the city's important location.

After the railroad is completed and wanting to see the Midwest, Newberry takes a year off, and traveling mainly by steamboats, tours the Great Lakes, and the Ohio, Mississippi and Missouri Rivers. During those travels, he recognizes the importance of river and lake transportation in addition to the railroad. Moreover, he is shocked by the number of boat accidents due to the lack of established standards and regulations. Consequently there are a number of expensive, extensive and complicated liability suits.

Upon his return Newberry abandons any more immediate railroad work in favor of studying maritime law in the Detroit law offices of Emmons and Van Dyke. In no time he becomes the acknowledged Midwestern maritime expert, publishing *Reports of Admiralty Cases in the Several District Courts of the United States*. Newberry wins his first important case, defending Captain Sam Ward, owner of the *Ogdenburg*, in his case against the *Atlantic*. He proves himself as the paramount admiralty law litigator in the Midwest. Establishing his own law practice, and having his office in the Rotunda Building on the corner of Larned and Griswold streets, in the heart of Detroit's growing financial district, he acquaints himself with all the important men of Detroit commerce.

John Newberry and James McMillan had taken Detroit's industrial development from a cool, spring daybreak, transforming it into a blazing midsummer's afternoon sun.

Although extremely busy with his flourishing practice, he is not too busy to fall in love. While in Buffalo on legal matters, he meets Harriet Newell Robinson, whom he weds in 1856. A son, Harrie, is born the same year. Tragically, ten days later, his wife of less than a year dies. Newberry saves all of her personal possessions and wedding gifts as remembrances for Harrie.

Three years later while on business in Cleveland, Newberry meets Helen Parmelee Handy, the daughter of a prominent banker. Marrying in 1859, they return to Detroit, first living in a rented house on the four hundred

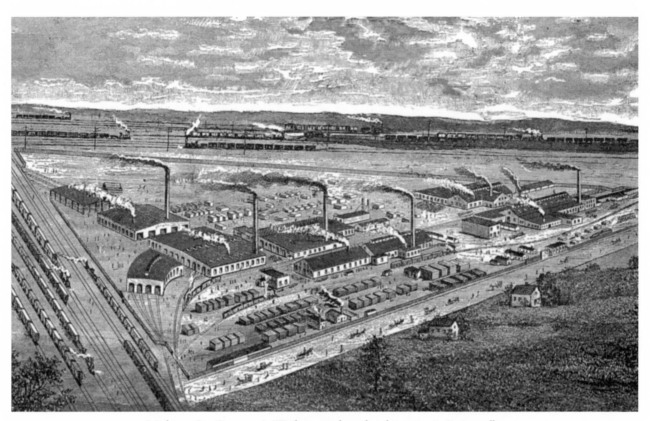

Michigan Car Company's Works, near the railroad junction in Springwells.
Illustration from Silas Farmer's History of Detroit and Wayne County and Early Michigan.

block of the soon-to-be-fashionable East Jefferson Avenue, making that street the place to live for most of Detroit's new, post-Civil War, manufacturing and financial class. Two sons, Truman Handy and John Stoughton Jr., and one daughter, Helen Hall, are born to that union. All three, making excellent use of their father's financial legacy, achieve their own successes in late nineteenth and early twentieth century Detroit and Grosse Pointe.

Canadian-born James McMillan comes from Hamilton, Ontario, to Detroit in 1855. Although an excellent scholar and qualifying for college, he too, like Newberry, chooses business instead. His father, William, works for the Great Western Railroad, both as it is being built through Ontario in the early 1850s connecting the east to Detroit, and in its freight and passenger business.

Taking the Great Western, young McMillan first sees Detroit's busy riverfront with its boats, wharves, warehouses and small factories, from across the river in Windsor. From there the sailing ship's spiring masts, spars, and web-like shroud lines resemble a dense forest, while the belching smoke from the steamboat's funnels and Detroit's few factories play hide and seek with the sun. Not seeing anything ugly about it, McMillan just sees the economic promise.

Carrying a letter of introduction attesting to his work habits and intelligence, he wastes no time looking for a job.

Stopping first at the hardware store of Christian Buhl and Charles DuCharme, he is immediately hired. But the job lasts only two years as the recession of 1857 forces Buhl and DuCharme to retrench, and McMillan is let go. Because of his father's influence and despite the recession, the 20-year-old soon hires on with the Detroit and Milwaukee Railroad.

That railroad is completing its 188 miles of track from Detroit to Grand Haven, where, to cross Lake Michigan, steamboat connections are made to Wisconsin. Samuel C. Ridley, the construction manager, employs McMillan as his materials purchasing agent. Although his two years with Buhl and DuCharme fully acquaint him with Detroit's industry, the Detroit and Milwaukee job significantly adds to both his knowledge and experience, which becomes very valuable.

McMillan performs his job so well that Ridley wants him for another job in Spain. McMillan declines, instead preferring to marry Mary Wetmore in 1860, the daughter of Charles Wetmore, a prominent Woodward Avenue merchant. They have six children.

etroit, now connected by railroad to both Chicago and the east, is still dependant upon eastern cities for the manufacture of railroad cars and locomotives. Trying to remedy that situation, Dr. George Russel establishes in 1853 on Gratiot Avenue a railroad car works, and at Congress and Larned streets the Detroit Locomotive Works, the first such factories east of the Hudson River.

In 1863, the Congress of the United States passes the Pacific Railroad Act committing the government to subsidize the construction of transcontinental railroads. That job, requiring million of tons of steel and tens of thousands of railroad cars, causes Newberry and McMillan — by now acquaintances through their membership in the Jefferson Avenue Presbyterian Church — to act quickly.

When Dr. Russel becomes ill, two of his employees, George Eaton and Edward Dean, lease his new Croghan Street shops. Then, because of expected sales increases, they buy an additional seven acres at Fourth Street and Larned, establishing there another car company, the Michigan Car Works. Because Eaton and Dean need additional financing, they join with the eager Newberry and McMillan. In addition to his own significant resources, Newberry is respected enough in Detroit's banking circles to get additional money.

Of the two, McMillan is the more outgoing, willing to take chances, able to meet railroad barons and secure contracts. Initially Newberry, the more experienced businessman, draws up better contracts for the new company. But, as their companies prosper through the 1870s and 1880s Newberry becomes more sanguine and conservative.

Shortly after the Civil War ends, they secure a contract from the new Union Pacific Railroad to build 700 freight cars. That railroad, taking advantage of the generous government land and cash construction subsidies, builds tracks westward from Omaha, Nebraska. They are hoping to hook-up somewhere out West with the new Central Pacific Railroad and build tracks eastward from California.

With the untimely death of George Eaton, and his widow not caring about continuing in the business and willing to sell her stock, Newberry and McMillan's combined 7,200 shares now greatly outnumber Dean's 3,600 shares. Consequently they rename the company and officially incorporate it in the state of Michigan as the Michigan Car Company.

Of the two, McMillan is the more outgoing, willing to take chances; Newberry, the more experienced, sanguine, and conservative.

Acting entrepreneurial, Newberry and McMillan send McMillan's brother, Hugh, to St. Louis, to establish the Missouri Car Company. As Detroit is becoming a center for railroading in the Great Lakes region, they fully expect St. Louis to do the same for the Mississippi Valley as well as become an entrepôt for goods going west and coming east. Soon that company does an annual $1,500,000 worth of business (at this time a basic freight car sells for $450). Moreover, fully recognizing the importance of the Canadian connection, they incorporate the Ontario Car Company in London, Ontario, which makes cars with an eight-foot gauge — as compared to the four-foot-eight-and-a-half inch gauge for American cars — for all railroads operating in that country.

By 1870, their impact on Detroit is evident. Industrial employment increases from 1,363 jobs in 1860 to 10,612, and the value of finished product increases from $2.1 million to $21.8 million. In 1873, Newberry and McMillan alone clear a little more than one million dollars in profits.

Meaning to take control of the entire railroad car manufacturing process in Detroit, in 1865 Newberry and McMillan incorporate the Detroit Car Wheel Company, capitalized at $250,000. At that time, poor wheels caused most railroad accidents. Determined to establish a reputation for making the best — although much more expensive — they insist upon using wrought iron which makes the best wheels. Initially Detroit Car Wheel produces just 20 wheels a day but within two years with 30 men working in the foundry, they begin producing three times that amount.

Not everything goes their way, however. Newberry and McMillan are forced out of the passenger car segment of the railroad car manufacturing business when George M. Pullman comes to Detroit in 1868. The king of the sleeping car and the ordinary passenger car, Pullman buys the abandoned Detroit Car Works of Dr. Russel at Croghan and Dequindre. Pullman reorganizes it as the Detroit Car and Manufacturing Works Company (located just east of the modern-day Chrysler Freeway, in downtown Detroit). Several years after the Civil War ends, Detroit rapidly starts leading the nation in railroad car building. Pullman buys some of his needed components from Newberry and McMillan.

Residence of John S. Newberry, 1363 East Jefferson Avenue. Built in 1875. Illustration from Silas Farmer's History of Detroit and Wayne County and Early Michigan.

With this industrial expansion, Detroit manufacturers need more steam engines to power their factories and other essential items made from iron. Fulfilling those requirements, Newberry and McMillan establish in 1867 the Fulton Iron and Engine Works on Brush Street. There they build steam engines, industrial anvils and vises, architectural iron works, mill work and many parts for railroad cars and locomotives.

So much western grain and Michigan lumber begins funneling through Detroit that in 1868 Newberry and McMillan incorporate the Detroit Elevator Company and the Detroit River Lumber Company. Eventually the elevator company employs 30 men servicing grain silos both in Detroit and Grand Haven on Lake Michigan. The silos, 135 feet high and having capacities of over one million bushels, are located on the water front close by the Detroit and Milwaukee Railroad depot located at the foot of Brush Street (the present-day site of the Renaissance Center).

In addition to greatly stimulating the growth of new industries in Detroit, Newberry and McMillan also influence the creators of those new industries to build their year around residences on East Jefferson and summer homes in "The Pointe" as it was styled 120 years ago.

A few of those joining Newberry and McMillan building homes on East Jefferson are: George Hendrie, president of the Detroit Car and Marshall Car Companies and secretary of the Detroit City Railroad Company; William B. Wesson, president of Hargreaves Manufacturing Company and of the Wayne County Savings Bank; Francis Palms, president of the Michigan Stove Company, the Peoples Savings Bank, and the Palms Gold Mining Company; and William K. Muir, president of Eureka Iron Company, the Cloud

Manufacturing Company, the Aikman Automatic Car Coupler Company, the Northwestern Rolling Stock Company, and of Detroit Car Loan Company.

Newberry and McMillan pay a thousand dollars an acre to buy Grosse Pointe's French strip farms. In 1875 they build their mirror-image, three-story "cottages" named "Lake Terrace," that turn the Pointe into an exclusive summer colony for Detroit's *nouveau riche*.

Some have preceded Newberry and McMillan, and are already enjoying Lake St. Clair's splendid scenery, cooling breezes, abundance of white fish, pickerel, trout, muskellunge and sturgeon, sailing its choppy, blue-green waters, and relishing a playful summer's respite from Detroit's ever increasing industrial hustle and bustle. They are Theodore H. Hinchman, a respected Detroit merchant; D. Bethune Duffield, a lawyer; Edmund Askin Brush, owner of Detroit real estate; Dr. Morse Stewart, one of Detroit's most respected physicians; Dr. Isaac Smith, who came to Grosse Pointe from California's gold fields in the early 1850s; G. V. N. Lothrop, a railroad lawyer; and Dudley B. Woodbridge, son of a Michigan governor and manager of a farm and Detroit real estate.

Some of those following Newberry and McMillan building summer residences are: T. P. Hall, who built "Tonnancour" in 1880, a commodities broker and grain merchant; John B. Moran who built "Bellevue" in 1882, president of the Peninsula Stove Company, and Detroit Electric Light and Power; Hugh McMillan, who built on Cloverleigh in 1882, secretary and treasurer of the Telephone and Telegraph Construction Company and Michigan Bell Telephone, president of the Commercial National Bank and of the National Electric Traction Company; H. B. Ledyard who also built on Cloverleigh in 1882, president of the Michigan Central Railroad; W. K. Muir who built "Otskita" in 1882; W. A. McGraw who built the "Poplars" in 1884, a

Residence of James H. McMillan, 1411 East Jefferson Avenue. Built 1873-80. Illustration from Silas Farmer's History of Detroit and Wayne County and Early Michigan.

"Lake Terrace." *The summer cottages of Newberry and McMillan, Lake Shore Road, Grosse Pointe. Built in 1875. Photo courtesy of the Burton Historical Collection, Detroit Public Library.*

successful real estate developer; and Joseph Berry who built "Edgemere" in 1882, a co-owner of Berry Brothers Paint and Varnish, president of Detroit Linseed Oil Company, and of Combination Gas Machine Company.

Getting to the Pointe is a pleasurable pastime. If Newberry, McMillan and their families are in town — living in neighboring residences on East Jefferson Avenue — and wishing to go to the Pointe, they order their carriages to take them the several blocks to their adjacent private yacht houses located on Atwater Street, to board their steam yacht. Depending upon their pleasure, the trip can take several hours. The men dress in white-duck trousers and blue blazers; the women in light pastel frocks reaching to their ankles, carrying parasols shielding themselves from the hot sun. Gliding past Belle Isle they admire the island's development into a beautiful park under the leadership of James McMillan, probably evaluate the progress of the new Detroit water works trying to meet the needs of the growing population, strain to see the racing at the Grosse Pointe Race Course, and then try estimating how many people are enjoying themselves at the new park on

Windmill Pointe. All the while bantering with those on sailboats playfully challenging them to race.

Upon arriving at the Pointe they land at a dock — jointly built with Alfred E. Brush — extending well into the Lake. Perhaps already moored there are Brush's yacht, the *Lillie*, and another, the *Leila*, mutually operated by many of the other summer colonists. Their summer carriages are called for and if they wish, before going to "Lake Terrace," they might take a drive on the Lake Shore Road enjoying the beautiful homes and admiring the landscape architecture.

The top of the carriage is down and they fancy the different trees from Japan, South America and from all over the United States both shading the drives to the summer homes and being artfully placed on the grounds to look natural. The musical sounds of all the birds singing in those trees entertain them. They watch the summer help — who are beginning to live year-around in the Pointe — manicure the lawns. When passing the old Vernier house with its double porch, still surrounded by orchards, they probably gossip about who might buy the place. They are charmed by the old curmudgeon Ferdinand Charles Rivard, still the largest French land owner in the Pointe, if he happens by challenging them to race — his love of horse racing is legend. Proceeding past the Hamilton Park built by James McMillan for racing and exercising horses, he especially looks to see who of his friends are using it.

Upon coming to the Protestant Church, — reorganized and enlarged by Newberry and McMillan for the expanding summer population — they wonder who Sunday's guest preacher might be. Then on to the Claireview Stock farm, owned and operated by George S. Davis, the executive officer of the Parke, Davis Pharmaceutical Company. The farm has 28 buildings, a blacksmith shop, 60 standard bred horses, 30 brood mares belonging to others, a herd of Jersey cows, all well tended by 25 employees. And, before returning to "Lake Terrace," they fulfill one of their special social obligations by inspecting a summer convalescent home kept for Detroit children.

Once Newberry and McMillan establish their domination of the railroad rolling stock industry, thereby creating a firm financial foundation, they quickly move to dominate the ship building and steamboat transportation businesses. The Detroit Dry Dock Company located at the foot of Orleans at Atwater Street is purchased in 1872, capitalized at $400,000 with James McMillan president. In 1879 they purchase the Clark Dry Dock Company located at the foot of Clark Street in Springwells not far from their West Detroit, Michigan Car Company plant. To supply engines for their boats they buy the Dry Dock Engine Works in 1886. Then a third ship building company is acquired, the Detroit Boat Works located on Atwater Street, where McMillan immediately orders a new steam yacht, the *Idler*, equipped with an electrical generator. Making their move in 1882 into the steam transit business, they buy into the Detroit and Cleveland Steam Navigation Company, making McMillan vice president. They also buy the Detroit Transit Company with McMillan as president; the Detroit Navigation Company is purchased, with Newberry vice president, and finally Star Lines Steamers is purchased, with McMillan president and Newberry vice president.

There is not a business to which they were not attracted. In 1873 they incorporate the Detroit Seed Company that competes with Dexter Mason Ferry's seed company. They specialize in garden seeds, flower seeds, field seeds, trees, plants and dried flowers. About a quarter mile from the city limits bordering Michigan Avenue they establish their seed farm and trial gardens. Although the Detroit Seed Company does well, making plenty of money, D. M. Ferry and Company absorbs it in 1880 — obviously with McMillan's blessings as he becomes vice president of the new company, remaining so until his death in 1902. So profitable is the new company that at the time of McMillan's death each share of stock is worth over $5,000.

No new invention escapes their financial eye. One year after Alexander Graham Bell demonstrates the practicality of his telephone at the 1876 Philadelphia Centennial, The Telephone and Telegraph Construction Company is incorporated at $500,000 with Hugh McMillan secretary. Not satisfied with merely erecting poles and stringing wire, Michigan Bell Telephone is incorporated in 1881 with Hugh McMillan as both secretary and treasurer. Believing it's time to take active control of the new telephone business, James McMillan becomes president of the Michigan Telephone Company with brother Hugh still secretary and treasurer.

In 1882, when Thomas Edison demonstrates he can generate a continuous flow of electricity to power his new light bulb and other electrically powered inventions, McMillan incorporates the Edison Electric company. To supply power for the city's new street lights, McMillan incorporates the Electrical Accumulator and Lighting Company with his son, William C. McMillan, as secretary.

Occasionally Newberry and McMillan's ambitions get the best of them. Believing there is a need for additional office space due to Detroit's rapid growth, they complete two office building complexes in 1879: the Newberry and McMillan Building at the corner of Griswold and Larned streets in the heart of Detroit's "Wall Street," and in the second block north of Jefferson Avenue on Woodward a much bigger office block comprising four adjoining addresses. But they misjudge the need for office space, and new rentals come in very slowly. Hoping then to attract occupants, they lower their rents and actively recruit tenants from other office buildings. One landlord losing his tenants to Newberry and McMillan is Christian Buhl.

> *There is not a business to which they were not attracted. . . . Occasionally Newberry and McMillan's ambitions get the best of them.*

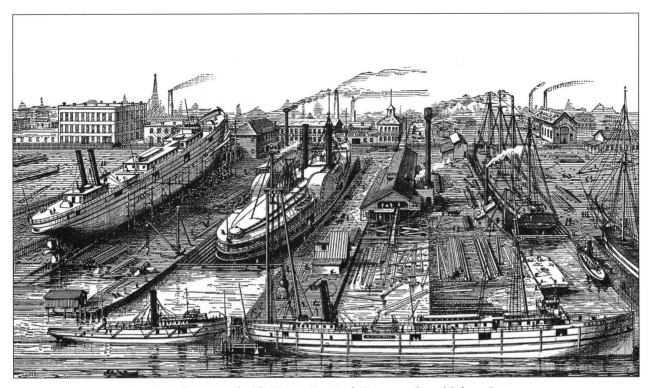

Docks and repair yard of the Detroit Dry Dock Company, foot of Orleans Street.
Illustration from Silas Farmer's History of Detroit and Wayne County and Early Michigan.

That was a serious mistake, for Buhl was not a man to fool with.

In addition to his hardware store and a wholesale fur business, Buhl owns or is a majority stock holder in: the Second National Bank, of which he is a vice president; the Peninsula Stove Company, of which he is the treasurer; the Detroit Copper and Brass Rolling Mills, of which he is president; and the Buhl Iron Works, of which he is also president. As revenge, Buhl finances Col. Frank Hecker and Charles Freer's Peninsular Car Company with his son, Theodore Buhl, as president to safeguard his father's interests. They buy Hiram Walker's buildings on Woodbridge near Joseph Campau streets for their factory. The investors are Buhl, Hecker, and Freer. Freer's $6,000 note is endorsed by Russell Alger and Hiram Walker. Although the 1880s is a very prosperous decade with great demand for railroad cars, Hecker and Freer are outstanding managers selling record numbers of cars. Within just five years Hecker and Freer are able to buy out Buhl and Walker. Then for $50,000 each they take on Russell Alger, James Frederick Joy and Allen Sheldon as their new partners. They move their factory to the Milwaukee Junction, and the new facility becomes so profitable that within just three more years Hecker and Freer can now buy out Alger, Joy and Sheldon for $150,000 each, keeping a 33-1/3%

dividend for themselves. Buhl gets his revenge as Hecker and Freer become more than just "mere" competitors for Newberry and McMillan.

By 1880 Newberry is suffering from Brights disease, an ailment of the kidneys. Undoubtedly preparing for his death, he begins keeping yearly trial balances of his net worth. In 1880 his investments total $2.5 million and his wife's, $281,840; in 1881, Newberry's worth is $2.9 million with his wife's $356,840; in 1885, $3.8 million (no separate figures for his wife); in 1886, $4.5 million (again no figures for his wife). With death approaching he also begins suffering from bronchial asthma. Refusing to confine himself to bed, he insists upon sitting in his chair so he can look out his bay window. On November 25, 1886 he signs his will making the comment, "That will make a nice present for the boys."

While sitting in his chair, Newberry passes away on January 2, 1887. Servants rush to James McMillan's house several doors away, but he can not revive his beloved and trusted partner of many years.

His funeral is the occasion for many tributes, but the one offered by his old Romeo friend and university classmate is probably the best. Judge J. Logan Chipman eulogizes. "With Mr. Newberry, as with all great men, there was indomitable will, energy, the great iron power that characterized his whole life." His estate is worth approximately $4.5 million, with investments in more than fifty different companies. To charitable organizations he leaves $650,000.

Perhaps getting a little tired of making money, perhaps missing his long-time partner, McMillan turns to politics in the late 1880s, getting elected to the United States Senate in 1889.

Upon arriving at the nation's capital, he is dismayed at its lack of beauty, style and grace. To correct that defect he gets himself elected as chairman of the District of Columbia Committee, and calls for a review of Pierre L'Enfant's original plans. Using the expertise gained as chairman of the Detroit committee overseeing the development of Belle Isle, McMillan immediately gets increased Congressional appropriations and hires professionals to make plans. The first change is the removal of railroad tracks and the railroad depot from the Mall, and rerouting trains into the city through a newly-dug tunnel into the Union Station. He has the White House enlarged, and groups new federal buildings into what is now called the Federal Triangle. Using European models, he supervises the widening of avenues, the expansion of the old and creation of new parks, and the building of Memorial Bridge to Arlington, Virginia.

Being exceptionally busy as a U.S. Senator and wanting to curtail his business activities, he employs the aphorism, "If you cannot beat them, join them." To Hecker and Freer, McMillan proposes a combination of their railroad car companies. They agree and five companies are consolidated in 1892 with a capital stock of $8 million and $2 million in bonds, under the name of The Michigan-Peninsular Car Company.

To assuage the fears of the new stock and bond holders, McMillan reassures them he will stay on for the next five years helping to guide the new company. But, the very next year a severe economic depression forces 5,000 companies into bankruptcy and drives over 600 railroads out of business, putting more than a million workers out of a job. The effect on the new Michigan-Peninsular Company is disastrous. The company waters its stock, hoping new orders can justify the practice. Instead, new orders never materialize and old orders are cancelled. The consequence is that the actual value of the stock and good will is reduced to $2 million.

The preferred stock holders are upset. They hold $5 million worth of 8% cumulative preferred stock, which they bought upon McMillan's strong recommendation. Because of the watered stock, fixed costs are too high, putting the new company at a competitive disadvantage. The interest on the bonds amounts to $100,000 a year. In 1894 they lack the $63,976 necessary to make the payments. Earnings in 1896 are only $35,000, not enough to meet fixed costs.

To extricate the new company from its morass of financial difficulties, McMillan returns to Detroit from Washington, D.C. and begins organizing the American Car and Foundry Company. The Chairman of the Board is James McMillan's eldest son, William C. McMillan. The company is capitalized at $30 million worth of 7% non-cumulative preferred stock and $30 million of common stock. James McMillan holds a considerable amount of stock in the new company, hoping he can live out the remaining years of his life on substantial dividends from that stock.

Such is not to be the case, for just three years after the formation of the American Car and Foundry company, McMillan dies on August 10, 1902, just past his sixty-fourth birthday. He suffers a heart attack at his new summer home, Eagle Head at Manchester-By-The-Sea, Massachusetts. Henry B. Ledyard, president of the Michigan Central, sends his private railroad car to transport McMillan and his family back to Detroit. As Russell A. Alger described him, "He had a will, and a purpose; he exercised the first and followed and conquered that which he sought."

Years later, when a new generation of industrialists began manufacturing automobiles in Detroit and desired both an economic climate and an elegant area in which to live, Newberry and McMillan had paved the way by creating foundries, shops, factories, a trained work force, plenty of capital and a graceful, very desirable, Grosse Pointe.

———————————❧———————————

For over thirty years Thomas A. Arbaugh has been a member of the faculty at Macomb Community College. He is presently a professor teaching American History and the History of Technology. His teaching and study of the industrial history of Detroit led to the research and writing of this article. Mr. Arbaugh is a long-time resident of Grosse Pointe Park.

———————————❧———————————

ILLUSTRATION CREDITS: Portraits of John S. Newberry (page 73) and James H. McMillan (page 74) from *Compendium of History and Biography of the City of Detroit.*

Sabbath Eve at Grosse Pointe

by Divie Bethune Duffield

D. Bethune Duffield was known as "one of the poets of the west" during the nineteenth century. He wrote for the New York Knickerbocker *magazine and published several books including a collection of poetry,* Stray Songs of Life, *from which this selection is taken.*

SABBATH EVE AT GROSSE POINTE.

Soft as the shadows of a heavenly day
Fades the mild radiance of our Sabbath eve;
The voiceful waves in sobbing murmurs grieve,
  Like drowsy children, borne from sport away.

High and afar the silver cloud sweeps by,
Bearing perchance, this soft and hallowed even,
Some band of loving angels home to heaven,
  In tender charge of one no more to die.

Below, and slowly o'er the darkening wave
Flits man's frail bark with white though shattered sail,
That tells the story of that stormy gale
  Betwixt his cradle and the waiting grave.

But higher than the cloud, or floating shroud,
Or golden stars that now drop down their rays,
Far through the upper depths in notes of praise
  Earth's pilgrims send, with chantings full and loud,
Their thankful chorus for God's Sabbath days.

SOURCE: *Stray Songs of Life* (New York: Anson D.F. Randolph & Co., 1889).

Divie Bethune Duffield was born in Pennsylvania in 1821 and came to Detroit in his early teens. He was an eminent lawyer who was familiar with Hebrew, Greek and Latin and was fluent in French and German. Duffield was elected Detroit city attorney in 1847 and served as commissioner of the U.S. Court. He was later president of the Detroit Board of Education and is known as the "father of the high school." A long-time summer resident of Grosse Pointe's Lake Shore Road, Duffield was a frequent visitor at Tonnancour and was a member of the community's literary circle. He was also one of the founders of the Grosse Pointe Memorial Church. D. Bethune Duffield died in 1891.

PHOTO CREDIT: Photograph courtesy of the Burton Historical Collection, Detroit Public Library.

Grosse Pointe of Old: As An Artist Saw It

by Jerry Sullivan

Photographer-turned-artist Frank C. Bracy sketched scenes along the Detroit River and Lake St. Clair in the 1880s. It is from these drawings that we have this view of turn-of-the century Grosse Pointe.

GLIMPSES of Detroit as it looked a hundred years ago are revealed in the drawings of one of the city's earliest photographers.

Frank C. Bracy came to Detroit in 1882 and opened a photo studio on Monroe avenue with J. H. Diehl as a partner. He claimed to be the first photographer west of New York City to do retouching, working with a magnifying glass on 16-by-20-inch plates lighted from beneath. Vaudeville stars were among his early patrons.

Bracy's portraits were painted in watercolors and crayons. Later, he turned to watercolor landscapes which were sold widely in New England through an agent.

Bracy was born at Watertown, New York, on February 12, 1851. His family traced their roots from New England. Bracy's great-great-grandfather drove an ammunition wagon at the Battle of Bennington, Vermont, in the Revolutionary War.

Frank Bracy's father, Edwin C. Bracy, moved west with the lumbering industry. The family settled in Augusta, Michigan, about 1857 where the elder Mr. Bracy set up a woodworking and cabinet shop. Young Frank left home at the age of 16 to travel with an itinerant photographer and eventually settled in Detroit.

The photo studio on Monroe was destroyed by fire and the partners set up a second one on Woodward avenue near Grand Circus Park. However, they felt they were too far from the main business district and sold the studio. It was then that Bracy turned to painting.

In the 1880s, Bracy took Sunday afternoon walks along the Detroit River and Lake St. Clair. It was on these leisurely afternoons that he painted the scenes shown here.

In 1887 Bracy married Olive S. Monchamp, whose ancestors had settled here in Cadillac's time with a land grant from the King of France. Their son, Arthur E. Bracy, also became well known as an artist. Frank C. Bracy continued to live and work in Detroit and died here on September 27, 1931 at the age of 80.

This portrait of photographer-artist Frank C. Bracy was taken on a 16 by 20-inch plate in a camera for which he paid $750 in 1882. Photograph courtesy of the Burton historical Collection, Detroit Public Library.

SOURCE: Originally published as: Sullivan, Jerry, "Detroit of Old: As Artist Saw It." *Detroit News Pictorial Magazine*, January 31, 1961, pp. 26-27.

REFERENCES:
Gibson, Arthur H., Compiler. *Artists of Early Michigan.* Detroit: Wayne State University Press, 1975.

This was Grosse Pointe as Bracy saw it in September, 1884. Steamers and a sailing vessel can be seen on Lake St Clair. A handsome carriage with coachman up front makes its way along the lakefront.

This idyllic scene of Grosse Pointe was sketched on a Sunday afternoon in September, 1884, and shows a couple strolling along the Lake Shore Road. In these pencil sketches, artist Bracy used the "wash" method.

ILLUSTRATION NOTES: "Grosse Pointe, September 1884, above Detroit, Michigan." Pencil sketches, Collections of the Dossin Great Lakes Museum, Belle Isle. These two drawings were used as endsheets in Volume 1 of *Tonnancour*.

The Wreck of the Julie Plante

Retold by Joe Grimm

During the 1930s and 1940s Ivan Walton, an English professor in the University of Michigan's Engineering school, traveled the Great Lakes collecting songs from the days of sail. One of the more popular types was the Scow song, and one of the most popular of these was "The Wreck of the Julie Plante."

Scow Songs

SMALL, FLAT-BOTTOMED vessels with a mast or two or a steam engine shuttled wood, stone, sand and building materials about the Detroit and St. Clair Rivers and on Lake St. Clair in the last half of the nineteenth century. Built without keels but with centerboards that the crew could lift straight up or crank up on a pivot, scows had very shallow drafts. This made them ideal for ferrying cordwood from points along both shores to the wood docks for fueling tugs and steamers and for householders in Detroit and nearby communities.

Family crews of two to four operated most scows and the captain's wife often served as cook. As the dialect in these songs indicates, these families were, more often than not, French habitants. As a family of songs, scow songs are most distinctive because of their dialect and their humor.

❦ ❦ ❦

The Wood Scow "Julie Plante"

The usual setting for this song is Lake St. Clair, but variations place it in northern Green Bay off Menominee, and Lac St. Pierre in the St. Lawrence near Montreal. Even Detroit-area versions contain references to Lachine Canal near Montreal.

Nationalistic debate surrounding the song's locale and authorship arose in the 1920s and again in the 1940s. Proponents of Canadian lineage waved copies of William Henry Drummond's 1897 volume of poetry, "The Habitant and Other French Canadian Poems," as the original version. Detroiters responded with recollections of singings and stage performances dating back to more than 50 years before that. They said that Drummond had merely picked up a song in public circulation and passed it off as his own composition. As with many folk songs, the true origin seems to be untraceable, and any argument for the one, authentic version runs contrary to the nature of folk songs passed along and kept alive by word of mouth, rather than by printed page.

———————— ❦ ————————

Walton intended to publish the songs he had collected, including "The Wreck of the Julie Plante," but he never completed the project. Joe Grimm, an editor at the Detroit Free Press, *picked up the project in the 1980s and has completed a manuscript, which he hopes to have published as* Windjammers: Songs of the Great Lakes Under Sail.

The Wreck of the "Julie Plante"

ON WAN dark night on de Lac St. Claire
De win' she blow, blow, blow,
An' de crew of de wood scow "Julie Plante"
Got scar' an' run below —
For de win' she blow like hurricane,
By'm-by she blow some more,
An' de scow bus' up jus' off Grosse Pointe
Ten acre from de shore.

De captain walk on de fron' deck,
He walk on de hin' deck, too —
He call de crew from up de hol',
An' he call de cook also.
De cook, she's name was Rosie
She kom from Montreal,
Was chambermaid on lumber barge
On de beeg Lachine Canal.

De win' she blow from nor'–eas'–wes',
De sout' win' she blow too,
W'en Rosie cry, "Oh, Capitaine,
Capitaine, w'at I shall do!"
De captain den t'row out de hank,
But still de scow she dreef;
De crew he can't pass on de shore
Becos' he los' hees skeef.

De night was dark like wan black cat,
De wave run high an' fas',
W'en de captain take hees poor Rosie
An' lash her to de mas'.
An' den he take de life preserve
An' jomp off in de lake
Say'n, "Au revoir, ma Rosie dear,
I go drown for your sake."

Nex' mornin' veree earlee,
'Bout half pas' two-t'ree-four,
De captain, scow, an' poor Rosie
Was corpses on de shore.
For de win' she blow like hurricane,
An' den she blow some more,
An' de scow bus' up jus' off Grosse Pointe,
Ten acre from de shore.

Now, all good wood-scow sailormen,
Take warnin' by dat storm,
An' go maree some nice French girl,
An' leev on wan beeg farm —
De win' may blow like hurricane,
An' s'pose she blow some more —
You can't get drown on Lac St. Claire
So long you stay on shore.

The Poetry of Alexander Blain

Alexander Blain is a literary man with a love of the wilderness. Here is a selection of his published works, poetry that reflects his insights into his lands and times.

PORCUPINE MOUNTAINS

Virgin hemlocks grow
where there are no bulldozers.
In the middle of lonely Mirror Lake
the loon cries.

IN ELMWOOD CEMETERY

Gray marble above ground
only your name and dates
next to my father.
Forsythia, wild roses
near the stone angel
her arms, wings outstretched
to the crosses of the
Grand Army of the Republic.
Mother, you who first held me
died in my arms
under the picture of a cedar waxwing.
Blossoms turn to flowers
in the center of the
city. Leaves turn green.
Dandelions frame your
name.

STOP

You can't dig here.
Beneath roots of these gnarled trees
lie the remains of my people.
Even the rocks scold.

No one may disturb my ancestors.
Their spirits have smallpox, crushed skulls,
knife wounds, arrowheads in their hearts.

Some even have scalps
taken from old enemies — Iroquois, Sioux.
Their remains can never be removed
from beneath these roots.

Fireballs have been seen, spirits of
disturbed dead, by people of the
Council of the Three Fires and of the Six Nations.

Last week I saw blood welling up here.
It comes from the other side of the earth
where all is holy.
Leaves fall, cover this shrine from winter snows.
Leave now. You can't dig here.

❦ ❦ ❦

LOOKING SOUTH

Across Lake St. Clair
lights of Canada
like stars near earth
gleam over water, a
benediction for Autumn.

No redwings among cattails
but ducks dive the shallows.
They hear the same
flute music we do.
It carries across water,
through cattails,

this sudden Spring between us.

❦ ❦ ❦

I BELIEVE

I believe in wilderness, ducks, grouse,
moose. I believe in
venison from deep swamps
aurora borealis
blue snows, blue blizzards
desert islands; the Virgins, Galapagos
Dominica tropical, lush. I believe it.

I believe in you, earth. I believe in the
uninhabited places.
Mountains, jungles, seas, black lava flowing
Tin cans, empty beer bottles and rusted machines
Everywhere screaming insults
I have seen it and I believe it.

❦ ❦ ❦

CHIPPEWA SCALP DANCE

tom toms throb
west of the Menominee
in the forest in the night
war whoops, cries of triumph and loud, loud weeping
Sioux scalps decorated with feathers of the war eagle
long black hair streams brandished in the firelight
in the forest in the night
west of the Menominee
tom toms throb

SPRING PEEPER

first warm spring rains
you hear him
in marshes
spring peeper

you hear him
powerful piping well into June
spring peeper
Hyla crucifer

powerful piping well into June
quiet nights you hear him a mile
spring peeper
in marshes

Hyla crucifer
quiet nights you hear him a mile
first warm spring rains
he bears his cross.

"Stephanie Nahdee, Chippewa" — *Alex Blain,
Sculptor. Stephanie Nahdee is a descendent of Nahdee,
Tecumseh's lieutenant at the battles of Fallen
Timbers and the Thames.*

❦ ❦ ❦

GHAZALS
IV

A conversation, dialogue between the waves
and this rocky shore.

We have listened to this dialogue.
It continues but we are hundreds of miles away.

Even from a distance we know the conversation
gets rougher during high winds.

When the winds die
there is only a whisper.

We can still hear a whisper
about how things were between us.

Voices tell us what is happening to us.
When the night is silent you can hear stars falling.

❦ ❦ ❦

NOT FAR

Not far from where
Pontiac carried out
the ambush.

Not far from where
my grandfather found
the stone axe.

Not far from where
my father was born,
his grave

Not far from where
my ancestors sleep, I sit
their furious genes
in my daughters and sons.

———————— ❦ ————————

Grosse Pointer Dr. Alexander Blain was born in Detroit. His family immigrated from Scotland to Quebec, and finally to Michigan. Alex Blain was educated at the Detroit University School, Washington and Lee, Wayne State University, and the University of Michigan.

A well-known pioneer in vascular surgery, he was Chief of Surgery at the U.S. Army Hospital, Bad Kreuz-mach, West Germany, and chief surgeon at the Alexander Blain Hospital for twenty-five years.

In addition to his distinguished medical practice, Alex Blain has been active in a number of civic, social, and literary organizations, including: the Detroit Zoo Commission; Family Service Society of Detroit; Grosse Pointe Club; Detroit Racquet Club; Prismatic Club; and Waweatonong Club.

Alexander Blain is a life-long poet and has published several volumes of poetry and essays, among them: Prismatic Essays and an Ode; Clackshant; Shu Shu Ga; Prismatic Haiku Poems; and Partridge Springs Anthology. In addition to his poetry, Alex Blain is an accomplished sculptor and potter.

Blain's poetry shows a continuity between his Scots heritage and personal past in concrete, often witty language. Whether responding to Kirtland's warblers in Northern Michigan, the sparkling waters of Lake St. Clair, or the recollections of times from long ago, his poems convey feeling, curiosity and an irrepressible zest.

The Tug Champion
and the Calvert Lithographing Company

by Jennifer Williams

The cover art for this volume of Tonnancour *is from the noted nineteenth-century lithograph*
The Tug Champion. *The scene depicts the steam tug* Champion *and her tow of eight sailing*
vessels entering the Detroit River at the head of Belle Isle. Peche Island is seen to the right.
To the left is Windmill Point Lighthouse at Grosse Pointe. In this article Jennifer Williams
tells the story of this famous lithograph and the company that produced it.

THE TUG CHAMPION, painted in 1878 by Seth Arca Whipple (1855-1901), recalls a vanished era when sailing ships plied the straits of Detroit, still one of the world's most active commercial shipping lanes. Whipple's best known painting pays homage to the steam-powered *Champion*'s legendary ability to tow eight vessels at once. Great Lakes sailing ships depended on tugs like the *Champion* to guide them through the shallow waterways connecting Lakes Erie and Huron. Because *The Tug Champion* was reproduced as a popular color lithograph of the same name by the Calvert Lithographing Company of Detroit, it survives today as a valuable historical and visual document of what people valued in the visual arts.

The Tug Champion evolved from the tradition of nineteenth-century ship portraiture. Detroit artist Charles Wardlow Norton's (1848-1901) side-wheel steamer *R. N. Rice*, created at about the same time as Whipple's painting, is an example of this earlier style. Norton's work was also reproduced by the Calvert Company and may have served as advertising for the Detroit and Cleveland Navigation Company, owners of the *R. N. Rice*. The foremost requirement of the ship portrait was that it represent the ship in meticulous detail. Ship owners cared little about formal art and would have objected to atmospheric effects and perspectives that would have obscured their prize. Invariably the ship's port or left side was represented, since the name of the ship appears on that side. The wind and waves served as a minimal backdrop and did not distract from the ship.

Whipple's composition for *The Tug Champion* went beyond the draftsmanship of Norton and his contemporaries. Whipple's line of sailing ships disappear into the horizon using convincing linear perspective, and he tackled atmospheric effects of light on water in his use of color. Fluttering pennants, blowing smoke and a fisherman doffing his cap, all create a feeling of motion. The ships are being towed downstream into the Detroit River from Lake St. Clair. Peche Island, Canada, is on the right. The lighthouse in the background is the Windmill Pointe light at the head of the Detroit River, subject of another painting by Whipple, *Fishermen off Windmill Pointe* (reproduced in *Tonnancour*, Volume 1, page 82).

The Tug Champion. *Color lithograph, 26 x 38 in. Reproduced from an 1878 watercolor by Seth Arca Whipple.*
From the Collections of the Detroit Institute of Arts.

Whipple was a self-taught artist who also worked as a photo engraver, sailor and shipyard draftsman. In *The Tug Champion*, Whipple combined his intimate working knowledge of boats with an original artistic vision. Whipple may have been influenced by the luminist painter of marine scenes Fitz Hugh Lane (1804-1865), who also drew and published his own lithographs.

Whipple's tiny water color of *The Tug Champion* was displayed in a Detroit storefront, as was the custom, then purchased by the owners of the tug. It was later given to Henry Ford, and it remains in the collection of the Henry Ford Museum and Greenfield Village in Dearborn. It is the only surviving original design from which a Calvert company lithograph was reproduced.

The color lithograph, known as a chromolithograph, of *The Tug Champion* is several times the size of the original 9-by-12 inch watercolor. Despite Whipple's training as an engraver and draftsman, it is probable that his work was recreated as a print by a skilled lithographer. While capturing all the detail in Whipple's original, the lithographer softened Whipple's intense blue river to a translucent

green, with the tug reflected in its waves. The water has been so skillfully handled that it can almost be heard lapping at the passing ships. This reproduction of Whipple's work struck a chord with Detroit-area residents, who must have realized that life along the shore was changing and events like this would disappear. So popular was this print that two versions exist; it is not known if the Calvert Company produced both.

The print of *The Tug Champion* was produced by the Calvert company during the golden age of chromolithography, between the Civil War and World War I. Firms across the nation exploited a new technology to serve a growing appetite for visual imagery. During this 50-year period, the chromolithograph popularized fine arts, bringing reproductions of art into middle-class homes. At the same time, mass production of large, colorful images revolutionized the advertising industry. Eventually, chromolithographs suffered from their tremendous popularity and overuse, and were replaced by reproductions of photographs.

The Calvert Lithographing Company of Detroit is largely forgotten today. It was one of the nation's most successful commercial lithography firms and in business for over a century. The firm was established in 1861 by English-born entrepreneur Thomas Calvert (1828-1900) upon his arrival in Detroit. At that time Detroit was a growing city of 46,000 people and a major point of entry into the American frontier. From humble beginnings, when his office comprised only one man and his outfit was a small hand press, Calvert rapidly expanded his firm to meet the printing needs of a growing nation.

By the 1890s Calvert had become a wealthy man and an officer in the National Lithographer's Association. He employed over 300 people who operated twenty-two steam and fifty hand-powered lithographic presses and filled orders taken by sales offices in Chicago, St. Louis, and San Francisco. In 1903 the firm moved to a five-story building at the corner of Grand River and Elizabeth Streets. Company assets tripled between 1908 and 1920, totaling almost a million dollars. The company prospered under the direction of Claude Candler, who had been an original partner, and George Heigho and Frederick Heutwell, both of whom served the company from the 1890s until their retirement in the 1940s. The fortunes of the company declined after it was sold to outside investors in 1950, the Grand River building was torn down, and the Calvert Lithographing Company was absorbed by a Canadian printing firm in 1970.

Calvert transfer department, c. 1918.
Calvert workers carefully handle stones on which large lithographs were drawn. Photograph from the Collection of Joseph Davidson, Aaron's Archives.

The lithographic printing process had been developed in 1796 by the Bavarian Alois Senefelder (1771-1834) and the revolutionary technique soon spread to England and America, where the nation's first commercial lithography firm opened in 1825. The ease and economy with which images could be drawn directly onto the printing surface of a flat stone (or later metal) plate surpassed that of contemporary printing techniques. Lithography was the ideal mass communication medium of the industrial revolution.

Lithography is still used by artists today. It is a chemical printing process, based on the principle that oil and water do not mix. The image is drawn on a fine-grained limestone or metal plate with a greasy crayon. The entire plate is washed with a watery gum which adheres to blank areas but not to the image. Oil-based ink is rolled over the plate and sticks only to the image but not to wet areas of the plate. Printing paper is laid over the inked plate and passed through a press under tremendous pressure. The paper is pulled from the plate revealing a print which is a mirror image of the drawing on the plate.

Early lithographs were printed in monochrome and colored by hand. In the 1830s true colored lithographs, or chromolithographs, were devised by printing at least three individually drawn plates, each a different color, in sequence on a single sheet of paper. This process increased in technical complexity as perfect alignment, or registration, of the multiple images and a sophisticated understanding of color mixing were necessary to produce chromolithographs which often used twenty or more different plates.

Steam-powered printing presses, which supplanted hand-cranked presses by the 1870s, greatly increased production and transformed lithography from a craft to an in-

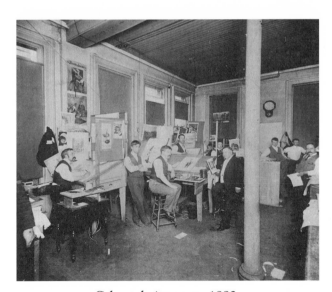

Calvert design room, 1892.
American photographer and designer John Baldwin Thomas (1856-1937) appears at far left surrounded by his work. Company founder Thomas Calvert leans on a stool in the center of the room. Photograph from the Collection of Jean Wyatt.

On the Warpath. *Color lithograph, 21¹/₂ x 29 in. Reproduced by Robert T. Bishop from an 1872 painting by John Mix Stanley. From the Collection of the Library of Congress.*

dustry. In the 1880s and 1890s new techniques allowed photographs to be reproduced in color and eliminated the need for much of the original art work used to that point. By World War I, such photomechanical reproduction had begun to replace chromolithography as a commercial medium for printing firms.

The Calvert company's reproduction of Whipple's *The Tug Champion* painting in 1878 was no doubt affected by an earlier, ill-fated project. In 1872 Calvert had collaborated with John Mix Stanley (1814-1872), a Detroit-born painter of the American west with a national reputation, to reproduce *On the Warpath*. According to an accompanying brochure *On the Warpath* portrayed "an army composed of Northern Tribes, *en route* to give battle to an insolent foe." In reproducing it, Thomas Calvert spared no expense as he tried to equal Stanley's earlier chromolithographs, which were created in Berlin. Calvert brought lithographer Robert T. Bishop from England to create twenty stone

plates that would capture the rich colors and detail of Stanley's oil painting. The original painting has since been lost, leaving chromolithograph as the only record of this composition.

Acclaimed as an artistic success, *On the Warpath* was a financial disaster for Calvert. Smoke from a fire in a nearby building ruined the plates when only 300 prints had been finished. Stanley died before the company could recoup its investment on future works. The following year, the worldwide financial panic of 1873 crippled the local economy, putting the twenty dollar *On the Warpath* out of the price range of local buyers.

No wonder the Calvert Company never again attempted fine art reproduction on so grand a scale. Though no recollection of *The Tug Champion*'s production remains, Whipple's work can be seen as a much safer choice for the company to reproduce. Whipple was a local artist and subject matter was dear to the hearts of local buyers.

Both *On the Warpath* and *The Tug Champion* catered to the persistent public taste for the style of art popularized by the Dusseldorf Academy. The German school was a mecca for American artists between 1840 and 1870, including John Mix Stanley. The paintings of these Dusseldorf-trained artists suited popular demand for idealized, narrative pictures told in super-realistic detail. This style fit the needs of chromolithographers as well because the artists worked in clearly defined areas of local color that lithographers could easily separate into individual color plates for production.

Less financially risky than fine art reproduction was the Calvert Company's commercial work. Though the bulk of this commercial printing was probably business forms and labels for canned goods, the company liked to emphasize the pictorial quality of its advertising.

A major Calvert client was the Detroit-based Ferry Seed Company. This firm was the first to provide merchants with complete, prepackaged assortments of vegetable and flower seeds suited to local growing conditions. With their promise of bumper crops, attractive seed packets and colorful posters and catalogs were crucial to the Ferry Seed Company's success. *The Ferry Seed Annual* must have been welcomed by customers as a harbinger of spring. This catalog cover featured the Belle Isle Conservatory designed by George Nettleton and Albert Kahn.

Then as now, brewing and tobacco advertising was aggressive. Eye-catching cigar box designs were essential in the fiercely competitive tobacco industry. Hundreds of cigar brands might compete against each other in a single store. In 1888, for example, the *New York Sun* had commented, "The label is often better than the cigar." The watercolor design for the *La Bois Blanc* brand cigar box advertised both the product and the development of Bois Blanc (Bob-Lo) Island as a recreational center.

The loose brush work and light-filled colors of this turn-of-the century watercolor reflect middle Americans' acceptance of the once revolutionary vision of the French Impressionists. Whether the freshness of this watercolor would have been retained in the finished chromolithograph is unknown since a finished label has not been found, but the gilded lettering and flourishes indicate this is a finished design concept.

La Bois Blanc and other circus and theater posters Calvert produced at the turn of the century may also have been influenced by entertainment posters produced by French commercial artist Jules Cheret (1836-1932). Cheret introduced the medium of chromolithography to artists and helped spark an end-of-century advertising poster craze. Works by Cheret (credited with inventing the

Ferry Seed Annual Cover, 1908.
Color lithograph, 9¹/2 x 6³/4 in.
From the Collection of the Detroit Historical Museum.

"right style of poster") were included in a nationally toured exhibition that came to Detroit in 1895.

Locally produced works of the Calvert Company were not part of this exhibition. While Parisian advertisements for everything from theater to bicycles were coveted by fine art collectors on both sides of the Atlantic, Americans ignored most domestically produced posters.

Despite the Calvert company's efforts to keep up with changing tastes, it was too late to change the popular perception of the American chromolithograph as a relic of the past. In 1895 a critic in *Scribner's Magazine* echoed the backlash against the Dusseldorf style in chromolithography:

Most lithographic draftsmen in this country are either Germans or German-Americans, and they adhere with persistence to the traditions of the German technique. . . Set before him, at the top of his little wooden desk, the most brilliant watercolor that Fortuny ever dashed off, and as he slowly separates its mystic tints into what he considers their

La Bois Blanc, c. 1900. *Watercolor, 4³/4 x 7³/4 in. From the Collection of Art Gallery of Windsor.*

component elements and reproduces them in his even, unvarying grain, that please him the better the more he makes it look like machine-work, he will pity the poor devil of a unskilled artist who didn't know how to finish up his work "nice and smooth."[1]

As tastes and technology changed, an entire body of work was dismissed as old-fashioned and tainted by its commercial associations. "Chromo" became a derogatory term for anything cheap and gaudy. Public and printer alike embraced modern photomechanical means of reproduction, and chromolithographs were abandoned as nineteenth-century relics.

Today chromolithographs like *The Tug Champion* are coveted by collectors. Unfortunately, little of the Calvert company's enormous output has survived a century of neglect. Chromolithographs were an important influence on public taste. The works Calvert produced brought the styles of European art academies to the general public both through reproductions of paintings and through commercial interpretations of contemporary styles. In addition, chromolithographs provide a fascinating glimpse into the past. *The Tug Champion* reminds us of the pride people felt in unique local events and of their support for artists who idealized these events.

———————— ❦ ————————

Jennifer Reed Williams is an Assistant Curator in the Department of Education at the Detroit Institute of Arts. She received her Bachelor's degree in art education from Ball State University, Muncie, Indiana and holds a Master's degree in art history from Wayne State University.

———————— ❦ ————————

1   H. C. Bunner, *Scribner's Magazine* (October, 1895) quoted in Keay, *American Posters of the Turn of the Century*, 1975.

BELLE ISLE:
The Story of an Island Park

By Lynda M. Lawicki

The French called it IIe aux Cochons, the English called it Hog Island. Today we call it

Belle Isle. Located at the head of the Detroit River where the waters of Lake St. Clair

pass the Grand Marais and Windmill Point, Belle Isle has had a long and colorful history.

Here the story of the beautiful island park is told by Lynda M. Lawicki.

BELLE ISLE IS many things to many people. It has a rich history filled with personal and historical significance. Belle Isle's heritage, as with much of American history, begins with the Indians. Their legends tell of the creation of the island and the snakes that inhabited its swampy shores. A spirit known as "Sleeping Bear" had a beautiful daughter whom he protected by keeping her in a box on Lake Michigan. The north and west wind spirits fought over the beautiful girl and created a great storm. The box broke loose and floated into Lake Huron and then all the way down to the mouth of the Detroit River. The girl was

*Built in 1863 by R. Storrs Willis,
the White House is today home for the Park's offices.
Photograph courtesy of the Friends of Belle Isle.*

The Belle Isle Lighthouse, 1927.
*Located on the site of the present-day Coast Guard Station,
this lighthouse began operation in 1882. Photograph courtesy
of the Dossin Great Lakes Museum.*

*A post card of the "Detroit Boat Club – 1902," with
the club burgee. Courtesy of the Dossin Great Lakes Museum.*

Page 97. *This view of the island dates from the turn of the
century. Upper left: Detroit Boat Club, 1894;
lower left: police station, 1893; upper right: canoeists on canal;
lower right, catboat; center: Detroit Yacht Club, 1895.
Illustrations courtesy of the Dossin Great Lakes Museum.*

rescued by the spirit known as "The Keeper of the Gates of
the Lakes. "The box then lodged in the mouth of the
Detroit River, broke into pieces, and became Belle Isle.

When French missionaries visited the Detroit area in
1670, they discovered an idol to the Indian god Manitou.
They destroyed the idol. When the Indians discovered
this, they gathered up the pieces and brought them to Belle
Isle where the spirit of Manitou had taken refuge. The
pieces were magically turned into rattlesnakes. This could
explain why many people have believed that the island
was first named Snake Island. There is no documentation
to back that claim, but it is known that the Indians called
it Wahnabezee, which means White Swan. The French,
who were the first Europeans to inhabit the area, called it
IIe aux Cochons, or Hog Island. Legend has it that the
swampy island, which is only two feet above sea level and
was infested with snakes, had hogs let loose on it to deplete
the number of snakes, and thus it became known as Hog
Island.

French settlers began farming on the 704-acre island in
1759, but a year later it became English territory. It was
then farmed by two British officers, Lt. George McDougall
and Sergeant James Fisher. In 1763 Chief Pontiac massacred the English farmers and their families after he had
staged an unsuccessful raid on the fort at Detroit. Lt. Mc-
Dougall was the only one who was not on the island at the
time of the attack and thus his life was spared. Later he
petitioned King George for ownership of the island. One of
the conditions of the purchase was that he had to obtain a
peaceful agreement from the Indians for the purchase of
the island. He made a deal with the Indians to purchase
the property for the price of five barrels of rum, three rolls
of tobacco, three pounds of vermilion paint and one
wampum belt. After the deed was signed, McDougall gave
the Indian chiefs three more barrels of rum and three more
pounds of paint. When McDougall died in 1780 the British
Government claimed the property. Through the Treaty of
Paris in 1783 the island became American territory.

William McComb purchased the island in 1794. David
McComb, his son, became the sole owner of the island in
1811, 15 years after his father's death. Barnabas Campau
bought the island from McComb for $500. He was the last
private owner of the island. He died in 1845. His widow
and her new husband, R. Storrs Willis, built a home facing
the Canadian side of the island in 1863. It remains the oldest building on the island. It was renovated in 1984 by the
Friends of Belle Isle organization. Originally the home was
named Insulruhe (In-Sul-Ru-A). It is now called the
White House and is home for the park's offices.

Ferry service to the island began in the 1840s and ran
three times a week. Alexander Campau, son of Barnabas,

Belle Isle Park – 1900.
Illustration courtesy of the Dossin Great Lakes Museum.

BELLE ISLE PARK

1.	Ferry Dock	24.	Michigan Fish
2.	Bath House		Commission
3.	Boat House	25.	Greenhouse
4.	Belle Isle Bridge	26.	Inselruhe
5.	Muir Fountain	27.	Barns
6.	Lily Pond	28.	Zoological Grounds
7.	Loop Canal	29.	Nashua Canal
8.	Sunset Drive	30.	Inselruhe Avenue
9.	Casino Way	31.	Ladies' Toilet
10.	Casino	32.	Police
11.	Detroit Boat Club	33.	Shelter Pavilion
12.	River Bank Road	34.	Athletic Field
13.	Marsh Run	35.	Detroit Yacht Club
14.	Muse Road	36.	Tanglewood Drive
15.	Electric Light	37.	Vista Drive
	Transmission House	38.	Lake Okonoka
16.	Shelter	39.	U.S. Light House
17.	Central Avenue	40.	Horse Shelter
18.	Men's Toilet	41.	Lake Muskoday
19.	Loiter Way	42.	Lakeside Drive
20.	Skating Pavilion	43.	Woodside Drive
21.	Lake Tacoma	44.	Oak Way
22.	Picnic Way	45.	Meadow Road
23.	The Strand	46.	Wildwood Pass

installed two docks, a hotel, bathhouse, archery galleries, croquet grounds and refreshment parlor on the island to attract city dwellers. Many gathered for picnics on the island in the summer. In 1845, members of the Detroit Boat Club and their female guests held a picnic on the island. The men did not feel that the name Hog Island fit the beauty of the location and decided to call it Belle Isle in honor of Governor Lewis Cass' daughter Isabella, who

was a member of their party that day. ("Belle" is French for beautiful.) The name wasn't officially adopted until August 25, 1881, when the Detroit City Council passed an ordinance changing the island's name. The City of Detroit purchased the island for $200,000 in 1879.

The first light from a new lighthouse built on the island shone on May 15, 1882. In 1939 a Coast Guard station was begun on the 1.25 acre lighthouse site. It was completed in 1942. The light from the original lighthouse is still in use on the top of the present station. It was originally known as the St. Clair Lifeboat Station. After the St. Clair Shores station was built, the island station's name was changed to Station Belle Isle.

The Detroit Boat Club, which was founded on the mainland in 1839, moved its permanent residence to Belle Isle in 1890. The elegant wooden structure, built on pilings in the river, burned on October 15, 1893. That next year a new club was built. Fire again consumed the club on October 17, 1901. The new building was then constructed with reinforced concrete to make the structure more fire-

The Belle Isle ferry at the "Steamer Landing," foot of Woodward Avenue, 1913. Post card courtesy of Cynthia Bieniek.

proof. The Detroit Boat Club boasts the prestigious distinctions of being the oldest rowing club in continuous existence in the world, oldest boat club in the United States, and the oldest social club in Michigan.

In the early days of the Olympic games, the athletes were sponsored by athletic clubs. The 1928 U.S. Olympic swimming trials were held at the Detroit Boat Club. The Detroit Boat Club was the home club for Johnny Weismuller, who became an Olympic medal winner in swimming. He is widely known as the star of MGM pictures' Tarzan movies.

In September of 1992, the Detroit Boat Club filed for bankruptcy. The decline in membership over the years and increased operating costs contributed to its dismal financial situation. On March 2, 1996, the Detroit Boat Club facility on Belle Isle was turned over to the City of Detroit for nonpayment of rent and back taxes. The Detroit Parks and Recreation department plans to open the marina and pool to the public. The fate of the deteriorating club house is yet to be determined. The rowing team, which is funded by the Friends of Detroit Rowing organization, plans to continue using the boat club facility.

The City of Detroit's purchase of the island in 1879 prompted the city council to seek the aid of Frederick Law Olmstead, the famous landscape architect who designed

Central Park in New York, as well as the Washington Mall, Boston Common, Grant Park in Chicago and Golden Gate Park in San Francisco. The series of interconnected canals on the island are a result of his master plan for the island park. The canals provided visitors with a fun and relaxing recreation. Canoes could be rented or brought to the island. Many of the canoes were elaborately furnished with pillows and victrolas, which visitors would bring in their own boats. Sometimes the canoes would be decorated and then linked into a chain. Paddling along peacefully through the canals became a wonderful pastime. In 1995 the canals were drained so that silt that had built up over the years could be dredged out and the canal banks could be reinforced. The clean-up is expected to be completed within the next few years.

The building of the canals served many purposes in the original master plan for the island. Some of the dirt was used to help fill in the swampy east end of the island and combined with dirt from the construction of the new casino building to help build the picturesque Cedar Mount at the west end. The beautiful Cedar Mount had a grotto underneath it, a bandstand on the top, and a beautiful waterfall cascading down one side. It was located near the casino building.

Above: *"Canoe Day, August 25, 1906." Canoeing has always been one of the island's most popular activities. Photograph courtesy of the Dossin Great Lakes Museum.*

Below: *A post card of the "Cedar Mount, Waterfall and Canoes, Belle Isle — one of the most beautiful parks in the United States." Courtesy of the Dossin Great Lakes Museum.*

Olympic swimmer Johnny Weismuller, Detroit Boat Club, 1928. Photograph courtesy of the Dossin Great Lakes Museum.

The island's second casino, opened in 1908. Designed by the noted architect Albert Kahn, the Casino is today the site of many of the social activities held on the island. Photograph by Joseph P. Messena.

Looking around the park today, the structures hint of the charm and elegance that are so much a part of this island's history. Some are the original buildings and others have replaced the ones that served their time or were destroyed by accidental fires. The casino building on the Canadian side is the second one built at the park. The original wooden structure was built in 1887. After it burned, the new casino, designed by Albert Kahn, replaced it.

The 1889 wooden bridge to the island caught fire in 1915 after several hot coals dropped off a city street repair truck. Several sections of the bridge burned and it was unable to be saved. It was reported that over 1,500 people were on the island and were forced to have to wait for ferries to take them back to the mainland. A temporary bridge was put in the following year. The new concrete bridge, which is still standing today, was completed in 1923. It included an underpass that allowed an uninterrupted drive onto the bridge from East Grand Boulevard. In 1942 it was named after Gen. Douglas McArthur. When the bridge was renovated in the early 1980s the underpass was eliminated and a new intersection was added to the entrance of the island.

The city landscape from the mainland and island entrances have changed over the years. In the early days there was a stone grotto that provided shelter for those waiting for a cart to take them across the bridge to the island. Some may recall the two amusement parks that used to be on either side of the bridge, or the Uniroyal plant, and

the enormous wooden stove. On the island, the first bridge entrance had a canal that came very close to the road off the bridge. When the new bridge was built east of the original one, the entrance changed. In the 1960s the floral clock that had been at Waterworks park was brought to Belle Isle. It remains the greeting point on the island today.

The 1893 skating pavilion was replaced in 1950 by the Flynn Memorial Pavilion. In 1994 Bert's Jazz Bar took over the pavilion and began operating there. Ice skating and sleigh rides were some of the winter recreational activities at Belle Isle. Ice skating was as popular in the winter as canoeing was in the summer, although it did have its dangers. On one occasion a teenager was daring enough to skate across a patch of ice that went across the river to Canada. Upon reaching the shore, he found that the ice had broken up behind him and he was forced to take a ferry back to Detroit, a street car to the Belle Isle bridge, and then walk back to the skating pavilion where he had left his shoes. Ice skating on the canals has since dwindled and there isn't a pavilion available anymore. Hart Plaza is the new location in the city where ice skates can be rented and an outdoor lighted rink is available for those who wish to skate at night.

The police station, which is still operating on the island, was built in 1893. In 1927 this police station became the first location in the United States to regularly broadcast to its police cars by radio. The upstairs room in the station served as the dispatch.

By the late 1800s, swimming had become one of the favored summer activities. Long dresses and suits were replaced by thick wool one-piece swim suits. In 1894 a bath house was built near the lower end of the island and was continuously expanded upon over the next 10 years. The bath house provided changing facilities, towels and swim suit rental. Swimming continues to be one of the favored attractions on the island during the summer. A new water slide is scheduled to open.

The Aquarium and the elegant Conservatory were built in 1904. The Aquarium is the oldest municipally founded Aquarium in the United States. One of the most popular exhibits there contains an electric eel, which, when being fed, releases an electrical charge that lights up a light bulb on the outside of the tank. The Conservatory in 1955 was named after Anna Scripps Witcomb, daughter of the owner of the *Detroit News*. Seasonal floral shows include the fall mum, Christmas, cyclamen, Easter, and summer flower exhibits.

In 1909, the first Detroit Zoo was established on the island. Jack Timmons was the Zoo keeper from 1920-1930. On June 1, 1924, Sheba the baby elephant was brought to the zoo, purchased with 200,000 pennies ($2,000) contributed by Detroit school children. The *Detroit News* donated the red cart that was hitched to Sheba so she could take children for rides. The first camels born in cap-

Visitors to the Conservatory, 1923.
Photograph courtesy of the Dossin Great Lakes Museum.

tivity were born at the Zoo on Belle Isle. The Belle Isle Zoo was moved out to the main Detroit Zoo in Royal Oak in 1956. It was replaced by a children's zoo, which was funded with a gift of the James and Lynelle Holden Fund. In 1980 the Safari Land Zoo replaced the children's zoo.

Many memorial statues adorn the island landscape. The first to be placed on the island was of a newsboy and his dog. It was brought there in 1897 and paid for by James E. Scripps, founder of the *Detroit News*. The newsboy has

The city fireboat James Battle *fights unsuccessfully to control flames as the Island bridge burns, April 27, 1915.*
Photograph courtesy of the Dossin Great Lakes Museum.

Built in 1925, the beautiful Scott Fountain is still one of the island's most prominent sites.
Photograph courtesy of the Friends of Belle Isle.

Yachtsmen and club members gather at the Detroit Yacht Club for the Harnsworth Trophy Race, August 31, 1929.
Photograph courtesy of the Dossin Great Lakes Museum.

been stolen twice. It was recovered the first time, but when it was taken in 1974 it was never found. The Major General Alpheus Starky Williams statue features him sitting on his horse and studying a map. This statue is in the middle of the Central Avenue-Inselruhe intersection. It was brought to the island in 1921 and was sponsored by the Michigan Commandery of the Military Order of the Loyal Legion of the United States. Other statues feature German writer Johann Friedrick von Schiller sitting and reading in a chair, the Samuel Francis Smith Flagpole, the Civil War Monument, James J. Brady Memorial Monument, the International Peace Monument, Spanish-American War Memorial, Dante Alighieri bust, Levi Barbour Fountain in the Conservatory outdoor garden, and the James Scott statue that accompanies the beautiful fountain.

The Scott Fountain, which cost one million dollars to construct, was built with enormous marble carvings, brass fixtures, and Pewabic tile. James Scott bequeathed the funds for the construction of the memorial fountain and statue to the city of Detroit upon his death in 1910. For several years the city council debated over whether to accept his donation. Mr. Scott was known as a gambling, heavy drinking womanizer and many did not want to have a statue of him accompany the fountain. In the end the donation was accepted. Cass Gilbert was the architectural designer of the James Scott Fountain. He won the commission over 93 other entries in a nationwide competition conducted in 1914. Fifty-one acres of fill dirt from the construction of new city streets was brought to the island to create a location for the fountain. Stones from the foundation of the first Belle Isle bridge were used to create a breakwater around the new edge of the island. The fountain was completed in 1925. At night, in the summer, the picturesque marble fountain is lit with colored lights.

Another of the distinguished structures on Belle Isle is the Detroit Yacht Club. The club was organized on the mainland in 1868. In 1895 the Detroit Yacht Club bought the Michigan Yacht and Club facility on Belle Isle. That building burned in 1904, and a new facility was built. In 1923, the clubhouse that is standing today was built at a new site, east of the original.

The Detroit Yacht Club has a lengthy history in powerboat racing. Gar Wood, nicknamed The Silver Fox, won the famous Harnsworth trophy from England and brought the race to U.S. waters. He was also the first Commodore at the new club location. The Yacht Club has hosted the Gold and Silver Cup races for years. As you look around the club there are trophies everywhere. One could easily mistake them for beautiful metal sculptures, but on close inspection you will find an inscription with the name of the recipient. In addition to the powerboat races the club also sponsors catboat and other small sailboat races.

The Great Lakes schooner J.T. Wing served as the island's first maritime museum. Photograph courtesy of the Dossin Great Lakes Museum.

The Dossin Great Lakes Maritime Museum is another major attraction on the island. It provides a location where people of all ages can learn about the numerous historical events that have taken place on and around the waterways of the Great Lakes. It is however, not the first maritime museum on Belle Isle. In 1945, the *J.T. Wing* was brought to dock at the island. It was a wooden schooner which carried lumber before it was brought to rest on the Canadian side of Belle Isle. Many artifacts were exhibited in the vessel and its deck was preserved as it had been when it sailed the Great Lakes. Unfortunately, by 1954, severe dry rot had set in. The *J.T. Wing* could not be saved and was burned.

The present museum was opened in 1960. It was greatly expanded in 1968 with the construction of the Aaron De Roy Hall. Today visitors can view exhibits of fine Great Lakes ship models, scan the river through a periscope brought from the submarine *U.S.S. Tambor,* and experience a true hands-on tour of the pilot house of the freighter *William Clay Ford,* which was opened in 1992.

Over the years Belle Isle has provided a location for some famous historic shows. The "Buffalo Bill Wild West & Pawnee Bill Great Far East Show" was invited to perform on Belle Isle by the Elks Club, which held its annual convention on the island on July 14, 1910. The parade and pageant took place on the grounds where the athletic fields are today. On November 27, 1906, Houdini performed his escape artistry off the Belle Isle bridge.

Above: *A family outing on Belle Isle, ca. 1900. Photograph courtesy of the Dossin Great Lakes Museum.*

Left: *The Livingstone Lighthouse guides freighters as they leave Lake St. Clair and enter the Detroit River. Photograph courtesy of the Dossin Great Lakes Museum.*

Below: *Pony cart rides were for many years one of the island's most popular attractions. Photograph courtesy of the Dossin Great Lakes Museum.*

Many other activities have taken place on the island. Family reunion picnics have been recorded as early as 1899 and are a big part of the activities during the summer. Older residents remember the fishing and the model boat ponds, or the bike shelter and boathouse, and still others recall the pony carts and horseback riding on the island. All these activities hold memories of a simpler time when families and friends gathered to enjoy the beauty of nature, breath the fresh air and soak up the sun at the island park. For years cricket has been played on the west side lawn by the Casino. The woods have for generations been a peaceful haven where you can feed the deer or just enjoy a tranquil drive through the forest. In the winter there is no need to venture into the woods to find the deer, for they come out to look for food and can often be seen in the picnic grounds.

The entire island is a peaceful retreat. The nature trails go through the woods and along the canals. Another path leads to the Livingstone lighthouse at the far east end of the island. Along the waters' edge there is a view of one of the busiest waterways in the world. During the winter, the ice fountain and the ice flows are some of the outdoor sights to see, as echoes of the carillon's chimes gently break the winter silence on the island. In the warmer months, there is a constant flow of freighters from all around the world passing by.

Some of the other unique structures on Belle Isle are the William Livingstone Memorial Lighthouse, the Nancy Brown Peace Carillon, and the Lee Remick Band Shell. The 58-foot-high lighthouse designed by Albert Kahn was erected in 1930 at the cost of $100,000, which was raised by The Lake Carriers' Association and Detroit businessmen. It is the only lighthouse in the world that is completely made of marble. The Nancy Brown Peace Carillon was built in 1940 with funds donated by readers of the *Detroit News* writer's "Experience" column. The carillon's 49 bells toll the time at the top of the hour, and its elegant chimes toll a song on the half hour. A short distance away is the Remick Band Shell, which was built in 1953. Many types of bands have played there over the years. Some of the most popular programs were those presented by the Detroit Concert Band under the direction of conductor Leonard B. Smith. In the summer of 1977, the NBC network recorded a television special called "Soul and Symphony," featuring musical artists from the Detroit Symphony and soul music bands to demonstrate their talents at this beautiful outdoor setting.

Right: *The world-class Detroit Grand Prix has become one of the motor city's premier sporting events. This photograph of the 1992 race, with the Detroit skyline in the background, was taken by Tony Spina. Courtesy of the* Detroit Free Press.

Hydroplanes roar past the Detroit Yacht Club, June 10, 1986, at the Gold Cup Races. Photograph courtesy of the Dossin Great Lakes Museum.

This Nike missile base was built at the east end of the island at the height of the Cold War. Photograph courtesy of the Dossin Great Lakes Museum.

This ariel view of Belle Isle, taken in the early 1950s, shows this beautiful island park much as it appears today. Photograph courtesy of the Dossin Great Lakes Museum.

Though the island is a tranquil park, it has also seen unrest. The city's 1943 race riot began on the Belle Isle bridge, and the violence escalated to encompass the surrounding neighborhoods. In 1954, a Nike guided missile site was built at the east end of the island near the Livingstone Lighthouse. Fortunately, there was never a need to use them and the base was removed from the island in 1969. In 1967, as a result of the 4,732 arrests made during the race riots, the National Guard made a jail out of the bath house. The bath house was never used again and was torn down a few years later.

Over the years various features on the island disappeared from its landscape. The ferries stopped going to the island in 1957. Eventually, the sleigh rides, pony cart rides and horseback riding became a thing of the past. Through neglect, many of the island's buildings fell into disrepair. For several years the island's grounds were not maintained as they should have been and the island had a sadly rundown appearance.

Fortunately, today, renovation has begun. With volunteers and funds, the restoration of the island to the elegance that previous generations remember has become possible.

In 1992, the Detroit Grand Prix was brought to the island after being held for ten years on the streets of downtown Detroit. The revenues from the event have helped to restore turn-of-the-century picnic shelters and renovations at the Casino. The Michigan Department of Natural Resources began its restoration of the canals on Belle Isle in 1995 and plans to complete the project within the next few years.

This isle is a beautiful haven where folks from all walks of life have come to picnic with their families and relax under the trees, while watching freighters glide down the river. The island has watched the City of Detroit grow into an industrial giant and has provided refuge from the hustle and bustle of the city with its beauty and serenity. Its history is rich with fact, folklore, and fame.

———————————— ❧ ————————————

Lynda M. Lawicki received her B. S. in Broadcasting from Grand Valley State University. With a life-long interest in local history, she co-produced with WDIV TV4 the documentary "Belle Isle: A Portrait in Time." It first aired on television March 30, 1996. She has also co-produced with WDIV an earlier documentary, "Boblo Memories." Ms. Lawicki is a long-time resident of the city of St. Clair Shores.

Let the Lower Lights Be Burning: A History of the Lighthouses at the St. Clair Flats

by Cynthia S. Bieniek

Located at the head of Lake St. Clair, the delta area popularly known as the "Flats" has been an obstacle to navigation since the first Native Americans explored the region by canoe. During the 19th century, as commerce developed on the Great Lakes, it became obvious that improvements were needed at the Flats. These navigational aids included charts, dredging of shipping channels, and lighthouses.

Early Navigators

IN TOPOGRAPHICAL TERMS, the area of the St. Clair Flats is a delta, consisting of multiple water channels running through an area of marshy vegetation. The Flats are about seven miles wide from shore to shore, and the waters of Lake Huron flow down the St. Clair River and discharge into Lake St. Clair through this fan shaped waterway. Father Louis Hennepin recorded in his journal, *A New Discovery of a Vast Country in America* that:

The streight between the Lake Huron and the Lake St. Claire . . . is very shallow especially at its mouth. The Lake Huron falls into this of St. Claire by several Canals, which are commonly interrupted by Sand and Rocks. We sounded all of them, and found one at last about one league broad without any Sand, its Depth being every where from three to eight Fathoms Water. We sail'd up that Canal, but were forc'd to drop our Anchors near the Mouth of the Lake. . .[1]

This description of Father Hennepin's voyage with the explorer LaSalle on the *Griffin* in 1679 paints an image of

---

[1] Father Louis Hennepin. *A New Discovery of a Vast Country in America*, 1972 (reprint), Vol I. p.11.

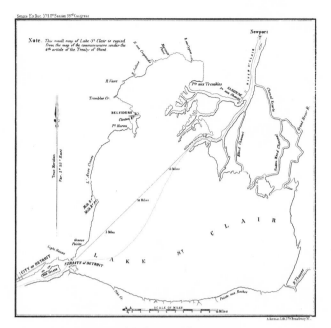

Map of Lake St. Clair, 1853.
*This 1853 map clearly shows the multiple channels
of the Lake St. Clair delta region known as the Flats.
Illustration courtesy of the Dossin Great Lakes Museum.*

the St. Clair Flats as much broader than our present day and filled with islands and rapids.

After the American Revolutionary War, Captain William Thorn, a British citizen living in Cottreville on the St. Clair River, became one of the first Great Lakes pilots.[2] He is credited with sailing the first schooner to the head of Lake Huron through the east channel of the Flats in 1770.[3] In 1814, he served as Colonel George Croghan's pilot during the unsuccessful attempt to recapture Fort Mackinac from the British.

Thomas L. McKenney in his *Sketches of a Tour to the Lakes* in 1826 described the Flats from aboard the schooner *Ghent*, with Colonel Croghan and Michigan Territorial Governor Lewis Cass as sailing companions, as follows:

> At eight o'clock p.m. we had passed up the strait (Detroit River), and through Lake St. Clair, where the wind left us, and we came to anchor, distant from Detroit about thirty-five miles. The river at this place is narrow. Extensive marshes on either side, through which it winds its way, produces immense quantities of mosquitos. These

annoy us very much. Yet there is no escaping, except the wind shall blow, not only fair, but strong enough to force us through the current, which is rapid, and runs, at this place at the rate of three miles the hour. [4]

Statehood: Topographical Engineers and Lake Surveys

The year 1837 marked statehood for Michigan and eager eyes were turned to profit as goods and people were transported westward. Passenger and freight vessels plied the lakes in increasing numbers on the long roundabout trip to Chicago. One of the major navigation problems at the Flats was the fluctuations of lake levels, and a call was made for a general lake survey to be performed and lake charts of the region to be drawn.

> A great rise of water took place in 1800, though of a corresponding fall in 1807, nothing is said. Another great rise took place in 1814, and in 1830, with a corresponding depression in 1839. They are at an unusual height the present season, covering parts of the river road and portions of the lower street and some of the wharves in Detroit . . . This unexpected inundation has spread over considerable tracts on Lake St. Clair and the straits (Flats), to the destruction of the crops and injury of roads. Time may develop facts more satisfactory, but we are inclined to attribute the concurrent circumstances to the fortuitous coincidence of time and fact, rather than to any settled law governing this apparent periodical fluctuation.[5]

In 1842, Captain William G. Williams of the U.S. Topographical Engineers mapped the St. Clair Flats delta and noted the velocity and amount of water pouring over the marshy ground, where "the sides of steamboats are swept on either side by the rushes." Cargoes frequently had to be lightered (partially unloaded) to get them over the Flats. One spot, called the "Old Crib," had been used for this purpose since the early French voyageurs passed through the Flats in their bateaux. This survey of the Flats cost $6,000 and the recommendation was made to dredge the South Channel to a depth of 12 feet and widen it to 500 feet.[6] This would allow the larger vessels being built for lake commerce to pass easily over the Flats.

2   Michigan Pioneer and Historical Society. *Collections.* Vol. 4 1881. p.310.
3   Michigan Pioneer and Historical Society. *Collections.* Vol. 5 1882. p.503.
4   Thomas L. McKenney. *Sketches of a Tour to the Lakes.* 1827. p.144.
5   John T. Blois. *Gazetteer of the State of Michigan.* Detroit: Sydney L. Rood, 1838. p.48-65.
6   John W. Larson. *Essayons: A History of the Detroit District U.S. Army Corps. of Engineers,* 1986. p.38.

In a letter dated May 15, 1846, to the House of Representatives' Committee on Commerce, James Barton, a Buffalo grain dealer, called attention to the need for lighthouses on the Flats, and that dredging the channels there would allow grain vessels to carry 1,000 barrels more flour per trip. The Steamboat Association wanted to borrow a dredge and start the work themselves in 1846, but they were unable to do so because of a lack of funds. [7]

The Clinton River Lighthouse

The Michigan Senate Appropriation bill of March 3, 1847, provided $30,000 to build the first lighthouse on Lake St. Clair at the mouth of the Clinton River where it enters the lake just west of the Flats. The combination light tower and keeper's dwelling constructed was a one story brick building with two rooms and a chimney on each end. The attic was divided into two rooms and a kitchen was attached to the structure. The official plans read as follows:

> On the centre of the house to be an octagon tower, thirteen feet high, above the walls of the house . . . on one side of the deck to be a scuttle, to enter the lantern . . . stairs to lead from the attic story of the house to the entrance of the scuttle . . . On the tower to be an iron lantern of an octagon form, with two spare lamps, five double tin oil canisters to hold 45 gallons each, lantern, canister and trivet, tin wick box, tin tube box, hand lantern and lamp, oil feeder, torch, six wick formers, two pair scissors, two files and one glazier's diamond. [8]

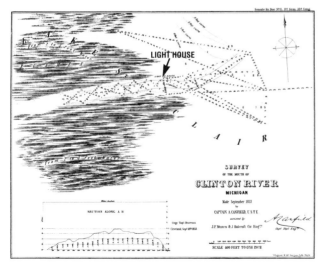

Chart of Clinton River, 1853.
A portion of the 1853 chart showing the location of the first lighthouse at the northern end of Lake St. Clair. Illustration courtesy of the Dossin Great Lakes Museum.

The demise of the Clinton-Kalamazoo Canal project soon changed the status of this light to a mere navigational aid. The heavy tow barge traffic that was the original impetus of the canal construction was rendered obsolete by the growing railroad industry. The lightstation and grounds were auctioned off in 1872 to be used as a hunting and fishing club. Records show there was still a light custodian in 1874. By 1880, Custodian Edgar Weeks was complaining that he had his hands full dealing with the club owners for access to the building. The lighthouse was eventually closed and the structure was destroyed by a fire in 1908.

The 1850s: Shipping and Commerce

On August 20, 1852, President Millard Fillmore signed a bill for $20,000 for improvements at the Flats. That same year $5,000 was also appropriated to repair ice and water damage to the pier and lighthouse on the Clinton River. During 1853, Captain Augustus Canfield, now in charge of the U.S. Topographical Engineers at Detroit, mapped the Flats and the mouth of the Clinton River as part of his survey work. On April 18, 1854, Captain Canfield died, and he was replaced by Lt. Colonel James D. Graham. The next internal improvements bill which would have funded the dredging of the Flats was vetoed by President Franklin Pierce on August 4, 1853. The Democratic platform did not favor the belief that Congress had the authority to remove river obstructions like their Whig counterparts in power previously.

During the 1850s water levels continued to be a problem at the Flats. The year of 1854 was a period of very low water, and an estimated $500,000 in damages from collision and lighterage costs occurred at the Flats. Michigan Senator Lewis Cass wrote to Secretary of War Jefferson Davis on September 16 that:

> . . . . fourteen vessels, steamboats and others are constantly employed in lightering vessels and in towing them through this difficult pass.

There was fear that the lower lake levels would continue into 1855 as well. But, 1855 was a time of unusually heavy rain fall and lake levels rose substantially, The investigation of Captain Amiel Weeks Whipple, of the U.S. Topographical Engineers, into the amount of commerce over the Flats for the year 1855 showed that in 230 days of navigation, the total value of merchandise and agricultural

---

7 Ibid. p.52
8 U.S. Customs House Bid for Lighthouse May 18, 1847.

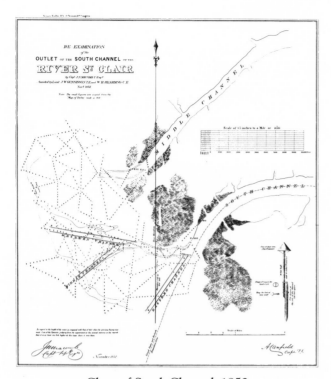

Chart of South Channel, 1852.
*An 1852 chart of the "Re-Examination of the . . . South
Channel . . ." site of the two South Channel lights.
Illustration courtesy of the Dossin Great Lakes Museum.*

The Lighthouse and Beacon of the South Channel

Along with new navigational charts and a newly dredged channel, the decision was finally reached to build a lighthouse at the South Channel of the Flats. Captain Whipple's Annual Report of 1859 to the Secretary of War described the new light station being built. The station was actually two structures, a lighthouse with attached keepers dwelling and a front range light or beacon. Captain Whipple wrote:

The towers have been erected with Milwaukee bricks; the caps and sills for doors and windows, and the cornices, being of well dressed stone from the Buffalo quarries. The lighthouse is nearly complete, with cast iron stairs and 4th order lantern. . . . The keeper's dwelling is supported by nine cut stone piers . . . bound together by strong girders of rolled iron upon which rest the walls of Milwaukee bricks. The floor is composed of brick arches resting upon iron beams, and covered with concrete. The house is two stories in height, and is covered by a firm slate roof. [9]

The fixed white light of the 4th order lanterns in the beacon and the lighthouse shone over the Flats for the first time on November 1, 1859. They were visible for 11 and 13 miles respectively. The front beacon tower was 23 feet high and the lighthouse tower was 37 feet high. The lighthouse tower was connected to the dwelling by a covered walkway.[10]

This lighthouse and beacon now allowed tugs with tow vessels (mostly converted schooners) to travel by night instead of anchoring at dark as had been the custom. Of the 72 lights shining on the Great Lakes by 1852, 68 were fixed lights and four were revolving.[11] The practice of making each lighthouse a distinctive flash was not the norm at this time. The 11th Lighthouse District took charge of manning and maintaining these new lights of the South Channel at the Flats.

Captain Whipple also commented in his report to the Secretary of War in 1859 that when the lake levels again receded, the Flats would again be obstructed. He recommended that a beacon be built at the sharp bend in the South Channel. However, this beacon was never built. In later years navigational buoys and pier lights would solve this problem. On February 1, 1860 President Buchanan

produce that passed over the Flats was $251,167,706. This translated to $1,002,033 per day! By 1856, the commerce passing the Flats amounted to over $300 million dollars.

With this increase in shipping through the Flats it was obvious that new and reliable navigational aids were needed. As a result, a survey party directed by Captain George Gordon Meade of the Topographical Engineers prepared drawings of the Flats in the spring of 1857. In the winter of 1856-57, Captain Whipple, in addition to his duties with the 10th Lighthouse District, was assigned to supervise the dredging of the west channel of the Flats. By July 1857, Captain Whipple was convinced that the middle channel was in fact straighter, and shorter than the west channel. However, no appropriations could be used to dredge this channel without Congressional approval. In June 1858, the House of Representatives passed their appropriate funding measure and in October the steamer *Northern Light* went through the newly dredged channel.

9 A.W. Whipple. *Report of the Chief Topographical Engineer Accompanying the Annual Report of the Secretary of War.* 1859. p.22.
10 George Scott. *Scott's New Coast Pilot For the Lakes.* Detroit, 1907. p.96-97.
11 Lighthouse Board. *Report of the Officers Constituting the Lighthouse Board.* Washington, D.C. Feb. 5, 1852.

South Channel Lights. *Two views of the South Channel lighthouse and beacon, ca. 1900.*
Photographs courtesy of the Save Our South Channel Lights Association.

Tug *Goldsmith* with tow of six schooners.
Steam tug Goldsmith *towing the schooners,* Fearless, York State, Even Fuller, Porter, Butcher Boy, *and* George Steel *through
the Flats at the turn of the century. Photograph courtesy of the Great Lakes Historical Society.*

vetoed the St. Clair Flats $55,000 improvements appropriation bill. This was the seventh River Improvement Bill vetoed by Democratic presidents from 1838 to 1860. The Republican party would favor these improvements as part of its election platform for Abraham Lincoln.

The Civil War

With the onset of the Civil War in April 1861, the officers of the Topographical Engineers on the Great Lakes were reassigned by the War Department. Captain Whipple was transferred June 1 to the Department of Northeastern Virginia and later fought at the Battle of Bull Run. He was mortally wounded at Chancellorsville on May 3, 1863 and was promoted to Major General of Volunteers before his death. Captain Meade was transferred to Washington and was later promoted to General and commanded the Union

forces at the Battle of Gettysburg against fellow engineer officer General Robert E. Lee. Of the 93 officers in the Topographical Engineers, 15 joined the Confederacy. In all, 55 engineering officers attained the rank of general during the war.

Colonel James Graham, Superintendent of Lake Harbor Improvements at Chicago, took over Captain Meade's post at the Flats during the war. With $1,600 left in his budget, Colonel Graham repaired the lighthouse piers damaged by the ice at the South Channel. He also conducted experiments on water levels and concluded that there were "lunar tides" on the lakes.

The battles of the Civil War were far away and did not touch the Great Lakes directly. The area, however, did furnish raw materials to aid the war effort. The development of iron and copper mines on Lake Superior also promoted economic growth in the Great Lakes region.

The Era of Reconstruction

On June 23, 1866, with the Civil War behind them, the Republican 39th Congress passed an $80,000 appropriation bill for improvements at the Flats. In August 1864, Colonel Thomas Jefferson Cram of the U.S. Army Corps of Engineers (the Corps of Topographical Engineers had been merged into the Corps of Engineers in 1863) was assigned to be in charge of river and harbor improvements on Lake St. Clair. Colonel Cram, like his predecessor Colonel Whipple, also objected to spending money dredging the old South Channel and proposed dredging the straighter Middle Channel 13 feet deep and 200 feet wide, from the mouth of the south pass out into Lake St. Clair, with two 7,300 foot long dikes of timber cribs. These dikes would keep the dredged earth from sliding back into the channel. The Secretary of War and the Corps of Engineers disagreed. Colonel Cram again requested appropriations, claiming that 86 vessels and one raft had passed the Flats daily in 1865 and accidents, towage and beacon maintenance were costing $500,000 annually because of the winding channel used. The estimated cost for the new project was $351,000.

The River and Harbor Act of March 2, 1867, finally appropriated the needed funds for the project and plans for dredging the new canal were begun. Bids were contracted for each task. Contractor John Brown of Thorold, Ontario, supplied wood and materials, while Moses Hill of Cleveland, Ohio, supplied iron. Brown sodded the dikes and planted willow trees in 1870. The new Ship Canal opened on July 25, 1871. The custodian of the Canal, William Mott, was assigned to ensure the safety of vessels entering the Canal, oversee repairs to the dikes, observe vessels and

U.S. Lake Survey Chart of the Ship Canal at the Flats, 1907.

This chart clearly indicates the locations of the two old South Channel lights (here identified as "St. Clair Flats Range Lights, Rear Lt. and Front Lt."); the twin lighthouses of the Ship Canal (here identified as the St. Clair Flats Canal Lower Lt. and Upper Lt."); and the "Custodian's Dwelling." Illustration courtesy of the Dossin Great Lakes Museum.

keep "loafers and evil persons" from abusing the channel. If this included fishermen and picnickers, it was never made clear. Also included in the appropriation was $60,000 to build two lighthouses on the new Ship Canal. [12]

Over at the old South Channel, the lighthouse and beacon were again in need of repair. A lake survey report dated May 18, 1873, revealed that the beacon had shifted over an inch in just two months. In 1875 repairs to the structures were made at a cost of $10,000. Officially the old South Channel would be in use for another 36 years by small boats and tow barges. The list of keepers of the lighthouse and beacon on the old South Channel is long, with names constantly changing. In all, from 1859 to 1907, there were 10 keepers and 24 assistant keepers.

The Twin Lighthouses of the New Ship Canal

The 1872 Annual Report of the Lighthouse Board states that the twin lighthouses of the new Ship Canal were lit November 15, 1871. These identical lighthouses were located at the ends of the dikes at opposite ends of the Canal. The original lights were fixed red 4th order lens with ruby chimney. The focal planes were 45 feet above water. The towers were octagonal red brick with cut stone bases. The keepers houses were built of red brick with slate roofs and green window "blinds." Each dwelling had ten rooms and water was piped from the lake to a hand pump in the kitchen sink. A white boathouse, red painted oil house, and whitewashed chicken coop completed the scene. The lighthouses were accessible only by boat.

At one of the new Ship Canal lighthouses, Andrew Rattray began as keeper in 1883 when he joined the Lighthouse Service at age 31. He stayed at this post for the next 36 years. He was born September 13, 1852 on Harsens Island of pioneer parents. Andrew and his wife Alice, had two sons, William and Radcliffe. A daughter Alice was born at the upper lighthouse. The family spent their winters

Ship Canal Twin Lighthouses, 1871.
Views of the twin lighthouses built at the two ends of the Ship Canal in 1871. These two lighthouses were identified as the Upper Light (northern end of the canal), and Lower Light (located at the southern end of the canal). Photographs courtesy of Gordon D. Amsbary (A and B) and the Institute for Great Lakes Research, Bowling Green State University (C and D).

12 John W. Larson. *Essayons: A History of the Detroit District U.S. Army Corps. of Engineers*, 1981. p.77.

Upper Light. *A (above) and B (below).*

Lower Light. *C (above) and D (below).*

Andrew Rattray. *Keeper of the St. Clair Flats Ship Canal Light Station from 1883 to 1919. Photograph courtesy of Gordon D. Amsbary.*

Burning of the Upper Lighthouse, May 13, 1934.
Photograph courtesy of the Institute for Great Lakes Research, Bowling Green State University

in Algonac. Their son William was temporarily stationed at the old South Channel light during November and December 1905 because of the sudden death of keeper John Sinclair. Andrew Rattray retired from the Lighthouse Service to a cottage at the Flats in 1919, and died in 1948 at the age of 96. The other lightkeeper at the new Ship Canal was Tom Lappin, who served nearly as long as Rattray. [13]

The difficulty in visiting these lighthouses by land probably contributed to the lack of images existing today of these structures. Although they were unique in being duplicates built from the same plans, they were never popular topics of postcards at the Flats, as were the hotels and hunting clubs which dotted the landscape in the 1890s and early 1900s.

The Twentieth Century: Automation

The twentieth century marked the end of the lighthouse keepers' way of life. In 1907, the old South Channel lights were deactivated. A navigation light was placed in the towers in 1915, according to the Lake Carriers Association Annual Report of that year.

Due to the larger vessels sailing the lakes, the construction of another new channel was approved. By 1908, the Ship Canal had been split and rebuoyed so that upbound boats used the east side and downbound boats the west side. In 1913, the lower light of the Ship Canal was changed from red to white and its intensity increased to 520 candlepower; by 1915 it was changed again to a flashing white signal with the rear light occulting white every two seconds. In 1927 the lower light of the Ship Canal was increased to 1600 candlepower. But automation was quickly displacing lighthouse keepers. The Lake St. Clair lightship that had been moved from Windmill Point to the Flats in 1911 was singled out as the most outstanding improvement of 1935 with its crewless automated light, fog bell and radio beacon controlled from its station eight miles away on shore. The green St. Clair Flats range lights appeared that year as well.

On May 13, 1934, the lighthouses at both ends of the north bank of the Ship Canal were burned as the quickest way to dispose of them. Then, the north bank was removed to widen the channel so a greater volume of shipping could be accommodated.

Patrick Garrity, last keeper of the light, has had to leave his post. He is still at the Flats spending his time in the

---

13 Gordon D. Amsbary. "St. Clair Flats Range Light Station." *Keepers Log,* Winter, 1994, p. 18-20.

Two Views of the "St. Clair Flats Range Lights," 1996.
Today, these two historic lights are being restored by the Save Our South Channel Lights Association.
Photographs courtesy of the Save Our South Channel Lights Association.

world renowned marshland that borders the lower reaches of the St. Clair River. [14]

After the Prosit Club toasted Prohibition at the old South Channel lighthouse, the dwelling was removed during the 1930s. As the years passed, the rear beacon became a "day mark," unlit, its ten sided cast iron lantern dumped into the lake. Today, an automated light keeps vigil on the front tower.

Freighters have replaced schooners and the era of shooting clubs, hotels and island amusement parks is gone from the St. Clair Flats. Lake surveys are still made, dredging occurs occasionally, and the Coast Guard tends the buoys and changes lightbulbs and solar cells to keep our waterways safe. Quietly these duties are carried out and taken for granted, as the faithful lighthouse keepers at the Flats went about their tasks so long ago.

The St. Clair Flats remains a vital link in the Great Lakes transportation system. Its buoys and range lights are still carefully maintained to allow safe passage of lake and river traffic. And one solitary navigation light still shines from its tower on the old South Channel, guiding vessels safely to their destination.

————————— ❦ —————————

I was greatly assisted in researching this article by the following groups and individuals: Chuck Brockman of the Save Our South Channel Lights Association; Gordon D. Amsbary of the Maritime Museum in Ashtabula, Ohio; Institute for Great Lakes Research at Bowling Green, Ohio; Great Lakes Historical Society at Vermilion, Ohio; and John Polacsek, Curator of the Dossin Great Lakes Museum at Detroit, Michigan.

————————— ❦ —————————

Cynthia S. Bieniek received her bachelors degree from Oakland University and her masters degree from Wayne State University. In addition to her full-time duties as librarian and archivist, she is a volunteer at the Dossin Great Lakes Museum and has an avid interest in lighthouses. Ms. Bieniek is currently researching and writing a history of the Old South Channel lighthouses at the Flats. She is also the author of "The Windmill Point Light and the Grosse Pointe Lightship," which appeared in Volume 1 of Tonnancour.

————————— ❦ —————————

[14] "Old Club Members to Miss Famous St. Clair Landmark." *Detroit Free Press,* May 20, 1934.

The St. Clair Flats: A Summer Place

by Michael M. Dixon

Since its earliest settlement, the development of Grosse Pointe has been linked to that of Detroit. The growth of Detroit and the prosperity of the late nineteenth century changed the Grosse Pointes from a quiet farming community into a fashionable summer resort. Concurrently, the St. Clair Flats delta developed rapidly as a nationally acclaimed summer resort. Most of the founders of the clubs, hotels and stately summer residences there were prominent Detroiters. Many of these same families were the founders of Grosse Pointe's summer colony and among the first year-round residents moving out from Detroit.

THE ST. CLAIR FLATS had much to offer during the era when it was acclaimed nationwide as a premier resort community. People came for the unexcelled duck hunting and fishing when the automobile and telephone had not been dreamed of and there were no country clubs or mechanized street cars. In the 1870s and 1880s, clubhouses with overnight accommodations and hotels with resort facilities, as well as grand private residences, began filling in along the banks of the St. Clair River delta, the area known as the Flats.

During the 1890s five palatial clubhouses lined the American side of the South Channel, with membership rosters that read like a Who's Who of Detroit society. On the North Channel and on the Canadian side of the South Channel similar clubs were organized. Additionally, seven public resort complexes and numerous small hotels were available. Among the most notable public houses were Gustav Trautz's, Joe Bedore's, The Riverside (Idle Hour), and the Star Island Hotel, which had the largest dining room in the state, reportedly having been able to serve 500 people in one seating. And in 1897 the Tashmoo Amusement Park opened and continued to attract excursionists until 1951.

Regular passenger steamship service between Detroit and Port Huron began in the fall of 1829 and was available as late as 1951. The first passenger steamship, the *Argo*, was little more than two 55-foot dugout canoes supporting a platform with a cabin and a four-horsepower steam engine capable of making the upriver run to Port Huron in two days. The last passenger steamship, the *Put-In-Bay*, was one of the finest excursion ships ever built. She measured

Steamer Tashmoo Entering the Saint Clair Ship Canal.

256 feet long with a 60-foot beam and included elegant lounges, a ballroom and first-class dining.

At the turn of the century, White Star Line steamers would make as many as three daily round trips to the Flats and on a typical Sunday evening 500 or more people may have been waiting at the dock of the Tashmoo Park and each club and hotel along the South Channel. Through most of the 1920s, passenger service continued to be regular, affordable and dependable. "Flatters" along the South Channel could catch the morning boat, be in downtown Detroit offices by 9am and return to their families on the evening boat. From 1898 until 1927, the passenger ships also provided the postal services along the South Channel, under contract with the U.S. Postmaster.

The North Channel also received regular passenger service. Ships provided freight and passenger service between Mount Clemens and Algonac until about 1915. By that time, the interurban passenger railway service had completely displaced the North Channel passenger ships. From the docks in Pearl Beach, Pt. Tremble and Algonac, ferry boats would shuttle passengers from the interurbans to cottages, clubs and hotels. During the feverish competition to build interurban lines the "Rapid Railway" promoted a rail

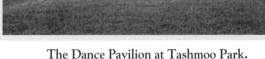

The Dance Pavilion at Tashmoo Park.

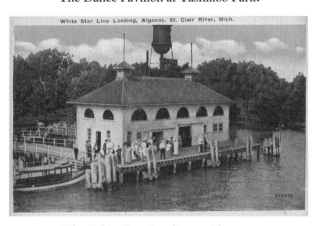

The White Star Landing at Algonac.

Opposite Page. *Illustration courtesy of Michael M. Dixon*

On the porch at the Old Club.

Gustav Trautz's Hotel.

line across Lake St. Clair. The line would have connected with the Gratiot line and crossed the lake beginning from a point near Metro Beach, run along the South Channel to Russell Island and there cross back over to the mainland to continue along the river to Port Huron. (Blue prints of the plan can be found in the Macomb County Library and the St. Clair County Lands Office). Construction of this project actually began before being abandoned, reportedly at the request of the passenger shipping interests.

In 1924, after overcoming great difficulties, roads connecting New Baltimore, Algonac and Detroit were completed, and automobile access for Detroit-area residents to mainland docks along the North Channel became available. From then on, the flexibility of traveling by automobile displaced both the steamers and the interurbans.

A number of factors contributed to the passing of the grand scale of the "Little Venice" resort community. Fire destroyed many of the area's landmarks. The Mervue clubhouse and Joe Bedore's hotel were both torn down, about 1948 and 1968 respectively, when they could no longer

Guide Map, St. Clair Flat.

Illustration courtesy of Michael M. Dixon

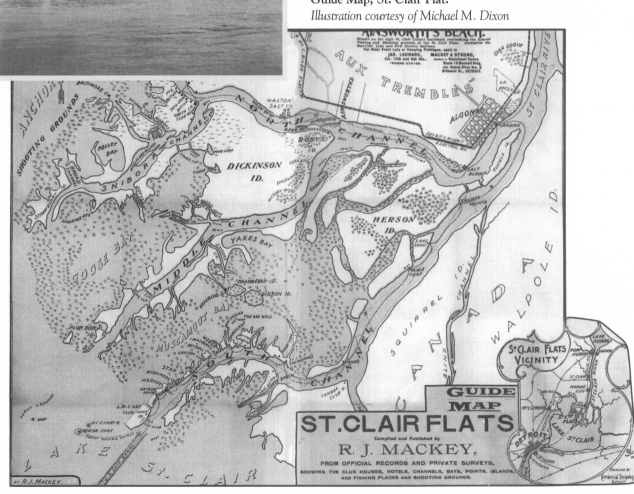

13866 MARSHLAND, STE. CLAIRE FLATS, MICH.

The Dock at the Marshland Hotel.

attract the clientele to support them. With the mobility provided by the automobile, people began going in all directions, and a ride in the country replaced excursion ships as an escape from the city's summer heat. Golfing clubs had become increasingly popular after the turn of the century. Prohibition and later the Depression and cyclical periods of high water dealt their blows to the mass popularity of the Flats.

Nevertheless, the St. Clair Flats maintains its hold on thousands of residents and visitors. Today, there are many fine private residences. The Old Club has continued as a private community since 1872, and the Idle Hour, which had been closed for several years, has been renovated and reopened as a private club. Gustav Trautz's resort, while greatly diminished in facilities, continues as Jacob Harson's Harbor Club. The North Channel Club has continued under various forms since the 1860s and the "Canada Club" has had a continuous history since 1875.

ꗣ ꗣ ꗣ

Post cards on pages 119-121 from the private collection of Robert F. Rinke.

Cottages at the Flats.

The Grande Pointe Hotel.

The following description of an excursion from the foot of Griswold Street in Detroit across the lake, and up the South Channel of the St. Clair Flats appeared in the spring edition of the 1906 *White Star Magazine*, and gives a fine contemporary account of a boat trip up to the Flats:

"Every morning at 8:30 o'clock (Sundays at 9:00,) and every afternoon at 2:30, (and 3:30 o'clock, except Sunday) during the season, the Tashmoo, City of Toledo, and Owana leave the White Star Line dock at the foot of Griswold street for their trips to St. Clair Flats, Tashmoo Park and the stopping places on the St. Clair River. Altogether there are twenty-four landings, two of them on the Canadian side of the border.

"The boat promptly leaves the dock on time, and, gliding out into the stream, quickly passes on the American side the Public Lighting and Detroit United Railway tall-chimneyed power houses, the Michigan and Detroit Stove Foundries, Parke, Davis & Co.'s great drug and bacteriological establishments, the Queen Anne Soap Works and Belle Isle. On the Canadian side can be seen Windsor, Walkerville, with its great distillery, and Peche Island, once the summer resort of Pontiac, chief of the once powerful tribe of Ottawa Indians.

"Just beyond Peche Isle, but to the left, is Windmill Point, from whence the course to the government canal, twenty miles away, is straight as can be. The channel is 800 feet wide, and twenty or more feet deep, and many buoys mark its limits. Half way between Windmill Point and the "piers," the local name for the government canal, a lightship serves as a point of observation by day and a beacon by night. The wooded shores of Lake St. Clair are still to be seen on the left, the foliage, both hiding and revealing the village of Grosse Point Farms, containing the costly summer residences of Detroit millionaires.

"On the lake there is a procession of freighters — "huge forms with breath of steam"—growing larger in size and increasing in number each year. As the boats keep to the comparatively narrow channel, tourists have close views of these great vessels, some of 12,000 tons freight capacity and with thirty or more hatchways, and their varieties and peculiarities become an interesting study.

"It is only a short run of an hour and forty minutes across Lake St. Clair to the willow-clad government canal, which is a mile and a quarter long, and dug and spiled to straighten the channel and shorten the route.

"It is at the piers that St. Clair Flats—America's Venice—begins, and it is the wonderland of natural and artificial beauties. The Flats is a delta formed by the silt dropping to the bottom of the lake at the mouth of the St. Clair River, and gradually filling up the channel until the deposits reached the surface. The flotsam began to catch on the bars, and after a while there was land on which hunting and fishing boxes could be built. There was only one or two of these on the whole Flats fifty years ago, but the fame of the spot for fishing and duck shooting rapidly spread, and, keeping pace with the population of Detroit and Michigan, first modest cottages and then club houses and hotels were erected, until today five thousand people can be fed and housed in America's Venice on short notice.

"Nowhere else can there be found such a summer resort. The houses are built upon piles driven in the silt, and often there is running water all around, the boats being moored to the very doorsteps. In the river and cuts are deep pools and swift currents, the home of the gamely bass or lively perch. Quantities of pickerel and pike are also caught here. There are everywhere facilities for bathing and boating, and though there is not much land, little is needed where there are so many other things to interest and amuse.

"This city in the waters with its liquid streets and roadways, has no gloomy antiquities or crumbling marbles like ancient Venice, but is sweet and fresh with summer homes. Here the clamor, and dust, and heat of the town is forgotten, for nature is kind to sweltering humanity when sweltering humanity has the sense to come, the cool breezes from the lakes tempering the atmosphere and make living a delight.

"So the Old Club and the Rushmere, Mervue, Star Island and Joe Bedore's, Marshland and the Riverside, Damer's and Trautz's (the German Village) and Muir's Landing, all stopping places on the Flats, have become the centers around which cluster cottages, each ministering to its particular class of patrons. Some are hotels and some are club houses, and the tourist will be made welcome at any of them."

——————————— ❦ ———————————

SOURCE: Portions of this article originally appeared in *The Flats Golden Era* (1987).

——————————— ❦ ———————————

Michael M. Dixon has had a lifelong enthusiasm for the Flats, as his family has been vacationing there since the 1860s. This interest has led Dixon to research and write about the area's history. As a result, he has published three books: Life At The Flats *(1985),* The Flats Golden Era *(1987), and* Marshland Memories *(1989). Dixon was educated at the University of Michigan and received his Masters degree from the American Graduate School of International Management (Thunderbird). A fourth generation Grosse Pointer, Dixon is a member of the Grosse Pointe Farms Historical Advisory Commission.*

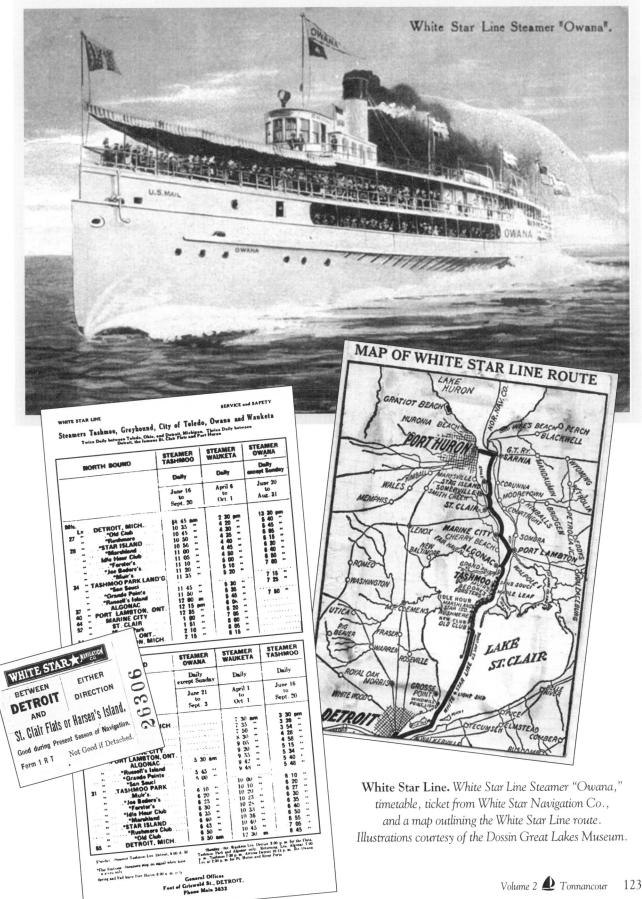

White Star Line. *White Star Line Steamer "Owana,"
timetable, ticket from White Star Navigation Co.,
and a map outlining the White Star Line route.
Illustrations courtesy of the Dossin Great Lakes Museum.*

A Beacon of Tradition: The Building of the Grosse Pointe Yacht Club

by James P. Gallagher

In this article James P. Gallagher tells the story of the Grosse Pointe Yacht Club and the building of its magnificent 187-foot tower.

SINCE 1929, SAILORS on Lake St. Clair and motorists on Lakeshore Drive have used the 187-foot tower of the Grosse Pointe Yacht Club as a navigation point. On clear days, it is visible from half way out into the lake and from Anchor Bay down to the mouth of the Detroit River. It was not always thus. An Indian, or a French voyageur, paddling a canoe north or south on the lake before the latter decades of the nineteenth century would have seen an essentially featureless shoreline from Gaukler Point all the way to Grosse Pointe. The shoreline was broken by no rivers or creeks or bays; it had only the most modest hills rising from the flat waterline; the only buildings were small farmhouses of French families who owned the strip farms that ran from the lake to a line approximately where Harper Avenue is today. A clump of tall trees or (after 1899) the belfry of St. Paul's Church would have been the only clues to location between the Detroit River and the St. Clair flats and Anchor Bay.

These early travelers were well respectful of the power of Lake St. Clair to kick up winds and waves that would be catastrophic to their heavily-laden canoes. When weather threatened, they often used a safer short-cut near Gaukler Point through the Milk River, a shallow stream that made its way into a swamp well back from the lake. Through this swamp, the Milk River connected with the Fox Creek, which ran southwest until it eventually brought the canoes back into the safety of the Detroit River at today's Alter Road.

Not that the intersection of Vernier Road and Lake St. Clair was uncharted wilderness. Since the early 1800s, the land there had been part of the 400-acre Vernier farm, Private Claim 156, granted and confirmed by the United States Commissioners to Jean Baptiste La Douceur, dit Vernier. It was one of numerous ribbon farms settled by French families after the United States won its independence from England. To provide each farmer with access to the river, the fastest and best highway to and from markets, the grants were narrow (from 162 feet to 600 feet wide), but deep (about three miles). Along the shore was a well-worn Indian trail used for centuries for movement between a famous salt spring near the mouth of the Clinton River and the various villages along the Detroit River. The Huron Indians' name for this beautiful lake of fresh water and abundant fish was *Oksiketa*, meaning sugar or salt, probably a reference to the salt springs at the lake's northwest corner.

Homestead farming was evidently not much more profitable or exciting than it is today, and in 1888, John

Vernier opened a roadhouse along the shore road on his property, catering to travelers moving north or south along the lake, or to venturesome Detroiters out for a day in the country. He was noted for serving chicken, fish, and frog leg dinners. In 1895, John Vernier sold the roadhouse to his cousin, Edmund C. Vernier, who was born on the family property on February 16, 1867, and lived there until his death in 1934. Edmund was one of the best-known pillars of the community, serving as township clerk, treasurer and supervisor for many years.

Shortly after he bought the business, Ed Vernier built a more pretentious place on the inland (west) side of Lakeshore, just south (toward Detroit) of Vernier Road. A history of the time says that the inn was celebrated for the hospitality of host Edmund Vernier, and was one of the most popular summer resorts of the Gay Nineties. This roadhouse, popular with both Detroiters and with the growing number of Grosse Pointe's summer resort community, lasted until 1915, when the Verniers built still another place, farther west of Lakeshore.

Fish, chicken and frog leg dinners were not to be the only claim to popularity or recreation for the Vernier/Lakeshore site. In the 1800s, none of the relatively warm wastewater poured into the lake from thousands of homes and businesses that today stretch back from the lake, and there was none of the chemical outflow from the St. Clair River and the industrial complexes near Port Huron and Sarnia. As a result, the lake froze almost from shore to shore during normal winters. This huge sheet of ice was used for the popular sport of iceboating, and about 1910, Frank Verheyden organized the Grosse Pointe Ice Boat Club, which held regular races throughout the winter, on a course as long as seven miles in one direction. A long pier was built out into the lake at the Vernier intersection, and the ice boat crews would come in from their races, tie up to the pier, and indulge in food and refreshments at the roadhouse.

According to the Works Projects Administration-sponsored history of the Grosse Pointes, written in the 1930s,

An architectural rendering of the club from the firm of architect Guy Lowell.

by 1918, the original Grosse Pointe Ice Boat Club was taken over by about two dozen men, who formed another organization that "was to form the nucleus of the Grosse Pointe Yacht Club." Since this date coincided almost exactly with the passage of the 18th Amendment (prohibition of liquor sales), the reader can draw whatever conclusion he or she wishes about the demise of the ice boating club and the rise of the yachting club!

The early 1920s are very murky concerning the GPYC, but we do know that the first emphasis remained on ice boating, rather than sailing, because the earliest minutes of the Club are devoted to acknowledging the winners of the ice boating races, and the prizes that they won. Rewards were not exactly generous by today's standards of athletic recompense. They included such items as a pair of leather gloves, or buckskin mittens, and a fancy sweater coat.

During the early 1920s, the Club membership was growing. The Grosse Pointes were slowly changing from a summer resort for wealthy Detroit businessmen and professionals and their families to a community of permanent year-round homes of the leading families of Detroit's booming automobile industry, plus many bankers and mercantile leaders. With that growth came an interest in the construction of a permanent clubhouse, a venture that fortunately was wholeheartedly supported by the municipal fathers of Grosse Pointe Shores, who had jurisdiction over the site. This support has continued until today. The building committee hoped for, and got, a lease of the outer end of the municipal pier, and Grosse Pointe Shores Supervisor George Osius welcomed the club and its plans. Not coincidentally, he was later honored by the naming of the lakeshore park after him. The boulder that bears the park's bronze plaque was taken from the shore where the GPYC now stands.

By 1926, the building committee was ready for serious planning, and one of its first happy duties was the acceptance of an offer by member Clarence L. Ayres of a parcel of land at the southwest corner of Lakeshore Road and Vernier, including the lake frontage and the associated

Ice-boating on Lake St. Clair.

Ice-boating was the real origin of the Grosse Pointe Yacht Club, as pictured here in this early 1900s photograph on Lake St. Clair.

riparian rights, for a total price of $28,000, to be paid as the Club found it possible to do so. Ayres realized that the Club did not have the means to buy the property, so when the land came on the market, he bought it with a clubhouse in mind, and transferred it to the Club at exactly his purchase price. At the same time, after negotiations with the Village, the Club leased the adjoining land, consisting of 90 feet along the lake, and 325 feet back from the shoreline.

Edsel B. Ford was named Commodore of the rapidly growing Club, and the Village granted the lease for 30 years (it was renewed in 1956, and again in 1986). In accepting the lease, the Club agreed to build a seawall on three sides of the property and to construct a clubhouse within the next two years, at a cost "not less than $50,000," a schedule and a budget that were to prove woefully inadequate.

1926 was a heady year in the United States and in Grosse Pointe. Members of the GPYC laid plans for the design and building of a clubhouse that would be grander than anything along the lake, one that would compare favorably with the two older clubs on Belle Isle in Detroit (the Detroit Boat Club and the Detroit Yacht Club), and one that would befit the social and financial prestige of the members. To finance the building and grounds, the plan called for membership contributions of $225,000, plus an additional $100,000 to be raised through the issuance of bonds. This sum was considered ample, because the land improvements and the clubhouse were budgeted at $200,000, a figure that rapidly became a wishful chimera, thus conforming to the adage that all building projects, back to the Pyramids and forward to the Renaissance Center, will always be over budget and behind schedule.

In August of 1926, the bids were opened for the construction of a seawall and for the area behind it to be filled

approximately 1,300 feet to the front of the present Village dock. The contract for the seawall was given to the A. J. Dupuis Company, and a second contract was awarded to the Liberty Construction Company for the fill and grading of the Club site. Unfortunately, the Liberty firm was unable or unwilling to do the work as contracted for the agreed price and schedule, so the contract was forfeited in July of 1927, and awarded to another firm, Dunbar-Sullivan Company, for the price of 90¢ per cubic yard of fill. No record is available as to where this huge amount of earth came from, but it is safe to guess that the bulk of it was provided by the enormous amount of excavation carried out from major downtown Detroit buildings that were being constructed during these years, like the Union Guardian and the Penobscot Buildings.

Another addition to the property was made in January, 1927, when the Bayer family agreed to sell the land immediately to the south (toward Detroit), which included a house, the lake frontage, and the riparian rights. Another example of the generosity of Club members: John T. Hurley bought the property for the Club, but refused any commission for his services. The examples of Clarence Ayres and John Hurley have been repeated over and over by others during the Club's history.

At the same January, 1927, meeting, an architect for the Club is first mentioned. The name suggested to the Board was that of Guy Lowell, FAIA, of Boston, Massachusetts, who was a graduate of Harvard College, the Massachusetts Institute of Technology, and the Ecole des Beaux-Arts of Paris. Lowell was a first cousin of poet James Russell Lowell, who was also an essayist and diplomat. Not mentioned in the minutes, but undoubtedly significant to his credentials, was his reputation as a leading yachtsman on the Atlantic

Coast. A blue-water sailor, Lowell had won the International Regatta at Kiel, Germany, with his boat *Cima*, and he had been a member of the U. S. sailing team at Barcelona, Spain.

Lowell had been interviewed by a committee consisting of then Commodore John H. French, George Hilsendegen, and Clarence Ayres. They were favorably impressed by his membership in the Eastern Yacht Club of Massachusetts, the oldest yacht club in the U.S. On a professional level, they liked his designs of the Piping Rock Club at Locust Valley, Long Island, New York, the New York County Courthouse in Manhattan, and country homes for such wealthy families as C. K. G. Billings, Clarence H. Mackey, and Harry Payne Whitney. Interestingly, there is no mention of consideration given to such local architectural giants as Albert Kahn (designer of the Detroit Athletic Club and the Grosse Pointe Shores Village Hall, across Lakeshore Drive from the Club) and Smith, Hinchman & Grylls (who were responsible for the University Club and the Players' Club).

The financial arrangement with Mr. Lowell for his professional services was that he was to receive a fee of 7^{1}/2% of the cost of the clubhouse construction, plus a $50 monthly salary for a clerk of the works (the architect's representative at the job site). There were several escape clauses for the Club, however; if the Club was not satisfied with the conceptual sketches and floor plans submitted, they could negate the contract upon the payment of a fee of 1^{1}/2% of the estimated cost. If the architect provided completed plans and specifications, and the building was then not built, the architect would receive a fee of 3^{1}/2% of estimated cost for his effort.

Oldest GPYC Membership Card.

The oldest Grosse Pointe Yacht Club membership card known in existence is that of one-time member Ignatius Backman, signed by then Treasurer William C. Roney in 1914. It was about that time that the Grosse Pointe Yacht Club was transformed from an ice-boating club to a yachting club.

A 1929 Architectural Plan.
From a 1929 Pencilpoints *architectural magazine, this plan shows the Club's south elevation.*

Here we run across a mystery and a correction of a historical error. Although Guy Lowell has been credited as the architect of the Club for the past 60 years, it is impossible that he provided any services beyond whatever rough sketches he submitted to the interviewing committee, and whatever limited discussions he may have had with his associates in Boston before the awarding of the commission. The calendar itself provides proof of this. On January 17, 1927, Mr. Lowell was engaged as the architect by the vote of the Board. Just 18 days later, on February 4, 1927, he died in the Spanish Madeira Islands, in the Atlantic Ocean off the northwest coast of Africa. Given the state of transportation in 1927 (a trans-Atlantic liner to Liverpool or Cherbourg, then some sort of smaller vessel to Madeira), it seems clear that almost all of the work after the committee interviewed Mr. Lowell was done by his senior associates. Ralph Coolidge Henry and Henry P. Richmond took over Lowell's work and became the architectural firm of Henry and Richmond, and all subsequent dealings were with these men.

The architects immediately noted the single outstanding characteristic of the site: "its apparently limitless extent of water surface, almost equally limitless and level terrain, and a rich vegetation." Given this, the designers sought an element of "Contrasting verticality in a region where all else is horizontal." Since both Lowell and Henry and Richmond were considering Venice as a prototype, their first thought was of a campanile, or bell tower, especially one of slender proportions and significant height.

Some months after the completion of the Club, Mr. Henry wrote in an article for the architectural magazine *Pencilpoints*, that "the entire building (is given) a lighter and gayer atmosphere than typifies the more solidly myste-rious prototypes of Venetian Romanesque and Gothic." Reflecting on the campanile, he mused "why not a large bell in the lantern to strike the hours and half-hours of the dial-less ship's clock; why not one with a modem aviation beacon at its apex?"

Anyone who assumes that the problems are over once the design has been approved and the architect engaged has never been involved in the building of anything larger than a doghouse. In June, 1927, the architects submitted floor plans to the Board, which approved them with only minor revisions, and they were ordered to prepare finished working drawings and specifi-cations for bidding. Only one month later, Board minutes give the first hints that may-be — just maybe — the mem-bership assessments would not be enough to cover the costs. These hints were borne out in October, when the bids came in at more than double the estimates. Instructions were given to the architects to scale back the design to get costs down to $350,000 (no more mention of the original $200,000!). This could well have been where the original north wing locker room and ladies' guest rooms were cut from the design. Back to the drawing board. In February 1928, the revised bids were opened, with the low bidder being Corrick Brothers Company, who offered a price of $380,000, plus a $20,000 fee. The same minutes mention, by name, architects Henry and Richmond, noting the first payment of architectural fees for $35,000.

Rising costs or not, construction was underway, and the harbor was opened for use in June 1928, giving boaters a gull's-eye view of the club that would be ready for their pleasure a year later. The outer harbor, 450 feet by 550 feet, is one of the largest protected harbors for small boats on Lake St. Clair. The inner harbor was shared with the village of Grosse Pointe Shores. The footings of the sea-walls and of the yacht club building itself are white oak piles with concrete cappings.

Bronze Statues *East Wind* and *West Wind*.
These are two of three bronze statues donated by Clarence Ayres, little more than one year after the Club's formal 1929 Grand Opening.

Fittingly, it was the Fourth of July, 1929, always one of the traditionally great holidays on the water, that was selected for the grand opening of the Grosse Pointe Yacht Club. In June, invitations went out to the membership and to selected guests. It was to be a lavish social occasion, and the Detroit newspapers devoted pages of text and pictures to the event. Capping more than three years of work and fundraising by the officers, Board, and members, what had originally been nothing more than a long wooden pier for ice boaters had finally been transformed into a landscaped peninsula, crowned with one of the finest private clubs in the country. Those first-day guests saw almost exactly what today's members see each time they turn off Lakeshore Road, with only the slight modifications that have been made in the landscaping, car parking, and some outdoor activity areas. Approaching up the long driveway, cars swung around the traffic circle to the main entrance in the north wing of what is essentially a U-shaped structure that faces west to the entrance drive and east to Lake St. Clair, and features an Italianate garden in the hol-low of the U.

The building itself is covered with a rough-troweled, warm-colored stucco, applied over walls of hollow terra cotta tile. All architectural trim is of stone, and the roof is a variegat-ed, red-brown clay tile. Every actor and actress knows that entrance is everything. The clubhouse itself, from the mo-ment one enters the front door, is designed to make the maxi-mum impression on the visitor. The broad, straight entrance foyer is 50 feet long, providing the setting for the most leisurely, or more stately entrance. This foyer culmi-nates in a 35-foot diameter Rotunda, the essential arrival point from which all other interior destinations are reached.

If the destination is the Main Clubroom (Ballroom), there is a broad stairway leading to it from the Rotunda. Any evening-gown-clad lady can rise like Venus from the sea, each step making her more visible to all in the Ballroom. If dining is the order of the evening, the Rotunda leads directly into the octagon-shaped Main Dining Room, with its colonnaded central area. The room is positioned so that five of its sides have an unobstructed view of the water.

Italian-styled Veranda.
The spacious Italian-styled veranda of the 1929 Grosse Pointe Yacht Club offered fresh air and fresh breezes from Lake St. Clair.
The Veranda has since been enclosed, remodeled and renamed the Binnacle — the Club's lakeside dining area.

Club Main Ball Room.
Conversational groupings of overstuffed furniture and rich oriental rugs reflect the decor of the late 1920s, early 1930s era.
The original chandelier, as seen in this early photograph of the Club Main Ball Room, still hangs in the same place today. The photo
was taken shortly after Commodore John H. French donated the massive 10-foot x 29-foot marine painting of the Sea Witch.

The Main Clubroom, which is the dominating mass of the building, is 86 feet long, 44 feet wide, and 29 feet high, with seven arched French windows leading to an open loggia (long since converted to the closed-in Binnacle). On the opposite wall are three high Gothic bays overlooking the Italian garden courtyard. The floor is polished oak for dancing, and the ceiling is timbered with girders, beams, and decorated plaster caissons. The focal point of the room is the Kadota-stone trimmed fireplace, crowned with a huge (10-foot x 29-foot) painting of three sailing ships pictured under full sail in an 1851 race from New York City around Cape Horn to San Francisco. This painting was a gift from Commodore John H. French on the occasion of the Club's opening in 1929, with the stipulation that it hang in this place of honor, a request that has been granted for almost seventy years.

The Rotunda (above).

The Rotunda is the central point of the Club, leading directly upstairs to the Ball Room, or to the Main Dining Room. Directly ahead are doors which lead to the East lawn.

Main Dining Room (right).

Smaller Dining Room, 1929.

"The more things change, the more they stay the same," the saying goes. A perfect example of this is found when comparing the Club's smaller dining room, now called the Spinnaker, as it was in 1929 (above), and the redecorated 1986 Spinnaker (opposite page). Although the present decor is a more luxurious and elegant setting, the furnishings almost duplicate the original ones.

The Spinnaker Room, 1986.

The Dining Room is one of the most cheerful large rooms ever designed, with east and north light flooding into the perimeter of the room, and with additional light tunneled into the center of the room through the round windows of the vaulted clerestory above. The central area is surrounded by marble columns, and was originally intended as a dance floor for the dining tables that surround it. Originally planned for the seating of 250 dinner guests, the dining room is directly connected to the kitchen and serving areas, which have been completely renovated, enlarged, and re-equipped in 1986 as part of the North Wing project.

At the west end of the kitchen is what was originally designed as a men's grill, an informal eating room that has evolved into the very popular Spinnaker Room, complete with bar, a casual counterpoint to the formality of the Main Dining Room.

By anyone's standards, the new Club was luxurious, but all the luxury was not without a price. By the early fall of 1929, just before the stock market took its Black Tuesday crash in October, the total of the loans taken out by the Club for the construction project reached $740,000, including fees to the builder of $458,757, more than half again the agreed-upon cost back in the optimistic, heady days of 1928. Although this debt might well have been manageable a few years earlier, the Club and its members had to carry this burden into the Great Depression, when overnight the financially solid membership became very unsolid, indeed.

The minutes of Board meetings during the first half of the 1930s are a saga of incredible effort and sacrifice on the part of the officers, Board, and members to keep the Club afloat. The primary duty of the monthly board meetings seemed to be accepting the resignations of members who could no longer afford the dues, let alone the special assessments and pleas for the purchase of bonds (at 6% interest, payable in gold). Somewhere in Grosse Pointe, perhaps papering the walls of a recreation room, there must be hundreds of these bonds, purchased in the hope that the Club could meet its obligations as well as keep up its services to members. Requirements for membership were broadened and re-broadened. Initiation fees were reduced again and again, and new categories of membership were established in the hope of attracting solvent initiates who could pay monthly dues and use the income-producing services of the Club.

But all was in vain, and the mortgages on the Club were foreclosed by banks that were themselves insolvent, the debt carried hopefully on the books as assets. The ownership of the Club passed from the members to their creditors, not to be regained until a new group of officers, optimistic about the economic climb back out of the depression and the following recession, bought back from the creditors the control and operation of the new Grosse Pointe Yacht Club.

The Grosse Pointe Yacht Club.
The club today, from a painting by member-artist Paul Gillan.

The gearing up of the nation for World War II, and the growing confidence of thousands of families moving into middle and upper-middle income brackets was the new base for the re-born Grosse Pointe Yacht Club. The sport of boating broadened its base among many Americans who heretofore thought of a boat only as something to be rowed or fished from. In a sense, the extension of both yachting and club membership to vast new segments of the population is what put the Club on the solid financial and social foundation it enjoys today.

But construction and maintenance had to be continued because of the changing needs of the membership for services and the vicissitudes of both high and low water on a site carved out of the lake bottom. Bowling alleys were installed on the lower level, the South Harbor was created, and the entire site had to be sheet piled against the intrusion of the lake during high water. In 1963, the tide had turned, literally, and the low level of the lake demanded the dredging of the harbors to provide the depth that the larger boats needed.

As early as 1984, the Board decided that the time had come to bring the Club to the highest standards of food service. The 1929 kitchen and serving area could no longer provide the level of service demanded by the quadrupled membership. So many dinners, so many receptions, so many banquets, so many lunches had passed through these areas that the time had come to renovate and upgrade the equipment and facilities.

Charles Terrence McCafferty & Associates were selected as architects for the million dollar improvement. They were asked to determine how the future requirements of the Club would be met within the constraints imposed by the existing Club facility. There was never any intention of tearing the place down and replacing it with Golden Arches or adding aluminum siding! The architects found immediately that the original construction documents were no longer available. The firm of Henry and Richmond had long ago gone out of business, and the successor firms had no idea what had happened to the plans.

This meant that before any new plans could be drawn, the McCafferty firm had to make detailed drawings of existing conditions as a first step in planning the renovation. Luckily, they had the complete and knowledgeable cooperation of a Building Committee composed of John Boll, Ted Smith, and Fred Schriever, who met regularly with the architect. When plans were ready, and bids accepted, the construction of what was called the North Wing Project was awarded to the firm of Edward V. Monahan, Inc.

The contract was a rigid one. Unlike the original construction that dragged out over several years, the schedule demanded that work start only after the close of the Club on January 3, 1986, and that it must be completed in time for the traditional Easter Brunch of March 30, 1986. Although there was the smoothest cooperation among the contractors and the various sub-contractors, the architect's office, and the Building Committee, the schedule was met only through the happy and unexpected blessing of Mother Nature, who provided a mild winter and temperate weather for those three months.

What was accomplished in the 90 days? The kitchen was more than doubled in size, new and more efficient equipment was installed, the basement area serving the kitchen was enlarged and improved, and the service courtyard was made much more usable, principally through the installation of an elevator to service the kitchen. Also, the popular Spinnaker Room was expanded, remodeled and completely redecorated. The focal point of the Club, the entrance foyer and Rotunda, was brightened and refurbished.

Like any tried and proven recipe, changes to the Club since 1929 have been made slowly and thoughtfully. Although the functional ability of the Club has been improved and modernized, it remains essentially the same Club that members saw on July 4, 1929, as they drove up the long driveway from Lakeshore Road. This architectural jewel remains a memorial to all those members and officers who sacrificed so much time, effort, and money to shape its character and stature. The heritage is here, in this special place on the shores of Lake St. Clair, and it will continue to be the symbol of excellence that is so cherished by its members.

———————— ❧ ————————

SOURCE: Originally appeared as James P. Gallagher, "Lakeshore Drive and Vernier Road: A Special Place," a chapter in, *A Beacon of Tradition: The Complete History of the Grosse Pointe Yacht Club* (Kelvin Publishing, 1986).

———————— ❧ ————————

James P. Gallagher is the former Director of Public Affairs for Smith, Hinchman & Grylls Associates. For 30 years he has been a writer with Time-Life and McGraw-Hill. Gallagher is the author of numerous articles and books including Smith, Hinchman & Grylls, 125 Years of Architecture and Engineering, *(1978), and* Renaissance of the Wayne County Building *(1989).*

Rumrunning on Lake St. Clair

by Philip P. Mason

Prohibition in the United States lasted from January 1920 to May 1933. The era brought about the wholesale smuggling of millions of gallons of Canadian whiskey and beer. No area was more seriously affected than the state of Michigan, especially along the banks of the Detroit River and the shores of Lake St. Clair.

PROHIBITION IN THE United States, which followed the passage of the 18th Amendment to the U.S. Constitution in 1918 and the Volstead Act, lasted for thirteen long years — from January 1920 to May 1933. Although it was later described by President Herbert Hoover as a "Noble Experiment," it was hardly that. Nor did it meet the expectations of its sponsors — temperance organizations, religious groups, and anti-saloon leagues — who predicted that Prohibition would bring about a new era in American life, a peaceful era when prisons would be empty, when the size of police departments would be drastically reduced, when workers' productivity would increase, and when men would spend more time at home with their families than in the saloons. Furthermore, the corrupt power of saloon keepers in state and local politics would end.

On midnight, January 16, 1920, millions of Americans and thousands of Grosse Pointers said farewell to legalized liquor. They welcomed the prediction of the evangelist and temperance leader Billy Sunday (already well known in Grosse Pointe circles)[1] when he issued an emotional cry of triumph:

> *Good Bye John. You were God's worst enemy. You were hell's best friend. I hate you with a perfect hatred. I love to hate you. The reign of tears is over, the slums will soon be a memory; we will turn our prisons into factories and our jails into storehouses and corncribs. Men will walk upright now, women will smile, and children will laugh. Hell will be forever for rent.*[2]

The prediction of drastic change was accurate, but not quite in the ways expected by Billy Sunday and other leaders in the campaign for prohibition. The 1920s did not characterize a decade of peace and tranquility, but of violence and crime, of gang wars and murder, and of the widespread violation of federal, state, and local laws on a massive scale.

---

1 In 1916, during his frequent visits to Michigan to campaign for statewide prohibition, Billy Sunday was often the guest of S. S. Kresge and John S. Newberry of Grosse Pointe. Roger A. Bruns, *Preacher: Billy Sunday and Big Time Evangelism* (New York: W. W. Norton & Co., 1992), 179.

2 *New York Times*, January 17, 1920.

Here is how young women smuggled liquor on a Windsor-Detroit Ferry. Photograph courtesy of Mrs. Nell Rhoades.

Although the smuggling of Canadian liquor pervaded all sections of the United States, no area was more seriously affected than the state of Michigan along the several hundred mile border separating it from Ontario. For thirteen years the struggle continued, pitting federal, state, and local law officers against rum runners. Yet, despite the concerted efforts of law enforcement agents, prohibition failed. Millions of gallons and hundreds of thousands of barrels of Canadian whiskey, beer, and wine were smuggled into Michigan during these thirteen years — an estimated 75% of all illegal liquor brought into the United States. The focus of the rum running operations centered on the Detroit River and Lake St. Clair. The greater Detroit area became the distribution center "to slake the parched throat of the American midwest." It developed the reputation of having "two major industries during the 1920s — the manufacture of automobiles and the distribution of Canadian liquor."

In order to fully comprehend the nature and extent of rum running, one must recognize the peculiar laws governing prohibition in Canada and the United States. The 18th Amendment and the Volstead Act prohibited the manufacture, sale, and consumption of alcoholic beverages except for scientific or medicinal purposes. In Canada, every province except Quebec had similar regulations. In Quebec the citizens voted to allow the manufacture and sale of liquor. The Canadian government did, however, license distilleries and breweries in Ontario and other provinces with authority to manufacture whiskey, beer, and wine for export to countries which did not have prohibition. Twenty-nine breweries and sixteen distilleries were licensed in Ontario alone — many located near or along the Michigan-Ontario waterway. Government-run export docks were opened in Ontario cities to facilitate the sale of alcoholic beverages. These arrangements became a bonanza for smugglers. Rum runners needed only to purchase liquor from those export stores and claim the destination as Cuba, Mexico, or Barbados. Even rum runners in row boats and other small vessels were never questioned or denied liquor.[3]

Not only were there adequate supplies of liquor readily available, but the Ontario-Michigan waterway was physically ideal for smuggling. The Detroit and St. Clair Rivers were narrow, with miles of deserted shoreline and islands to hinder detection. Lake St. Clair, which stretched thirty miles from Belle Isle to the mouth of the St. Clair River, also provided a haven for smugglers. Fishing and pleasure boating had always been popular in Lake St. Clair, but the number of licensed boats increased dramatically after the Volstead Act was passed by Congress. The sheer profits from rum running, as well as the challenge of outwitting federal and local enforcement agents, proved to be an overpowering incentive for residents living along Lake St. Clair and the Detroit River.

The methods devised to smuggle liquor into Detroit were well publicized in the local press, police and court records, and the accounts and reminiscences of those involved. Liquor was hidden on individuals, under coats, in hot water bottles and lunch boxes. Baby carriages and dog cages became useful receptacles as well. Enterprising rum runners rebuilt automobiles and boats with hidden compartments for liquor. Funeral hearses became vessels of liquor rather than deceased bodies. Each of these innovative means carried a constant supply of liquor into the Detroit area by ferry and, after 1929, via the Ambassador Bridge.

Railroad freight cars provided unlimited opportunities, especially because of their size. Liquor was hidden in shipments of grain, wood, agricultural produce, and, on one occasion, Christmas trees. A very popular practice of alter-

---

3   Canadian distillers had to pay a federal tax of nine dollars for each gallon of whiskey manufactured. The tax was returned if they provided documentary proof that the liquor was delivered to a country which did not have prohibition.

Grosse Pointe Police manned ice boats to pursue rum runners on Lake St. Clair, Photograph courtesy of the National Archives.

Above: *Police inspect steel cable, which ran from Peche Island, Ontario, to a cottage near the foot of Alter Road. Metal cylinders filled with Canadian whiskey were attached and pulled across. Photograph courtesy of the National Archives.*

Left: *This beer-laden smuggler's truck was too heavy for the ice on Lake St. Clair in the winter of 1933. Local residents, some on skates, came out to witness the accident. Photograph courtesy of the Detroit News.*

Jalopies were used to pick up contraband Canadian liquor from vessels on Lake St. Clair during the winter months. Photograph courtesy of the Dossin Great Lakes Museum.

ing the seals on freight cars enabled the transfer of liquor into Michigan to go undetected. Airplanes, despite their limited cargo space and the shortage of landing strips, were especially popular after 1929 when the Coast Guard increased its patrols on the Detroit River and Lake St. Clair.

Other ingenious devices included sleds laden with gallons of liquor which were dragged across the bottom of the Detroit River by powerful cables. In 1931 the U.S. Coast Guard discovered a steel cable attached to a metal drum full of liquor being hauled under water between Peche Island, off Belle Isle, and Alter Road in Detroit.[4]

Lake St. Clair offered unlimited possibilities for smugglers. Not only was it large and difficult to patrol, but it was also a popular body of water used by thousands of fishing and pleasure boating enthusiasts. A profusion of canals, boat slips, and boat house lined the shore from Grosse Pointe to New Baltimore. During the frigid winter days when solid ice covered the lake, caravans of jalopies laden with liquor crossed from Canada to the U.S. and unloaded their contraband in waiting trucks and autos. Even ice boats were used to outrun local police agents.

A *New York Times* reporter described the scene on Lake St. Clair in the winter of 1925 as "a new and strange phenomenon that rushes on the wings of a nor'easter through the friendly darkness, bringing contraband liquor from the Canadian shore."[5] A year later, the *Times* reported that U.S. Customs officials "headed off a wandering nag on Lake St. Clair and confiscated twenty-five cases of Canadian whiskey besides a horse and cutter."[6]

"Joe sent me," the popular phrase used during prohibition, gained a customer entrance into a speakeasy, blind pig, or joint where beer, wine, and hard liquor were readily available. Thousands of these establishments operated in the greater Detroit area during Prohibition, catering to the well-to-do, the blue collar workers, college students, secretaries — in fact, anyone who could afford a modest price for a drink. They were located in all parts of Detroit and in all of the surrounding communities. The Grosse Pointes were no exception, although the limited number of restaurants in these affluent communities somewhat curtailed the operation of these illegal establishments. But regardless of their location, residents of the Pointes had no trouble finding liquor if needed. Most of the restaurants along East Jefferson Avenue provided alcoholic beverages for their trusted

Blossom Heath Inn, located on Jefferson Avenue near Ten Mile Road in the Village of St. Clair Shores, was one of the areas most popular speakeasies. This post card view dates from 1923. Illustration courtesy of the St. Clair Shores Historical Commission.

patrons. Among the more popular such watering holes were the Woodbridge Tavern, Little Harry's, Pinkeys, Club Royale, Doc Brady's, Lefty Clark's, D'Emilio's French Club, Lidos, and the Aniwa Club on Van Dyke off Jefferson.

Of special attraction to Grosse Pointers — at least according to local police records — was the Blossom Heath Inn in St. Clair Shores. This popular restaurant featured nightly dancing as well as excellent cuisine. In May 1926, six hundred people, many of whom were Grosse Pointers, attended the opening of the Lantern Room, decorated to represent the streets of the Montmarte district of Paris. Bouncers carefully interviewed all newcomers who entered the restaurant, reviewing frequently a photo album of undercover customs and police prohibition agents. Liquor was readily available to trusted patrons as was access to roulette, crap, poker, Black Jack, and other games of chance located in the upstairs rooms.[7]

Blossom Heath became so well known to state and local authorities that it was often the target of police raids. In a state police raid on July 12, 1931, the restaurant lost "one slot machine, one Black Jack table, one crap table, and several hundred poker chips" and, of course, a large supply of Canadian beer and whiskey. The owner of Blossom Heath was arrested and fined one hundred dollars plus forty-five dollars in costs. The following month, on August

---

4 Larry Engelmann, *Intemperance: The Last War Against Liquor* (New York: The Free Press, 1979), 43.

5 *New York Times*, January 18, 1925.

6 *New York Times*, February 23, 1926.

7 Mary Karshner, "Blossom Heath," *Muskrat Tales*, 2 (Spring, 1981), 2-17.

The main dinning room at the Blossom Heath Inn. Illustration courtesy of the St. Clair Shores Historical Commission.

31, the police again raided the club and this time confiscated "three roulette tables, one crap table, one klondike table, and two thousand poker chips" and a large supply of alcoholic beverages. Each patron arrested was fined fifty dollars plus fifteen dollars in costs for "frequenting a gambling place." State police records confirm that Grosse Pointers were well represented at these social gatherings, although there is also evidence that secret passages at the Blossom Heath allowed many influential citizens to hurriedly depart undetected.[8]

Other local area speakeasies did not have the amenities of the Blossom Heath, Pinkeys, or Little Harry's, but they did provide a welcome service to local residents. A group of friends living on Finland Street in St. Clair Shores decided that their neighborhood needed a more continuous and reliable supply of beer and whiskey. They came up with an imaginative solution. They set up a still in one house to manufacture beer, next door, a distillery and bottling operation, and in the third house, a blind pig. The familiar assembly line concept, so well known to the automobile industry, was utilized to meet community needs.[9]

Grosse Pointe police department records also reveal that a number of blind pigs operated within the Pointes. They were notified of such illegal acts by neighbors who disliked the congestion, the odors of the stills, or just the thought that a neighbor might be violating the Volstead Act. On other occasions, it was the constant sound of gunfire which prompted complaints to the local police. On July 30, 1928, Grosse Pointe Park police received a complaint from an irate resident that his neighbor on Wayburn was not only "running a blind pig" but also "using the back yard for a toilet."[10]

Brys Drive in Lochmoor Village, now Grosse Pointe Woods, was the scene of a fire in the spring of 1932 caused by an exploding still. According to a neighbor, "the whole back side of the house was gone." She also reported that helpful neighbors arrived on the scene immediately to carry away the "milk cans full of alcohol."[11]

Grosse Pointe residents did not have to rely upon stills or local speakeasies, however, to provide a continuous supply of beer, wine, and whiskey. Given access to the proper phone numbers, which were readily available, single bottles

---

8 Capt. D. S. Leonard's Squad, "State Police Records," 1931, Michigan State Archives.
9 William A. Crouchman, "The Police Logs," *Muskrat Tales*, 6 (Winter, 1993), 8.
10 Grosse Pointe Parks Police Records, 1928.
11 Mrs. Richard Gale to Philip Mason, December 26, 1925. In possession of author.

or several cases could be ordered for prompt delivery to home or office, day or night.

The location of the Grosse Pointes along Lake St. Clair also resulted in rum running related incidents. U.S. Customs and Prohibition agents patrolled the shoreline waiting to apprehend smugglers, especially when they received advance warning of an impending shipment. They made many arrests as the boats of rum runners were being unloaded. Others followed high speed automobile chases along East Jefferson, Charlevoix, and other local thoroughfares. Serious injuries and deaths often resulted from these encounters.

Even more numerous and life threatening were the incidents involving prohibition agents and Grosse Pointers off shore on the lake. Poorly trained, yet overly enthusiastic, these enforcement officers often chased and opened fire on innocent fishermen and pleasure boaters who either did not understand their signals to stop for inspection or who got in their way during a chase.

Grosse Pointers became increasingly concerned about their safety on Lake St. Clair and on the Detroit and St. Clair waterways as such incidents were reported and appeared in the local press. Public concerns and outrage increased sharply in May 1927 when the death of James Lee

Above: *St. Clair Shores Police were kept busy twenty-four hours a day by rum runners. Photograph courtesy of the St. Clair Shores Historical Commission.*

Below: *Grosse Pointers could have contraband beer and whiskey delivered to their homes at night or during daylight hours. The cartoon reflects this popular practice. Illustration courtesy of the Dossin Great Lakes Museum.*

East side, west side,
All around the block,
The Bootlegger's
rushin' bizness
At all hours
of the clock.

The Crusaders, founded in 1929, helped elect repeal candidates to local, state, and national offices. Photograph courtesy of the Library of Congress.

without stopping to see if help was needed. The public outrage resulted in strong protests against prohibition enforcement practices.[12]

Another well-publicized incident involved federal prohibition officers firing at the launch carrying the two sons of Charles F. Fisher, vice president of the Fisher Body Company, and the son of prominent Detroiter Charles Walker. The boys were on a ride on the Detroit River when they were approached by a federal patrol boat. Not understanding the signal to stop, they waved and continued on their way. The federal agents opened fire, hitting the hull of the boat, just barely missing the occupants. Charles Fisher, irate at the episode, demanded that "innocent people who use the River be protected."[13]

Wealthy Grosse Pointers had other grounds for opposition to federal agents. Many owned waterfront property with boat houses and docking facilities, which were used extensively by rum runners to dock and unload cargoes of contraband liquor during nighttime hours. They were pursued by federal patrol boats and often gunfire erupted on shore.

Henry B. Joy, the retired president of the Packard Motor Company, was especially incensed at the actions of federal prohibition agents. He acknowledged that his boat docks were used by rum runners to unload their shipments of Canadian whiskey. And, although he made every effort to stop this activity, he charged that federal agents constantly harassed him and his watchman. When he could get no assistance from the Detroit Deputy Prohibition Director to curtail the harassment, he appealed directly to his friend, Andrew Mellon, the Secretary of the Treasury. When even this course of action failed to bring redress of his grievances, he dismissed his watchman and gave up the struggle. He admitted that he could not protect his premises "against use by smugglers or against marauding federal offi-

and his eleven-year-old daughter, Mildred, was announced. They had been pleasure boating on the Detroit River along with several other boaters when they crossed in the path of a federal patrol boat which was chasing a rum runner. The federal agents rammed the Lee boat, cutting it in two and killing Lee and his daughter. They sped from the scene

"Five Votes for Repeal" was the theme of this photograph, led by Mrs. Fred Alger (center). Photograph courtesy of the Burton Historical Collection.

Julius Stroh poured the first glass of legal beer at the American Legion Convention in Detroit on May 10, 1933. Photograph courtesy of the Associated Press.

cers." He also later admitted that he preferred the visits from smugglers because at least they did not damage his property.[14]

Other Grosse Pointers and groups joined Henry Joy in his campaign against federal prohibition officials. The Detroit Yachting Association, representing many wealthy and influential citizens of the Pointes sent a vigorous protest to Congress describing the "dangers of innocent persons being killed or wounded by indiscriminate shooting on the River and adjoining lakes." Even the Automobile Club of Michigan entered the fray, demanding that Congress investigate the "overzealous" actions of U.S. Customs agents for their "reckless searching of automobiles on the Detroit-Windsor ferries."[15]

As the decade of the 1920s neared its end, the opposition to Prohibition increased sharply. Local newspapers ran daily accounts of the violence, crime, shootings, and murders associated with prohibition. Many individuals who had actively supported the passage of the 18th Amendment now called for its repeal. Governors Fred Green and William Comstock, Senator James Couzens and General Motors President Alfred Sloan, were among those who now favored repeal.[16]

Grosse Pointers were not only active in the campaign for repeal of the 18th Amendment, but they provided leadership. Henry B. Joy campaigned nationally and contributed financial backing. Mrs. Fred Alger of Grosse Pointe formed and headed the Women's Organization for National Prohibition Reform.[17]

In February 1933, the U.S. Senate and House of Representatives passed, by the necessary two-thirds majority, a Constitutional Amendment repealing the Prohibition Amendment. Michigan endorsed the Amendment on April 10, 1933, by a vote of 99 to 1—the first state to take such action. The state legislature, aware that the national convention of the American Legion was being held in Detroit, authorized the sale of beer beginning May 10, 1933. Grosse Pointer Julius Stroh removed the bung from a gilded keg of Stroh Bohemian Beer and filled the first glass of beer to be served legally in fifteen years. Before the eight hours of festivities ended, three hundred barrels and five hundred cases of Stroh's beer were consumed by a happy throng of Legionnaires.[18] Thus prohibition—the "Noble Experiment" described by President Herbert Hoover—passed into history.

———————— ❦ ————————

Philip P. Mason is Distinguished Professor of History at Wayne State University and the former director of the Archives of Labor & Urban Affairs at the Walter P. Reuther Library. Professor Mason received his Ph.D from the University of Michigan. He has done extensive research in the fields of Detroit and Michigan history and has published numerous books and articles. His latest book, Rumrunning and the Roaring Twenties, *was published in 1995.*

———————— ❦ ————————

12 Engelmann, *Intemperance*, 100.

13 Ibid., 99-100.

14 Ibid., 102-103.

15 Philip P. Mason, *Rumrunning and the Roaring Twenties* (Detroit: Wayne State University Press, 1995), 147.

16 Ibid., 148.

17 Ibid.

18 Ibid., 150.

"Gentlemen, Start Your Engines!" Motor Racing at the Grosse Pointe Track

by Mark A. Patrick

From 1901 to 1904 the Grosse Pointe Race Track was the scene of exciting automobile racing. Here, automotive historian Mark Patrick takes an intriguing glance back to that early era of the motor car.

BEFORE THERE WAS an Indianapolis 500-mile automobile race, or even a 24-hour race at LeMans, there was the Grosse Pointe Race Track. Some of the biggest names in auto racing were drawn to this mile course to prove their mettle. Automobile manufacturers entered automobiles with hopes of winning and thereby making a strong reputation for their product. But to the spectators, the racing events were the extreme of excitement, adventure, and wild abandon.

The Grosse Pointe Race Track was constructed in 1894-1895. Of course, it was and remained a horse racing track throughout its short history, but in 1901 the turns were banked for automobile racing. The track was operated by the Detroit Driving Club, whose secretary was Daniel J. Campau, Jr. Daniel Campau was the scion of the Campau family who had arrived in Detroit with Cadillac in 1701. Daniel Campau, Jr., was quite successful in business, espe-

cially in real estate, and he had a passion for fast horses. Campau had a forceful personality and was a natural leader of men, as evidenced by his active role in the politics of the city of Detroit, the state of Michigan and the Democratic party. It was natural, then, when he was made president of the Detroit Driving Club, that Campau eclipsed the other officers and in effect became the club's prime mover.

One of Campau's first acts as president was to clean up the image of horse racing in Detroit. It had come to be associated with race fixing, organized crime, spectator drunkenness and other kinds of base behavior. One goal of the club's campaign was to move the races from an older track in Hamtramck Township (off Jefferson Avenue near Water Works Park), to a new track in a more bucolic, serene setting. It so happened that Campau owned a large tract of land, just outside the then Detroit city limits between Jefferson Avenue and the Detroit River and sand-

J.E. Peters in a Darracq racer.

wiched between Chalmers and Alter roads in an area known as Grosse Pointe Township. This is where the new oval horse track was built.

Of the track, the *Detroit Journal* reported in the May 5, 1901 issue, that "... all things considered (it) is the handsomest in the country in location, construction, and nature of the ground, its accessibility and the grand river and land view from the stands." Others commented on the park-like setting and beauty. The *Detroit Journal* went further — calling the track a "... monument to Campau's tireless persistence and successful contention for honest racing by honest men for honest purses, honestly paid." The Grosse Pointe Race Track was an oval eden, but then Campau let in the speed demons and for a few years Grosse Pointe was known for its wild motor car races.

Automobile racing officially began in Detroit on October 10, 1901. William E. Metzger of Detroit became perhaps the first automobile dealer in America when he opened his automobile agency in Detroit at 254 Jefferson Avenue and started selling assorted steamers and electrics. Metzger schemed and agitated and hyped the first organized automobile races in Detroit and convinced his friend and occasional associate Campau to lease the Grosse

Pointe track to them. Metzger talked up the 25-mile race with $1,000 prize money in the press. He predicted an enormous crowd on race day, claiming to a reporter that it would eclipse other significant racing events. On race day, businesses and official offices shut down — even courts were adjourned — and reports on the threatening weather

*Looking towards the grand stand
at the Grosse Pointe Race Track.*

Ford passing Winton in the seventh mile of their ten mile event, October 10, 1901.

Map of Grosse Pointe Race Track.
This turn-of-the-century map shows the Grosse Pointe Race Track south of Jefferson Avenue between Chalmers and Alter Roads. Illustration courtesy of the St. Clair Shores Public Library.

A Packard 25 horse power "Gray Wolf" racer.

An Oldsmobile "Pirate" racer on the track.

conditions moved to the front page: "Clouds Will Go!" pronounced the *Detroit News*. A parade snaked its way from downtown out to the track. By turn of the century standards, the crowd of more than 8,000 ticket buyers was enormous.

There were several races on the slate that day. A one-mile race for electrics was won by a Baker out of Cleveland. A one-mile race for automobiles under 1,500 pounds was described as uninteresting in press accounts the next day, but it was won by a Lytle of Toledo, easily beating a Duryea entry.

The final 25-mile race pitted Henry Ford, a local man already known to the Detroit automobile crowd, against the reputable Alexander Winton. The big race was reduced from 25 miles to ten because the racing slate had taken longer than expected. Right from the start it was exciting as the two racers fought it out. The Winton racer held the lead through seven miles with the Ford close behind. As audience tension grew, the Winton began to succumb to mechanical failures and lose power. A great roar came from the stands as Henry Ford caught and passed the Winton. Ford finished the race first, clocking the ten miles in 13 minutes and 23 seconds. Henry Ford, who within ten years would change the face of industry forever, was known first in the nascent automotive industry as a speed demon!

Many early speed records were associated with the track, but all of these records fell soon after they were set — some within days. Barney Oldfield raced the famous "999" to a one minute, six second mile on the track in October of 1902. In 1904, a Packard Model L set an endurance record of 1,000 non-stop miles in 29 hours, 53 minutes and 37 seconds.

Motor racing ended at the track around 1905. The track was razed soon after and a tract subdivision sprang up and the area was later annexed by Detroit. One must surmise that Mr. Campau, with his real estate instincts, felt the time was right to develop the land. Perhaps, too, he grew bored with the sport. Whatever the reason, just like that, speed, guts, and the glory of motor car racing came to an end in the Grosse Pointes.

Sincholle and the Darracq make tracks.

Racecar driver Tom Cooper at the tiller of Henry Ford's famous "999."

———————— ❧ ————————

PHOTO CREDITS: The photographs in this article, courtesy of the Detroit Public Library's National Automotive History Collection, capture some of those early moments in motor racing at the Grosse Pointe Race Track, 1901-1904.

———————— ❧ ————————

Mark A. Patrick is the Curator of the National Automotive History Collection, Detroit Public Library. With a bachelors and masters degree from the University of Michigan, Mr. Patrick has done considerable research and writing about the automobile and early motor racing. Mark Patrick and his family reside in Chelsea, Michigan.

Beaupre Service, 1952.

The Gas Stations of Grosse Pointe: Then and Now

by Michael Mengden

The automobile has been around for a hundred years, and the first drive-in gas station opened in Detroit in 1910. Not long ago, it seemed that there was a gas station at most every major street intersection. Today, most of those neighborhood service stations are gone. In Grosse Pointe, a handful of these old-fashioned gas stations still survive.

GROSSE POINTE PARK

Jess's Service Center, Inc.
15302 E. Jefferson
Jesse Rose, owner

The site has been a Sunoco station since the early 1920s, with the present building the third one. The station was known as "Breaux Service," during the 1930s. In 1951 the current station was built, at the time one of the most modern in the area. The original Trombley School was bought and demolished in the early 1950s in what is now parking area for the station. According to Mr. Rose, the building is virtually unchanged, with the exception of the ceiling, which was a bank of lights throughout, originally.

Though there are no other buildings in the Park being used for gas station purposes at this time, there are fascinating glimpses of the past still available from Neil Muir, considered the local station expert. Mr. Muir worked on Kercheval decades ago in what must have been the Park's station "strip," with several stations on corners. For example, there was a Shell on Wayburn, at Maryland there was a Hupmobile, at Lakepointe a Sinclair. At the Beaconsfield/Kercheval corner alone there was a Standard station (now The Brake Shop, with a period facade) as well as a White Star, which later became a Mobil (1930s). What is now Pointe Printing was a City Service known as Rogers and Fritz, with a car wash on the alley. Mr. Muir recalls the gas war of the late 1930s, when gas went for as little as twenty gallons for a dollar. For many years the price was apparently 20¢ per gallon, until the "war" started, with six gallons going for a dollar.

Also in the park, a former gas station (filling station) from at least the early 1920s still stands at Charlevoix and Lakepointe. The building and the grounds are well maintained by Tom McDonald, of the adjacent Crown Realty.

GROSSE POINTE CITY

R.C. Krausmann Service, Inc.
16820 Kercheval
Dick Krausmann, owner

This has been a station serving the carriage trade since at least the 1920s. The current building was opened in September 1956, as Krausmann Brothers Service, with Gulf gasoline. It currently is a Rent 'n' Ride and Havoline Oil Change use, but gas is still sold (Union 76). Mr. Krausmann is known as the neighborhood crossing guard for school children at Kercheval and Cadieux. He humbly rejects attention on this score, but proudly shows off his station, little changed since it was built 39 years ago.

Breaux Service, 1935.

Jess's Service Center, 1996.

R.C. Krausmann Service, 1956.

R. C. Krausmann Service, 1996.

Village Service, 1970.

Village Service, 1996.

Beaupre Service, 1947.

Beaupre Service, 1996.

Breaux Service, 1935. *"Can I check your oil?"*

GROSSE POINTE CITY (*Continued*)

Village Service
16821 Kercheval
Phil Zoufal, owner

Standard had a station at what is now Damman's, Kercheval and St. Clair. They bought the current Village Service corner in 1955 and built a station. Mr. Zoufal bought the station in 1969, adding ten feet in the back for storage. In 1981 it became a Mobil, in 1989, a Marathon station. The owner is proud of the huge covered drive, the latest computerized monitoring system, and the fact that Marathon is American owned and operated.

Beaupre Service, Inc.
18184 Mack
Chester (Chet) Yavor, owner

Beaupre Service opened March 2, 1946, and has remained a Mobil station, very little changed, ever since. Mr. Yavor bought the station from Mr. Beaupre in 1980, and knows a lot about Pointe-area stations and the industry in general. He spots former station locations readily, probably because he has grown up in the business.

GROSSE POINTE FARMS

Standard On the Hill
66 Kercheval
Tom Onofrey, owner

This station was originally at Kercheval and Hall Place, where an office building now stands. It moved about ten years ago to its current location of Kercheval and Mc-Millan. Mr. Onofrey bought the business from Tom Pitlock in the early 1980s. The existing station had been a Sunoco for many years, until it was closed and boarded up in the 1970s. The station has the same configuration as before it was reopened, with slight changes to Amoco specifications. Mr. Onofrey believes the building was built in the 1930s. He is the brother of Michael Onofrey of T & M Service Center in Grosse Pointe Woods.

GROSSE POINTE WOODS

T & M Service Center
20675 Mack
Michael Onofrey, owner

This is currently an Amoco station, and was for many years a Standard station known as Connolly Brothers. The building is essentially unchanged from the 1940s, when it was built. The owner is the brother of Tom Onofrey of Standard On the Hill — hence the T & M Service.

GROSSE POINTE SHORES

There are no gas stations of any kind in this village.

———————— ❦ ————————

With a long-time interest in automobiles and local history, Grosse Pointe Farms resident Michael Mengden undertook a survey of local gas stations in August 1995 and donated his findings to the Grosse Pointe Historical Society. This article represents a portion of that survey.

———————— ❦ ————————

PHOTO CREDITS: All "then" photos courtesy of each station; all "now" photos courtesy of Michael Mengden.

Standard On the Hill, 1996.

T & M Service Center, 1955.

T & M Service Center, 1996.

Detroit is right proud of her brand new two-storied motor 'buses, which ply between Grand Circus and Gladwin parks.

Double Deck Bus #509, June 27, 1920.
This photo of #509 appeared in the June 27, 1920, Detroit Free Press. To experiment with right-hand drive DMC purchased 20 (numbered 501-520) from Fifth Avenue. Not satisfied with them, they were gone by 1929. All double deck buses originally had open upper decks, which eventually grew in disfavor because, well this is Michigan. Need we say more?

Double Deck Bus #704, Mid-1920s.
*Double deck #704 also a Fifth Avenue Coach, operated with two men, a driver and conductor. In this mid-1920s photo, the original open upper deck has been partially enclosed to protect passengers in bad weather. A canvas cover would go over the center aisle, which the conductor would lower when passing beneath a railroad viaduct in Detroit.
Bidigare Collection.*

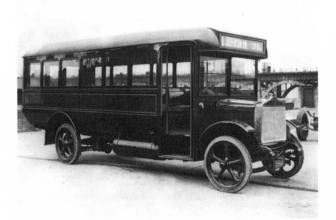

Motor Bus #135, 1922-1924.
*This photo of #135 illustrates the original appearance of the 100 series buses built by the Fifth Avenue Coach Company. DMC purchased 67 vehicles between 1922 and 1924.
Courtesy Motor Bus Society, Inc. Library.*

Motor Bus #129, 1931.
*Note the major changes in this 1931 photo of #129 from the earlier photo of #135. Lake Shore Coach Lines purchased 27 of these 100 series buses from DMC to start operations in 1932.
Schramm Collection.*

The Motor Bus Comes to Grosse Pointe

by Jack E. Schramm and William H. Henning

For over 75 years the motor bus has been an important part of our transportation system. Here, authors Jack Schramm and Bill Henning tell the story of the motor bus companies that have operated in the Grosse Pointe and St. Clair Shores area.

ONCE UPON A time in Grosse Pointe, and probably elsewhere throughout the country, buses contributed significantly to people's sense of community.

One such community were the "bus people"—those employed by the bus companies—who formed tight networks of support long before formal support groups came into vogue.

Mildred Bedford Naar, who wrote a "Michigan Memories" piece in the July 18, 1991, edition of the *Detroit Free Press*, recalled how the bus people became neighbors. In 1920, when she and her family arrived from New York at Detroit's train station, they transferred to a double deck bus, one of 29 that ran up and down Jefferson Avenue. It was owned by the Detroit Motorbus Company (DMC), and her father, Thomas Bedford, was to become one of its new employees. Twelve years later he started the Lake Shore Coach Lines.

"Because the bus company was being formed during a boom time in Detroit, we had arrived in the midst of a housing shortage," Naar wrote. "The bus people who were already here helped find places for the new arrivals." Over time, many of the bus company employees lived in the same neighborhoods, their wives became friends, talking over back fences, and their children played together.

Motor Bus News, a DMC employee newsletter, reported in 1930 that during the winter, riders were almost solely made up of residents from the east side of Detroit who worked and shopped in Detroit. When summer arrived, however, the atmosphere on the routes changed tremendously. Buses then catered to a crowd "anxious to shake the dust of the streets from their shoes and enjoy the beautiful scenery of the Lake Shore Drive on their way out to what is probably Detroit's finest playground, Jefferson Beach Amusement Park" (today the location of Jefferson Beach Marina and Brownie's restaurant).

The article continued. "Each bus load leaving the city limits has its quota of family parties with the usual accouterments of lunch baskets and suitcases filled with bathing apparel and sporting goods." The buses emptied their loads of pleasure seekers at Nine Mile Road and Jefferson, then turned around and came back down Jefferson Avenue.

There was a time during the 1940s when secretaries on their way downtown to work rode the Mack Avenue bus line with such regularity that a mobile community on wheels was created. Everyone knew everyone. They became such a close-knit group that occasionally bridal showers would be held *en route*.

Likewise, a sense of community developed among the housekeepers who rode out from Detroit to work in Grosse

Pointe's mansions. The continuity of community was enhanced by having the same bus driver each day. He often knew his passengers so well that he would let them off mid-block, closer to their destination.

Looking at the chronology of bus companies that have operated in the Grosse Pointe/St. Clair Shores area, one can't help but notice how many bus lines went in and out of business over the years. Many early companies were run by promoters who leased the buses and received permits from the Public Utilities Commission to operate specific routes. When revenue failed to provide enough funds to make payments on the buses, they returned them and went out of business. Auto companies were underwriting these operations and wrote the losses off as a business expense.

Today motor bus ridership has greatly diminished as has that very unique "sense of community." However, buses still provide an important transportation service to eastsiders.

Chronology

Bus Companies That Have Operated in the Grosse Pointe and St. Clair Shores Area

APRIL 12, 1923

Soren Jensen, John Baker, Louis Wisser, Cyrus and Frank Cadieux made application to incorporate the Grosse Pointe Bus Co. and issued 600 shares of stock at $10 each in order to obtain buses. Their seating capacity is not known, but early buses usually seated from 20 to 25 passengers. One of the advantages of buses over streetcars was that they were self-propelled and needed no tracks or wire.

Lake Shore Coach, 1940.
A Lake Shore coach turning off Woodward onto Jefferson in 1940. DSR Files.

APRIL 24, 1923

Grosse Pointe Bus Co. application approved. The route followed the interurban's route from Jefferson and Alter via Jefferson, Fisher, Grosse Pointe Boulevard, Moross, Kercheval to Weir Lane. (Note: An interurban was larger than the city-type streetcar which operated between cities such as Detroit and Mt. Clemens.)

MAY 29, 1924

The Detroit Motorbus Co. (DMC) purchased the Grosse Pointe Bus Co., naming the line *Grosse Pointe*.

MAY 2, 1927

A third company, Village Utilities Inc., began in St. Clair Shores where Village officials were working to force the interurbans off its streets. The original bus service operated from the Hart loop at the end of the Mack streetcar line in Detroit, out Mack to Defer Road (now Nine Mile Road). After going out of business, new owners bought the company and extended the line to Mt. Clemens via Jefferson Avenue and Crocker Boulevard. The company went bankrupt by December 1, 1926, and with the interurban's franchise about to expire on June 21, 1927, St. Clair Shores Village officials started their own company. After selling $30,000 in stock, mostly to local citizens, the Village Utilities Inc. began operation. The route was from Deanhurst via Jefferson, Defer Road, Mack, Cadieux to Kercheval where passengers could transfer to the DMC Kercheval bus, then to a Jefferson bus to go downtown. On May 19, 1927, after receiving Grosse Pointe Park's approval, the line was extended to Jefferson and Alter where passengers could transfer directly to the Jefferson bus. When Jefferson Beach opened, Village Utilities Inc. decided to sell rather than expand. It was purchased by DMC, which operated it as a separate division.

MAY 1, 1928

When the interurban was forced to discontinue operating in Grosse Pointe, the Grosse Pointe line was extended to Gaulkers Pointe where the Edsel and Eleanor Ford Estate stands today. Later, the line was extended into downtown Detroit, terminating at Grand Circus Park.

MAY 1930

By 1930, DMC had a fleet of about 450 buses with the double deckers carrying 48, 52, 60 or 66 passengers, depending on the make. Single deckers carried 23, 27 and later models, 33 or 40 passengers.

Coach #54, October 18, 1940.
October 18, 1940, coach #54 is loading passengers in front of the Grosse Pointe Candy Box at Jefferson and Wayburn. DSR Files.

Coach #93, October 18, 1940.
October 18, 1940, LSCL coach #93 is transferring passengers to coach #58, probably on their way to downtown Detroit. DSR Files.

Coach #89, October 25, 1940.
In this photo, taken at the intersection of Mack and Moross on October 25, 1940, LSCL coach #89 built by Ford has just turned off Mack and is heading east on Moross. Today the gas station has been replaced by Kinkos. The small building visible ahead of the bus was recently torn down to make room for a parking lot. DSR Files.

Boarding Coach #58, August 10, 1943.
Passengers boarding LSCL coach #58 in downtown Detroit at Grand Circus Park on August 10, 1943. From the Collections of Henry Ford Museum and Greenfield Village.

Grand Circus Park.
After World War II, LSCL began purchasing General Motors coaches similar to this one loading at Grand Circus Park. This has been the Detroit terminal for Grosse Pointe buses since the days of DMC. Courtesy Motor Bus Society, Inc. Library.

Cold Snowy Day.
Looks like a cold snowy day as these LSCL drivers and inspectors pose for their photo by the GMC coach. SEMTA Files.

CIRCA 1931

A short-lived fourth line, named *Windmill Pointe*, was started by DMC, operating from Jefferson to Lake Shore Road. The exact route is not known, nor the date it was started. According to Grosse Pointe Park records, it was discontinued on June 30, 1931. However, in the early 1930s, someone operated a seven-passenger Packard on this route which went from Barrington via Jefferson, Balfour, Windmill Pointe Drive to Marine Hospital (on the Detroit River across the bridge from Alter Road). It returned via Windmill Pointe Drive to Barrington to Jefferson. The fare was ten cents for adults, five cents for children.

JANUARY 1, 1932

In order to protect its investment in the Department of Street Railways (DSR), the Detroit City Council withdrew permission for the successful DMC to operate within the city. This action caused two new companies to emerge: Lake Shore Coach Lines (LSCL) on the east side and Dearborn Coach on the west side. The Grosse Pointe line became *Jefferson* or *Jefferson Beach* (presently the location of the Jefferson Beach Marina and Brownie's restaurant), and although those buses were allowed to continue to run downtown, they were prohibited from picking up inbound or discharging outbound passengers once they left their end points of Grosse Pointe and Grand Circus Park. This resulted in the creation of an express line, much like an express elevator that skips floors, allowing passengers to reach their destination more quickly. (The same restriction applied later to SEMTA and SMART until recently, when it was lifted in preparation for the Detroit Department of Transportation and SMART to combine their lines.) The portion of the *Kercheval* line within Detroit became part of the DSR; the portion outside was added to the Village Utilities line, later rerouted on Moross and Kercheval in place of Mack and Cadieux, retaining the name *Kercheval*. The DMC garage at Terminal and Edlie streets in Detroit was rented by LSCL for maintenance and storage facilities and still stands.

The routes changed very little during the years *Jefferson* was being extended to Jefferson Beach. Kercheval's route was from Deanhurst via Jefferson, Nine Mile Road, Mack, Moross, Kercheval, Wayburn to Jefferson, with a transfer to the Jefferson or Charlevoix lines required to go downtown. In later years, some trips continued to Crocker Boulevard via Jefferson.

MAY 1, 1935

Charlevoix was started at this time from Fisher Road via Charlevoix, Wayburn, St. Paul, Maryland, Jefferson to downtown Detroit. All routes going downtown terminated

GMC Bus, 1960.
*In 1960 LSCL purchased nine of these GMC "new look"
buses. Courtesy Detroit News.*

SEMTA Coach #8201, 1971.
*In 1971 SEMTA had taken over LSCL and here SEMTA
coach #8201 is passing the Renaissance Center.
Courtesy GMC.*

at Grand Circus Park. By 1937, the line was extended via Charlevoix, Moran, McMillan, to Mack, returning via Fisher to Charlevoix and then the regular route. It was extended again later via Fisher (inbound via Moran), to Chalfonte, to Moross, to Mack. By 1943, it operated a loop in Grosse Pointe Woods via Mack, Vernier, Marter, Brys Drive and Mack.

OCTOBER 24, 1955

A short-lived shuttle started at this time. Its route was from Jefferson via Nine Mile Road, Harper, Twelve Mile Road, Little Mack, Ten Mile Road, Harper, Nine Mile Road to Jefferson. The fare was 15 cents, ten cents for school children. Attempting to increase ridership, it was rerouted on November 26, 1955, from Edsel Ford Court via Jefferson, Nine Mile Road, Harper, Masonic Boulevard, returning the same way. Unable to attract riders, the line was discontinued on December 23, 1955. Another shuttle on Eight Mile Road was started in 1957 between Mack and Eastland Shopping Center at Kelly Road.

SEPTEMBER 7, 1971

Southeast Michigan Transportation Authority (SEM-TA) took over the Lake Shore Coach Lines, becoming the Lake Shore Division. There has since been some rerouting and extensions, and the Eastland Shuttle now is part of another line. Today, the *Jefferson* continues on Lake Shore/Jefferson to Marter, Vernier, Eastland Mall, while the *Jefferson Express* continues out Jefferson to Crocker Boulevard to Mt. Clemens. The *Kercheval* continues on Moross to Harper, Eight Mile Road, Eastland Center and Macomb Mall.

The second branch goes via Mack, Nine Mile Road, Jefferson, to Masonic Boulevard to Macomb Mall.

Charlevoix also has two branches, both traveling to Mack and Vernier; one continuing on Greater Mack, Ten Mile Road, Little Mack to Macomb Mall; the second going via Vernier, Marter Road, Jefferson to Masonic Boulevard.

JANUARY 19, 1989

SEMTA was renamed Suburban Mobility Authority for Regional Transportation (SMART), pursuant to Public Act 481 which reorganized public transportation in southeastern Michigan.

SOURCE: Originally published as "Buses: Mobile Communities," *Moorings,* Vol. 11, No. 3, Fall 1994.

Jack Schramm and Bill Henning have an appetite and passion for the history of transportation, particularly of the motor bus and the interurban railway. They are co-authors of Detroit's Street Railways, Volumes 1 & 2, *and* When Eastern Michigan Rode the Rails, Books 1-4. *They are also the authors of* A Street Car Named Grosse Pointe, *which appeared in* Volume 1 *of* Tonnancour.

Yachts of the Auto Barons

by John F. Polacsek

During the 1920s and 1930s the waterways of Lake St. Clair were the home of a number

of yachts owned by auto barons—those who amassed their fortunes by either assembling

automobiles, or by providing parts for others to create the horseless carriage.

In this article John F. Polacsek tells the story of these magnificent floating mansions.

YACHTING HAS ALWAYS been one of the costliest diversions in the world, as it takes a bankroll of royal proportions to purchase a steam or motor yacht, and to keep it spic and span. In the 1920s the waterways of Lake St. Clair and the Great Lakes were the home of a number of yachts owned by auto barons—those who amassed their fortunes by either assembling an automobile or by providing parts for others to create the horseless carriages. There were two factors that occurred in the 1920s that made possible these floating palaces that were mirrors of the mansions on shore—the diesel engine and the interior decorator.

There was a great desire among yachtsmen to own a spotless vessel. A large steam yacht might need a crew of 50 men, but a diesel yacht needed only one third that size crew or less. The advent of oil burning engines to replace the coal burning steam engines in the 1920s and 1930s was evident in the port of Detroit. In 1925 there were three steam yachts registered in Detroit and 58 motor yachts, by 1939 there were only two steam yachts while the number of motor yachts rose to 136.

The motor yachts were equipped with diesel engines and required a crew of 7 or 8 men to operate the vessel. Additionally, the absence of smoke, hot boilers, and a coal bunker altered the design of the vessel and more living space was the result. Hulls were designed with ample draft

and stability and were able to sail through the roughest weather that the Great Lakes or Atlantic Ocean could produce. On yachts 150 feet in length, two diesel engines provided between 800 and 3,200 horsepower, and matched propellers could produce a speed from 12 to 16 knots. The oil in the tanks inside the hull allowed for a cruising range of 2,000 miles or more, double that of the steam powered vessels.

As early as 1907 one of Michigan's auto barons, Ransom E. Olds, owned a yacht and was a member of the Detroit Boat Club as well as the Detroit Yacht Club. Mr. Olds organized the Olds Motor Vehicle Company in 1897, and reorganized it in 1899 as the Olds Motor Works in Detroit. In 1901 a fire destroyed his Detroit plant and the company moved to Lansing, Michigan. A few years later Olds sold the Motor Works and organized the Reo Motor Car Company. By the early 1920s he was ready for his fifth yacht.

In February 1922 Olds received a letter from Harry Defoe of the Defoe Boat & Motor Works in Bay City, Michigan. Defoe had heard that Olds was contemplating building a yacht and he requested to bid on the job.

The Defoe Boat & Motor Works was a well equipped steel ship building plant especially adapted to the construction of medium-sized vessels. The company began in 1905

REOMAR III, starboard view.

by building fishing skiffs. With the closing of the Frank Wheeler Shipbuilding Company in 1911, Defoe was able to grow using the pool of experienced shipbuilders who were in the Bay City and Saginaw area. They could construct a vessel from the design of any naval architect. Vessels up to 125 feet in length were built under cover, larger boats were built out in the open.

Mr. Olds contacted the Detroit naval architects Cox & Stevens and had them draw up the plans for a new steel hulled yacht. On December 30, 1922, Olds entered into a contract with the Defoe Boat & Motor Works for a new 97'5" vessel. The blueprints and specifications were delivered to the Defoe shipyard. Work commenced immediately as the yacht was to be delivered in the Saginaw River at the plant on or before the first day of June 1924. It was mutually agreed upon that any changes in the plans would need the approval of the builder and the owner. The agreed price for the vessel was $25,000, and the owner was to pay all federal taxes assessed on the luxury yacht.

In February 1923 the Defoe Shipyard wrote to Olds stating that the revised set of plans and specifications had

arrived from Cox & Stevens. However, the shipyard had been advised not to proceed until hearing directly from the owner as there was a distinct possibility that he might wish to change something else.

The shipyard was ready to create a scale model of the yacht and they wanted Olds' approval before any additional changes were made. If there were to be any changes in the lines of the hull, this might also be reflected in the amount of steel plate and frames that were needed. It was June before a letter from the Reo Motor Car Company arrived with instructions to order the steel from the Joseph T. Ryerson & Son firm of Chicago, Illinois. The steel was to be billed to Olds' account, but Defoe had some reservations about what kind of steel was coming under the classification of "warehouse stock." He was of the opinion that the warehouse stock would probably be inferior due to the ordinary open hearth steel making process, and he suggested a better quality ship's steel. In July the steel arrived after being purchased from the firm of Jones & Laughlin of Cleveland, Ohio, and Defoe was satisfied that it was good quality.

REOMAR III, main salon.

REOMAR III, interior with organ.

REOMAR III, stateroom.

REOMAR III, aft deck.

The joiner work for the interior was being created and would be installed as soon as the hull was ready for it. In September Olds decided to have the deck house made out of teak wood for an additional $500 charge. Olds did not like the look of oak. He preferred a darker appearance along with natural mahogany. He noted that it was vital that the very best varnish be used and that the outside varnish should be the best Valspar—nothing else would do.

As the joiner work came on board so did Olds' new interior designer, The Grosvenor Company of East 48th Street, New York City.

The interior designer recommended that no glass knobs be used anywhere on the yacht, and that the hardware in the owners cabin be of white brass. It was suggested that the finish on the mahogany in the owners stateroom be in a French gray or stain. Olds suggested that the shipyard try out a piece and he would look it over when he came up for an inspection. Olds was not satisfied, and had the interior designer send a sample of wood showing the exact finish that he wanted for the mahogany doors, trim in the state rooms, passage way, and the lobby of the yacht. The colors for the walls in the various rooms were forthcoming, and the Defoe Shipyard accommodated Olds' wishes. In addition, Olds requested that the lounge cushions and seats on the deck be made of brown pantesote, and the designer was to forward a swatch to match.

Work progressed on the vessel and in early June 1924, the yacht was in the final stages of completion. Olds wrote to Defoe, noting that he had ordered in May, from the Wanamaker Company of New York City, the table linen, bed linen, etc, and he wanted to be sure that it was all set aside and under good care.

On July 24, 1924, Olds sent a note on stationary embossed ON BOARD REOMAR III to the Defoe Boat & Motor Works. He stated that he was "very much pleased" with the yacht, and he thought that the shipyard had done a credible job.

Mr. Olds was pleased with his yacht, and as the seven-man crew got underway, he came down to meet them at the Detroit Boat Club on Belle Isle in the Detroit River. Olds used the REOMAR III for sailing north, up the lakes, then back down and out to the Thousand Islands and the St. Lawrence River. During 1925, Olds cruised about 2,500 miles aboard the REOMAR III and used about 2,000 gallons of oil as fuel. The vessel was wintered in Charlevoix, on Lake Michigan. Olds noted that he had a number of chances to sell the REOMAR III, but he held on to the yacht until 1931, when it was sold to Alex J. Groesbeck of Detroit, a former governor of Michigan. Groesbeck renamed the yacht RENMAR.

William C. Rands came to Detroit in 1891 and engaged in the bicycle business. In 1903 he bought out the Wheeler Manufacturing Company and was soon producing windshields, tops, lamp brackets, etc., for various automobiles. The company grew into the Rands

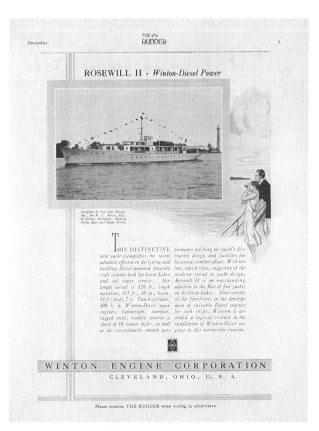

Advertisement – 1931.

ROSEWILL II, main salon.

Automotive Company, which in 1916 was combined with the Motor Products Corporation, a major source in the automotive industry. Rands was also one of the original founders of the Automobile Club of Michigan and held card number three.

In October 1923, Harry Defoe wrote William C. Rands of the Motor Products Company of Detroit asking to bid on the new yacht that Mr. Rands was contemplating building. Defoe mentioned that the hull of Olds' large steel yacht was about completed, and he was proud that Olds had chosen his Bay City shipyard to build his yacht. Rands was invited to visit the Defoe shipyard to inspect their work, or to visit the Detroit Boat or Yacht Club where Defoe products were at the docks.

In December 1925 Defoe was still trying to bid on a yacht for Mr. Rands, and he wanted the job because this was to be Rands' first vessel. Defoe was proud that he had been in the boat business for 20 years, and had given up the construction of a cheaper class of boats and was working exclusively on high quality vessels. Defoe stated that he would like to place another boat in Detroit that would prove the quality of his shipyard's work. He recognized that he had an opportunity with Rands and was willing to cut a deal. The price of the new boat was to be reduced to $29,500. However, this did not include the engines, electric equipment, the upholstery, or the small craft used to shuttle the owner and guests from the dock to the yacht.

A deal was struck, and the naval architectural firm of Hacker & Fermann, Inc., of Detroit, Michigan, designed an excellent 80-foot steel hulled vessel. The yacht, named the ROSEWILL, was completed late in the summer of 1926. Per Rands' request, the leather and cloth for the upholstery came from the Fisher Body Company of

Detroit, and the furniture and cabinet work were completed under the direction of the Andrew Sisman Company, well-noted craftsmen of Detroit. The yacht was 79'9" in length, with a 14'8" beam. The crew of four handled the vessel and she spent much of her time at the dock of the Detroit Yacht Club. Rands owned the vessel only a year, when she was sold to David Wende of Buffalo, New York, and was renamed the RESTLESS II.

Rands was a booster of the Defoe shipyard, and in 1931 a new 126-foot yacht named the ROSEWILL II was delivered to him in Detroit. The yacht was designed by the naval architects Cox & Stevens, Inc., who now had offices in New York and Detroit. The yacht had a low sleek design, in order to insure the proper clearance for canal navigation on the fall trip to Florida where the boat was wintered.

On the main deck was a dining salon with the galley up forward, followed by a large navigation room, and the owners stateroom, aft. The main salon was large and airy, measuring 12 feet wide by 25 feet long. Arrangements below decks included heads (sometimes known as bathrooms), dressing rooms, lockers, etc., all carefully worked out for the owner's family requirements.

The crew of eight managed the vessel. The engine room housed twin eight-cylinder 300-horsepower Winton Diesel engines which produced 16 knots. When the engines ran at top speed they were practically vibrationless. On board, a pair of two-cylinder 10 k.w. Winton Diesels generated electric current for the whole boat.

The ROSEWILL II was listed as being owned by Rands, Inc., and was operated on the Great Lakes until 1937, when the yacht was sold to Emma Burlington of Cincinnati, Ohio and the name was changed to the BURLANIA.

ROSEWILL II, owner's stateroom.

ROSEWILL II, port bow.

ROSEWILL II, starboard view, May 23, 1931.

COMOCO, dining salon.

COMOCO, engine room.

COMOCO, pilot house.

COMOCO, port view.

In 1926, Rands was instrumental in securing Defoe a bid on a new yacht for Ross Judson of Detroit. Judson was leaning towards having the vessel built on the lakes, and Rands extolled the merits and quality workmanship that was available in Bay City. After a tour of the ROSEWILL, Judson was convinced.

A month later Rands wrote Defoe, noting that, "I was very pleased to know that you were able to secure the order for Judson's boat." He suggested that Defoe pay a visit to the Detroit firm of Hacker & Fermann as Rands was aware that another of his business acquaintances was about to place an order for a yacht.

Ross W. Judson was president of Continental Motors Corporation, a company which he had founded in 1903. He observed that most American cars were using one- and two-cylinder engines, and was convinced that a practical four-cylinder engine could be developed, which he did. His firm had plants in Muskegon and Detroit. He was the owner of a large number of pleasure boats, sailing the Great Lakes in the summer and cruising off the Florida coast during the winter.

The naval architectural firm of John H. Wells of New York City received a check for $25,000 in October 1926 as down payment for the new Judson yacht COMOCO. Soon

after, Defoe requested the lines of the yacht so that a scale model could be made for Judson's approval.

Judson was a stickler for details and one day dropped into the New York office of Wells and decided that the smoke stack needed to be cut down one foot in height. He also planned a trip for himself, Wells, and Mr. Raphael, the designer, to be in Bay City to coordinate everything. Raphael provided sketches and details of a music roll cabinet which was to be located in the port side of the main salon. It was noted that the style of leaded glass in the sketch was merely an indication of what he thought was suitable, "but need not be followed absolutely in detail."

Judson had an objection to the telephones in the staterooms. They were the wall type and he considered them unsightly. He preferred the European type with the mouthpiece and transmitter in one piece. Raphael recommended that the cornices and window trim be covered with cornice valances under which the headings of the drapery could be concealed, especially in the dining salon and main salon.

The yacht COMOCO was launched on May 21, 1927, and slid out onto the Saginaw River. By July 1 COMOCO was ready to leave the dock and start on her trip down the lakes to Detroit. By August, word reached Wells that the COMOCO was "creating a great deal of favorable

COMOCO, **main salon.**

COMOCO, **owner's stateroom.**

COMOCO, **aft deck.**

comment." Judson met Defoe at the Detroit Yacht Club and told him how pleased he was with the vessel. There were some modifications that Judson suggested regarding the electrical generators, and Defoe told Wells that he may "rest assured that I will in any event do whatever is necessary to satisfy him in every way."

By October 1927 the COMOCO left the lakes and sailed out the St. Lawrence to the Atlantic Ocean. She proved seaworthy. Early in December Defoe met with Judson in his Detroit office to discuss some problems with the vessel. Judson was convinced that nine-tenths of his troubles were due entirely to the crew. He was also considering selling the COMOCO as she was, and building another yacht 15 feet longer. Before the end of 1927 the COMOCO was sold to James Whitin of North Ukbridge, Massachusetts. The COMOCO spent the rest of her years on salt water, and was destroyed by fire on July 11, 1956 at Canton Island in the Pacific Ocean.

In 1927, Judson solicited bids and designs for a 165-foot yacht. In mid-July the naval architect John H. Wells and Defoe submitted a quote of $300,000 for the new vessel. A week later Wells wrote Defoe stating that he "did not have the heart to tell you that Judson has decided to turn all of us down and have the boat built by Lawly at a price which he says is way below the figures we quoted him." Wells was, "disgusted with the whole thing, as it indicates that there is no gratitude after giving a man a good job." A small newspaper article later noted that the new COMOCO owned by Judson was launched May 15, 1929, at Neponset, Massachusetts, reportedly at the cost of $525,000!

E ven though Defoe lost the bid on the second Judson yacht, his business was still booming. He began the construction of the yacht LUANCO, which was 96'9" long and built solely as a display model. This steel hulled beauty was complete in every detail and as finely furnished and finished as anyone could possibly wish. A special feature was that she was built for salt water as well as fresh and could transit the New York State Barge Canal by lowering her mast and taking off the top section of the stack.

In May 1928 C.F. Kettering of Detroit came to Bay City to inspect the workmanship of the Defoe Shipyard. According to Defoe, Kettering bought the LUANCO with no sales effort on his part. He "took her about as you or I would go out and buy a Ford car." A crew of seven men took over the vessel, which was renamed the OLIVE K.

Charles F. Kettering organized the Delco Laboratories in 1905 and perfected the electric self-starter that appeared in the 1911 Cadillac. In 1916 he sold his interest in Delco to the United Motors Corporation. In 1920 he became the

OLIVE K, pre-launch, September 5, 1929.

OLIVE K, launch, September 5, 1929.

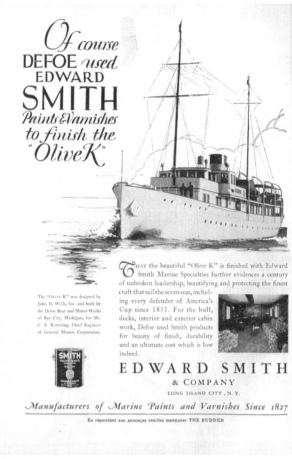

Advertisement - 1930.

head of General Motors Research Laboratories and acted in the capacity of vice president and director of research until 1947.

Kettering was soon in the market for another yacht. Less than three months after the purchase of the OLIVE K, Defoe called at Wells' New York office on a hunch that a new 165-foot yacht was to be built. Wells stated that the deal was going through and that he had been instructed to say nothing about the job. He did tell Defoe that the new yacht was for Kettering, and that he had given him the design and specifications for the 165-foot yacht that Judson had turned down. Wells stated that the cost of the vessel would run approximately $300,000 with engines, but without decorations or designer fees.

Mr. Kettering was doing his homework and went to the Winton Engine Company of Cleveland, Ohio to inquire what types of diesel engines would be appropriate for the new vessel. Another meeting was held with Wells and Defoe in October, and Kettering accepted their original figure of $300,000, without asking for competitive bids from any other shipyard.

The new OLIVE K had a number of specifications added to the original contract due to Kettering's special work and Mrs. Kettering's taste.

- All staterooms were to have an ivory colored ceiling with the prevailing colors to include turquoise blue, peach, linen blue, orchid and rose.
- A second refrigerator, a 'Frigidaire' unit model AP-18 complete with compressor, motor and pumps, was to be installed in the engine room.
- All metal work exposed to view was to be chromium plated.
- A work bench measuring about 7 feet by 4 feet was to be installed in the engine room on the starboard side.
- Some machine tools, such as a small lathe, drill press, etc., were to be installed in the upper grating of the engine casing.
- The radio and automatic victrola were to be located in the library with speaker outlets in six other locations.
- A fathometer, which tells the depth of the water under the keel of the vessel, was to be installed.
- Stainless steel wire cable was to be used for hand rails and standing rigging.
- The linens and blankets were to come from the James McCutcheon Company of New York City.
- The china racks were to be made large enough to hold two dozen sets of dishes of various sizes. The pattern was to come from the yacht china department of Ovington's in New York City.
- All fixed seats were to have real leather cushions from the John Reilly Co., Newark, New Jersey.
- A gun cabinet was to be built into a shallow cupboard capable of holding 18 guns.
- A still from the F.J. Stokes Machine Co. of Philadelphia, and registered with the Treasury Department, U.S. Prohibition Service, District 25 - Michigan, was to be installed (for scientific purposes).
- A special request to carry an airplane on the yacht, with a weight not to exceed 1,100 pounds, was dropped from the plans.

In August 1929 the registration of the original OLIVE K was changed and an official request went to the Collector of Customs in Detroit to have the yacht renamed ROY-ONO. The new owner, J.B. Ford, Jr. of Detroit, was to receive delivery of the yacht on or about September 5, 1929. At that time Kettering took all of the marked articles — the silver, china, bedding, and linen — off the

OLIVE K, library.

OLIVE K, dining salon.

OLIVE K, owner's stateroom.

OLIVE K, port view.

boat and transferred them to the newly completed OLIVE K. The ROYONO was turned over to Ford and then dry docked in Detroit at the Great Lakes Engineering Works for repairs to the vessel's rudder, and to have the bottom painted. The new OLIVE K was used by Mr. and Mrs. Kettering on a number of excursions around the Lakes and to Florida. The vessel was eventually sold in 1940 to the United New York Sandy Hook Pilot's Association and was used to place pilots on inbound and outbound foreign commercial vessels.

The auto barons made their fortunes based on the principal of the assembly line and mass production. Their private yachts were another matter. Here there was no assembly line, no mass production. These motor yachts were unique — not one of a class, but in a class by themselves. There was no need to justify the great expense of maintaining and operating these vessels — if you could afford one, you could afford to have it customized. The auto barons used their yachts for discussions of finance, for entertaining executives and guests, and for just some well-deserved relaxation — in their magnificent floating mansions.

John F. Polacsek is Curator of the Dossin Great Lakes Museum on Belle Isle, a position he has held since 1982. Polacsek received his BA and MA degrees from Bowling Green State University and has written several articles on a variety of Great Lakes maritime subjects.

PHOTO CREDITS: All photographs courtesy of the Institute for Great Lakes Research, Bowling Green State University. 1931 Advertisement on page 159 from: *The Rudder*, Vol 47, #12, Dec. 1931, p.7. 1930 Advertisement on page 166 from: *The Rudder*, Vol. 46, #3, Mar. 1930, p.14.

COUNTRY CLUB
(DETROIT)

The Game of Golf
Comes to Grosse Pointe:
The Founding of the
Country Club of Detroit

by David Robb

Sometime around 1893, the first game of golf was played in Grosse Pointe, and a

short time later the first formal golf course was built on Windmill Point. Then, in 1897,

a new course was built on the grounds of the old Grosse Pointe Club, and a new

club was formed. Here, David Robb recounts the story of those early days

of golf, and the founding of the Country Club of Detroit.

IN 1884, UNDER the leadership of Louis Campau, Detroiters with a fondness for outdoor sports organized the Grosse Pointe Club. Then, in 1886, the members built an impressive clubhouse on property fronting on the lake off of Jefferson Avenue at Fisher Road. Although the beauties of Grosse Pointe were recognized by the original pioneers, this charm was insufficient to offset the terrors of riding a steam launch which made infrequent trips from the city to a dock near the clubhouse, or required a half day or the greater portion of the night on horseback or by carriage over impassable roads. As a result, interest waned and two years after it was opened, the clubhouse was closed. Shortly afterwards, it

was reopened as the Grosse Pointe Casino for summer residents and continued for another five years.

Coincidentally during this time, if you had been a young man who played baseball on Saturday afternoon at Senator James and Philip H. McMillan's property at Hamilton Park, their private race track on property embraced by Touraine-Vendome Roads, you would have been introduced to the mysteries of golf. It was about 1893, when the McMillans returned from a trip to Wales with a desire to play and to interest others in the game. One Saturday morning, they organized a group of farmers to cut the grass and lay down tees and greens for a golf course of either six or nine holes at Hamilton Park. The course was laid out in

Country Club of Detroit (old Grosse Pointe Club building), ca. 1898.
Photograph courtesy of the Burton Historical Collection, Detroit Public Library.

the morning and was played on in the afternoon. This exercise went on for a couple of seasons: golf, with no green fees and no dues, but never on the Sabbath because the McMillans would not have approved.

Finally, in 1895, a group led by the McMillan sons, William C. and Philip H., along with W. Howie Muir, Benjamin S. Warren and Cameron Currie, decided that they could no longer infringe on the hospitality of the McMillans and asked James Foulis, an old school Scots professional at the Chicago Golf Club, to come over and consider land lying south of Jefferson Avenue along Fox Creek (at Alter Road) just inside the city limits of Detroit for a golf course. It was recalled by Ben Warren that when Mr. Foulis arrived, they waded the "course" in hip boots and decided that it might be utilized.

The club was imaginatively and appropriately named the "Wanikan Club" (or "Wanikin") which is an Indian phrase meaning "Hole-in-the-Ground." It was a nine hole course which ran from Jefferson Avenue toward Lake St. Clair and back with the so-called clubhouse being a small structure on Jefferson with one dressing room for the men and one for the women. The new club soon had 100 members.

The members played home-and-away matches with golfers from other cities, such as Cleveland and Grand Rapids. They were royally entertained at the clubs in those cities and on the way back from one of these matches in Grand Rapids decided that they should organize, obtain enough land for an 18 hole course, and find a clubhouse. Also, they felt that the proposed club should provide other athletic activities, including horseback riding, yachting, baseball, tennis and football.

Some members of the Detroit business community interested in forming such a country club in Grosse Pointe boarded the Newberry yacht at the Third Street Station in downtown Detroit, breakfasted aboard ship and went to view the Grosse Pointe Casino and property owned by Joseph H. Berry and the McMillan and Newberry estates lying on both sides of Fisher Road, which was available for lease. In addition, there was an old barn at the southwest corner of Jefferson and Fisher, where the Detroit United Railway waiting room was later built, which was available to serve as a stable for the horsemen and horsewomen.[1]

A meeting was held at the Detroit Club on October 1, 1897 for incorporation of the Country Club of Detroit.

Those who signed the Articles of Association were John H. Avery, Edwin S. Barbour, Joseph H. Berry, Bethune Duffield, Charles F. Hammond, Frank J. Hecker, James H. McMillan, Truman H. Newberry, Henry Russel, Martin S. Smith, John S. Sweeney, J. Harrington Walker, Benjamin S. Warren, William H. Wells and Frank S. Werneken. The articles were filed on October 20th.

Negotiations were entered into with the syndicates composed of those who owned the Grosse Pointe Casino and the 404-foot lakefront property running to the Fisher Road-Jefferson Avenue area, which was purchased. Property that contained 25 acres extending along Fisher Road embracing the area now occupied by Grosse Pointe South High School and the Gabriel Richard Elementary School was also leased. The Casino was converted into a clubhouse and the leased land formed the golf course.

Ninety eight members of the Wanikin Club joined the new club as did others who belonged to the Detroit Athletic Club and the Detroit Riding Club. The active membership was 200, each of whom would pay a $50.00 initiation fee and an annual subscription of $25.00.

The 18 hole course was designed for players to tee off near the clubhouse and play to the first green, located on what is now the Grosse Pointe War Memorial parking lot. The first nine holes terminated near the present-day Gabriel Richard School. Returning toward the clubhouse, players passed over the present-day Grosse Pointe South High School property, through Beverly Road to the 18th green near the southwest corner of the clubhouse. The fairways were like present-day rough and playing length was 4,816 yards. The description of the course contained in the August 1898 issue of *Golf*, the official bulletin of the United States Golf Association, states that the tee for the second hole "is on Mr. Berry's private ground and members have the privilege of walking through some of the most beautiful gardens in America."[2] The course opened for play in June 1898 and had for its first professional W.H. Way, whose British heritage was required for a recently created golf club.

The 1898 issue of *Golf* went on to describe the new Country Club of Detroit as follows:

About eight miles from the City of Detroit, Mich. in the beautiful suburban settlement of Grosse Pointe Farms, has been established one of the handsomest country clubs in the "Middle West." The clubhouse is on a point jutting out into Lake St. Clair, and its spacious verandas are kept cool

---

1 A picture of the DUR waiting room will be found in *Tonnancour*, Vol 1, p. 116.

2 Views of the Berry estate "Edgemere" will be found in *Tonnancour*, Vol 1, p. 117, 130.

Baseball at the turn-of-the century was one of the most popular activities at the Country Club. Photograph courtesy of the Grosse Pointe Historical Society.

Tennis was a sport enjoyed by both men and women at the Country Club, ca. 1900. Photograph courtesy of the Grosse Pointe Historical Society.

Lining up a putt at the Country Club golf course. Photograph courtesy of the Grosse Pointe Historical Society.

Country Club of Detroit, side view.
Club house designed by Albert Kahn, 1907.
Photograph courtesy of Albert Kahn Associates.

by the refreshing lake breezes. At this peaceful spot the choicest spirits in Detroit society adjourn for relaxation, and the club is reached in thirty minutes from the heart of the city by a special switch that runs the electric cars right into the club grounds.

Within the house itself every care has been taken to afford the seeker of comfort and rest a haven of delight; and under the efficient management of steward Dwight A. Whitney, the club has the reputation of being the most recherché establishment in Michigan.

For the next few years the club flourished as golf became increasingly popular. Yet sailing was also very popular. A bathhouse was built for members and sailboats were purchased. Two cat boat sailing races were held every Saturday afternoon as well as summer races between yachts of club members. On the west side of Fisher Road were riding facilities, including a steeplechase course.

As the activities of the club became more popular, the membership grew to more than 400, and at its annual meeting in October 1904, the Board recommended the erection of a new clubhouse. The Board called attention to the condition of the old building, which was in need of extensive repair. It was estimated that at least $20,000 was needed for repairs and that so large an outlay on an old building would not be wise. Sketch plans had been prepared by architect Albert Kahn, which were exhibited in advance of the meeting for inspection by the members.

In 1906 the Board retained Kahn to draw up final plans, construction was begun, and on May 30, 1907, the new clubhouse building was christened. This brick clubhouse opened to rave reviews. The following comment by W. Hawkins Ferry comes from his fine book *Buildings of Detroit*:

Considerable perspicacity was shown in the selection of Kahn as architect, for no one but a man of his imaginative

endowments could have responded so admirably to the beauty of the surroundings. Without indulging in the pretentious or falsely picturesque, he was able to combine monumental simplicity with formal charm.

The new clubhouse was a truly imposing structure with every detail planned for the comfort of the members. Rooms on the lower floor were furnished tastefully and luxuriously and of large size. This floor included the central hall or lobby, living room, card room, dining room, ladies room and a number of smaller apartments. The dining room, located on the east end of the building, was finished in light colors. Wide glass-enclosed verandas extended the full length of the building and on the west end a recessed porch overlooked the tennis courts and baseball field.

A massive staircase led to the floors above. On the second and third floors were sleeping rooms, twenty single rooms and nearly as many guest rooms. The guest rooms had a bath for every two rooms in a suite. The fourth floor contained accommodations for 40 bachelors. In the basement was a tap room, furnished in Old English style, a games room, heating plant and large kitchen. For the convenience of automobile owners a large garage was constructed on the northwest corner of the grounds.

The *Detroit News* also reported on the events at the new clubhouse on opening day, May 30, 1907:

Early in the morning automobiles began to arrive and by noon hundreds were lined up in front of the club house. Gay crowds all on pleasure bent filled the grounds and building. Golf, boat racing, tennis, base ball and several other sports were on the list to be participated in by the pleasure seekers. The ball game was a spirited contest, won by the "Blues" under the captaincy of A.I. Lewis, who defeated P.H. McMillan's Reds, 15 to 8. The score would

Lobby with Reading and Card Rooms adjoining.
Country Club of Detroit, 1907.
Photograph courtesy of Albert Kahn Associates.

Country Club of Detroit, front view.
Club house designed by Albert Kahn, 1907. Photograph courtesy of Manning Brothers.

Country Club of Detroit, rear view.
Club house designed by Albert Kahn, 1907. Photograph courtesy of Albert Kahn Associates.

A view along the first floor.
Country Club of Detroit, 1907. Photograph courtesy of Albert Kahn Associates.

View of the lobby with the stairway to the second floor.
Country Club of Detroit, 1907.
Note the Pewabic tile over the fireplace at right.
Photograph courtesy of Albert Kahn Associates.

A corner of the parlor.
Country Club of Detroit, 1907.
Photograph courtesy of Albert Kahn Associates.

Baseball game on the grounds of the Country Club of Detroit, August 27, 1910.
Photograph courtesy of the Burton Historical Collection, Detroit Public Library.

have been different had not several of the outfielders hid behind the automobiles to escape catching flies.

There was to have been a yacht race between four 21-footers, Cleveland of C.Y.C., Otsiketa and Ste. Claire of the Country Club and Borealis, of the Tawas Beach Yachting Association. The race was not pulled off on account of lack of wind but the prize for this race being a box of cigars, Dr. C.G. Jennings, captain of the Otsiketa, flipped a coin with the others and pulled off the championship.

A noticeable feature of the opening was the array of steam yachts among which were Pastime, owned by D.H. Walker, Galatea, E.S. Ford, Truant, T.H. Newberry, and D. Ferguson's Vita. R.A. Alger's motor boat Hunch was also on hand and its beauty was commended on every side.

During the 1900s the Country Club burgee, with its signature "Fleur de Lis" became a symbol of sailing excellence among the members of the Inter Lakes Yachting Association, and the cat boat races and annual regatta were considered leading events of their kind on the Great Lakes. Some of the fastest boats on fresh water flew Country Club colors, including the *Ste. Claire, Borealis, Otsiketa, Gamble,* and *Shake.*

The majestic Kahn designed building and its surroundings became a focal point for Grosse Pointe social and sport activities. Situated on the shores of the lake with an unobstructed view for many miles, the constantly passing procession of members yachts and other vessels, the adjoining tennis courts, baseball field, and golf course only a short distance away, the setting in the summertime was unparalleled. In the winter there were balls, parties and other social activities within, while members' ice boats skimmed across the lake in front of the clubhouse.

Within a short period of time, due to the greater accessibility of Grosse Pointe and the increase in land values, the golf course, which was on leased land, became too valuable and the club began to look elsewhere. In 1906 the club was unable to renew its lease on the Joseph Berry property (now McKinley Place) through which ran the second hole, and golfing was made more difficult when the first tee was moved to the southeast corner of the present-day Grosse Pointe South High School property.

In 1910 the Board decided to buy the Weir Farm, a property which ran from what is now Irvine Lane to a point north of Provencal Road and extending from Lake St. Clair to Mack Avenue. On the advice of Harry Colt, a well known English golf architect, the club bought the Lewis Farm for $55,000, a 106 acre strip which ran from Kercheval Avenue to Mack Avenue and was bounded on the south by present-day County Club Drive. In February 1911 blueprints of the property were sent to Mr Colt, construction was begun, and the course opened for play in 1912.

From 1912 until 1923, the club operated from two locations. While a locker room and pavilion had been built at the golf course and a polo field and stables in the trees beyond the original polo field were constructed (now a maintenance building), the clubhouse on the lake remained the focal point for other social activities, sailing, baseball and tennis. The Polo Team was organized in 1915 and the ponies were stabled at the Grosse Pointe Hunt Club. When matches were held at other cities around the Great Lakes, the ponies were transported aboard D & C boats.

Sailing and yacht racing were always one of the most popular activities during the early years of the Country Club of Detroit. Photograph courtesy of the Grosse Pointe Historical Society.

Having social and athletic activities at one site and the golf course located at another proved difficult, and at a meeting of the members of the club on September 16, 1920, authorization was obtained to issue bonds to "build a suitable club house adapted to the needs of golf, tennis and other sports to be built on the upper property and that the grounds of that property be laid out with a view of concentrating there all sports except water sports." The bond issue was secured by 450 feet of property on Lake Shore Drive, about 80 acres north of Mack Avenue, and the triangular section adjoining Grosse Pointe Boulevard and the golf course. The plans however did not contemplate the sale of the old clubhouse property (the corner of Fisher Road and Jefferson Avenue). The 450 foot frontage described was located "on the north side of Lake Shore Drive between Provencal Road and Weir Lane."

In the end, the sailing enthusiasts lost the battle to remain on the lake and the golfers prevailed so that Albert Kahn was again commissioned to design a new clubhouse. The clubhouse property at Fisher Road and Jefferson Avenue was sold to Mrs. Horace Dodge and became the site of her mansion, Rose Terrace. It was reported that after the construction of the clubhouse on the golf course, it was intended that a causeway would be built on the 450 feet of property at the end of Provencal on the lake shore so that yachting, swimming and other aquatic sports which had been removed from the club program by the sale of the old clubhouse on the lake would be restored. However, such a program was never implemented and the sailing enthusiasts built their own clubhouse on the lake adjacent to the old clubhouse property, and named it the Grosse Pointe Club ("Little Club"), which today enjoys an equally attractive setting, proud heritage, and membership.

In reflection, the move of the Country Club continued a proud architectural and social history, and a legacy of prominence in the affairs of Grosse Pointe. At its time by the lake, the Country Club of Detroit, in whatever season, possessed attractions seldom equalled and never excelled.

———————— ❧ ————————

David Robb, who served as Mayor of the City of Grosse Pointe, is a graduate of the Detroit University School, the University of Michigan, and the Law School of the University of Virginia.

The Children's Home of Detroit

by William C. Rands III

Still known to many Grosse Pointers as the Protestant Children's Home, its name when it moved to Grosse Pointe Woods in 1951, this is one of the enduring and treasured institutions of Grosse Pointe and possibility the oldest existing social service agency in Michigan.

WOODLAND SHORE ROAD leaves Lake Shore in Grosse Pointe Shores at the point where Stonehurst once stood, the stately mansion of the Schlotman family. The old stone wall facing the lake still stands, now greeting visitors to homes which are smaller but still grand. The gently winding road continues into Grosse Pointe Woods and makes a curve to the right, then intersects with Cook Road. On Cook Road the graceful tree-lined beauty of Grosse Pointe continues but the traveler encounters an area of civic activity. The Grosse Pointe Hunt Club is first to be seen, then University Liggett School, and, on 15 acres of green tranquillity, the Children's Home of Detroit, affectionately known to its friends, staff and trustees as "CHD."

The Children's Home broke ground March 1, 1950, for this beautiful campus, with 6 cottages that can house 72 children aged from 6 to 17, ample space for a school building which is staffed by the Grosse Pointe School System, a health center, and a separate administration building, an ultra-modern innovation for its time. The land had been purchased in the Village of Grosse Pointe Woods in 1946, four years before the village incorporated as a city, when on any fine afternoon horsemen and horsewoman from the Hunt Club could be seen riding all around the area.

There are many institutions of longer standing in Grosse Pointe, and on this scale CHD is a relative new-comer. But the Children's Home was organized in 1836 as the Ladies' Orphan Association of Detroit, when the Michigan Territory was at war with Ohio, Detroit had a population

Groundbreaking ceremony for the Cook Road Campus of the Protestant Children's Home, 1950.

of 6,927 and Pottawattamies and Ottawa were almost as common on the streets as Europeans. It is believed to be the oldest social service organization existing in Michigan today. The founders were 13 women who met at the Presbyterian Church on Woodward Avenue to consider "ways and means of caring for destitute and homeless waifs surviving after a frightful cholera epidemic." In June of 1837, the same year Michigan became a state, the first children were moved to a house in Detroit obtained from Messrs. Hastings, Kercheval, and Newberry. All three of these are family names that appear on Detroit and Grosse Pointe streets today. In 1840 a new building was built at the cost of $6,833, and 15 orphans were moved in.

The series of events that brought CHD to Grosse Pointe exemplifies perfectly both the willingness of Grosse Pointe families to rally in support of worthwhile social causes and the historical linkages with the city of Detroit. A Building Fund Campaign was launched in May of 1949 under the leadership of Charles A. Kanter. By the end of the year $678,000 had been successfully raised, and Mrs. Kanter, in the position of First Directress, which would now be called Board President, was able to dedicate the campus the following year. Mr. and Mrs. Kanter were members of the third generation of trustees belonging to the family represented on today's board by Mrs. Robert (Margie) Garbarino, a fifth generation trustee of the Children's Home.

For its first 115 years CHD had operated at various locations essentially as an orphanage, its last building being at 3270 East Jefferson Avenue, Detroit. The evolution of its mission toward a more activist approach to treating children therapeutically began in the early 1940s with a three-year strategic examination by the Executive Director Valmer J. Goltry. His first recommendation to the Board was "to extend our program to the care of children who

require study and observation before a permanent plan is made for them," a statement which pointed clearly away from the old paradigm of custodial care.

Goltry also recommended a change to a cottage system, which would afford ambiance for the children superior to that of an institutional building, and also much better opportunities for recreation and exercise. As commented in the pamphlet "Our Last Fifty Years," written for CHD's sesquicentennial in 1986 by John A. Hammel, retired principal of Montieth School, "The full implementation of this goal would not be achieved until many years later." Almost exactly ten years after the Goltry study was launched, the move to the open campus on Cook Road was complete.

The fundamental mission of CHD has evolved and been restated in its Articles of Incorporation from time to time. It currently stands as filed in 1990:

"to promote the health and well-being of children, particularly those with social, emotional or educational problems, by providing services and assistance to the children and their families . . . ."

CHD has essentially pursued this same objective for the entire time it has been in Grosse Pointe Woods, but providing a calm, nurturing image for the children has never been easy. It has required a great effort on the part of the community. Leading families of Grosse Pointe have given freely of their money and of their time as volunteers and board members. Citizens in general have extended their good will in endless ways, through the Garden Club, the Bridge Marathon, the Rotary and other clubs, and direct volunteer efforts such as the mentoring programs at CHD Community Services.

Over the years the list of volunteers and board members has included many familiar names: Ford, Shelden, Book, Hinchman, Van Dusen, Du Charme, Holley, Thurber, Caulkins. Trustees until very recently had no term limits, and many have devoted decades of service to the Home.

Cook Road Campus under construction.

The Protestant Orphan Asylum moved into its first home in 1840. Mrs. Charles C. Trowbridge served as the first directress. Illustration from The Detroit Free Press, *May 14, 1911.*

Four current Honorary Trustees were on the board when CHD moved to Grosse Pointe: Mrs. Frederick S. Ford, her daughter-in-law, Mrs. Frederick S. Ford, Jr., Mrs. William Clay Ford and Mrs. Arthur G. Reeves. Mrs. Frederick Ford, Jr. chaired the Education and Recreation Committee, today called the Child Care Committee, during the 1950s when educational facilities were established on the Cook Road campus. Mrs. Reeves represents the fourth Generation of the Kanter-Reeves-Garbarino family whose involvement for almost a hundred years has already been mentioned.

An effective fundraising effort has been constantly maintained, and although no regularly recurring special event has been associated with CHD, The Moonlight Ball in 1960 and the gala reception at the home of Trustee Mrs. Archie Van Elslander in 1994 will long be remembered. Named as patrons on the program for the Moonlight Ball were Mrs. Charles Wright III, an active trustee today, and Mrs. George R. Fink, grandmother of current Associate Trustee Mrs. Horace N. Carpenter. An Honorary Trustee until her death in 1994, Mrs. Edgar A. Guest gave many years of service to the Board. Edgar Guest contributed this poem, which was printed in the Board's long range plan brochure in 1949:

> He who for the children cares
> In the Master's labor shares.
> "Suffer them to come to Me
> And forbid them not," said He.
> Still to us the children plead!
> Still our tender care they need.
> His disciples once forgot.
> He replied: "Forbid them not!
> Suffer them to come to Me."
> As He answered: so should we.

Influenced no doubt by the Board and by the effective Administration of Herbert J. Shanks, Executive Director, a tone of acceptance and cooperation between CHD and the official institutions of Grosse Pointe was set very quickly in the 1950s. Grosse Pointe School System plans called for the children to attend Montieth Elementary School, another Cook Road neighbor, and Parcells Junior High, but neither was yet completed when CHD arrived in 1951. Special arrangements were made for the children to attend Mason School and a portion of Parcells was temporarily made available that first year. This strong beginning paved the way for an even closer relationship with the school system, culminating in 1957 with the construction by CHD of the Barnard School building on the Cook Road Campus. To this day Barnard School is staffed and operated by the school system. Other extensions of support were made available, by St. Michael's Episcopal Church, which offered meetings for the older children and places in the choir, by the Young Marrieds of Grosse Pointe Memorial Church, the Boy Scouts, the Girl Scouts, and many more.

Although the ties with the Grosse Pointe communities had always been strong on the level of working relationships, Board support and fundraising, there had never been a program offered especially for Grosse Pointe residents.

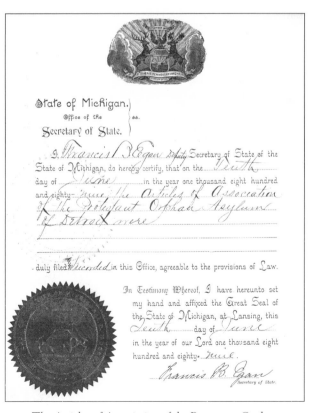

The Articles of Association of the Protestant Orphan Asylum of Detroit, as amended, June 10, 1889.

Children from the Cook Road Campus on their way to the Grosse Pointe Woods Lakefront Park for an afternoon of swimming.

Children and staff enjoying a Christmas party, ca. 1970.

Friends and families gather for a capital campaign openhouse, 1992.

The children at the Cook Road Campus have historically been referred by various branches of the Michigan social services system, the Department of Mental Health, or through the court system, and their homes are spread over a half-dozen counties. A compelling chance to change that situation occurred in 1991 when an old and respected organization in Grosse Pointe known as the Family Life Education Council, or "FLEC," announced that it was going to close for lack of funds.

For decades FLEC had conducted a "Youth Assistance Program," which made a solid contribution to law enforcement in the Grosse Pointes and Harper Woods, by avoiding the necessity of placing children committing minor offenses into the Wayne County juvenile system. The municipalities had felt strongly enough about the program to help fund it, and CHD'S Executive Director and Board felt that the civic value that would be saved by taking responsibility for the program exceeded the extra effort that would be required to take on the fundraising burden. The Youth Assistance Program has continued to develop under CHD, forming the basis for a whole area of activity under the title "CHD Community Services," which represents an important and expanding opportunity to benefit the towns that welcomed CHD in 1951.

During the years CHD has been located in Grosse Pointe, the predominant feeling has not always been one of success. In the mid 1980s, the Administration and the Board recognized the trend toward increasing competition and had attained the high achievement of certification by the Joint Commission on Accreditation of Health Care Organizations. But State of Michigan Mental Health programs had become a significant part of CHD's budget. Perceived political pressure to keep down the reimbursement asked of the State per day per child, combined with inflationary cost pressures, resulted in a series of budget deficits that threatened CHD's ability to remain financially solid and able to develop new programs as needs arose.

An attempt to work more closely with the staff of the Michigan Department of Mental Health on a program specifically for hearing-impaired children had been derailed by politics at DMH. Also, the Executive Director, H.E. Tammelaid, was making the Trustees increasingly aware that many children could not be served because the open campus on Cook Road lacked facilities to handle children too disturbed to allow the staff to follow normal methods of supervision. All of these factors led to apprehension about the future of CHD. In 1989 a new Executive Director, Michael Horwitz, had replaced the retired Mr. Tammelaid. Once again the Board of Trustees, the administration, and the community pulled together to move CHD forward. Just as it had in the 1940s, the Board embarked on a two-year planning process that led to the opening of a Secure Care unit in Warren, Michigan, which could serve children with a much broader range of emotional impairments. The Secure Unit opened in 1991 with 10 beds, and has been expanded twice. It now has 64 beds and annual revenues exceeding those of CHD on Cook Road. The Board also launched a new capital campaign to modernize the Cook Road Campus. Under the leadership of Mrs. Robert L. Nugent and Benjamin Burns, $1.5 million was raised and a new wing was added to the administration building to provide conference, office, and therapy space appropriate to current treatment practices. The cottages and the health center were completely renovated and significant additions were made to Barnard School.

This same long-range planning effort also brought to fruition long-standing efforts by a group of Board members toward offering substance abuse services for children and juveniles in the Grosse Pointes and Harper Woods. Having met as an *ad hoc* committee for years and formed working relationships with the counseling staff of the school system, this group proposed and the Board accepted plans for assessment and referral services to be housed on Mack Avenue with CHD Community Services.

In November 1994, CHD took the opportunity to add once more to its array of services, as it had with FLEC, by

Office of CHD Community Services at 20171 Mack Avenue.

taking responsibility for a project that was started elsewhere. An innovative program still in its formative stages, the Institute for Trauma and Loss in Children was publishing training materials for educators and clinicians. Affectionately known as "TLC," the institute was dedicated to teaching people how to help children whose lives have been touched by sudden trauma. TLC's products were extremely well received but it was struggling for funding.

This pencil sketch of the Protestant Children's Home on East Jefferson, was drawn by Edlore L. Knaggs, "one of our boys," in 1932. Sadly, Pvt. E. L. Knaggs was killed in action in Europe in the fall of 1944.

Volunteers planting flowers around the state historical marker erected to commemorate CHD's 150th anniversary in 1986.

The Institute brings CHD to a new level of stature in child care education and certification, and reaches beyond Michigan to a national audience. In its first year TLC had formal contacts with over 3,000 child-care professionals, and is scheduled to start an assessment activity that will involve direct clinical services to children.

Now in 1996 the Children's Home of Detroit is a much more complex and diversified organization than it was when it moved to Grosse Pointe, but it has the same basic mission of helping children and their families. As CHD approaches the twenty-first century, its outlook as an organization is colored by awesome threats as well as strengths which cannot be ignored—a statement that could perhaps have been made at any time during its 160-year history. Under current trends in government, the flow of reimbursement from state programs is constantly threatened, and CHD has come to depend significantly on this money. CHD's strengths include the proven record of its success serving children and their families innovatively for over a century and a half, and a unique tradition of calling on, and receiving, the support of the community. It has grown from just one location on Cook Road to three, with the addition of CHD Community Services and the Secure

Unit, and to national prominence with the Institute for Trauma and Loss in Children. Whatever the future, CHD has been for almost half a century a part of the caring tradition and the community life of Grosse Pointe.

———————————❧———————————

William C. Rands III is a Chartered Financial Analyst and conducts a portfolio management and consulting practice locally. He is managing general partner of Sagres Partners L.P., a limited partnership growth fund. A native Grosse Pointer, Rands was a volunteer working with the children on CHD's Cook Road Campus during college summers and has been a Trustee since 1983. He was President of the Board of Trustees during 1990 and 1991, and most recently served as chairman of a task force exploring possibilities for the development of outpatient services, including those of the Institute for Trauma and Loss in Children.

———————————❧———————————

PHOTO CREDITS: All photographs courtesy of the Children's Home of Detroit.

Movies at the Punch:
A History of the
Punch and Judy Theater

by Carrie Jones

To many Grosse Pointers, an evening at the movies meant a trip to the Punch and Judy Theater. Here Carrie Jones tells the story of one of Grosse Pointe's most familiar landmarks.

THE TRANSITION FROM silent to sound motion pictures took place, roughly, between October 5, 1927, when *The Jazz Singer* opened in New York, and 1935, the first year in which all motion picture theaters in the United States had been wired for sound films. In the midst of this transformation, on January 29, 1930, a small motion picture theater called the Punch and Judy opened at 17937 (now 21) Kercheval in Grosse Pointe Farms. Rumors cite the Punch and Judy as the first theater in Michigan, or even in the entire United States, to have been built specifically for talking pictures; however, this honor has never been documented. The Punch and Judy was certainly not the first theater in Michigan to exhibit

"Punch and Judy Theater," from a print by Jerry Crowley, 1985.

talkies; that distinction belonging to the Temple, Lafayette, or Madison theaters, depending on the source.[1] Nor was the Punch and Judy even the first motion picture theater in the Grosse Pointes. The Grosse Pointe Park theater (later re-named the Aloma), just inside the Grosse Pointe border on Charlevoix, was operating at least as early as 1923 and showing talking pictures over six months before the Punch and Judy opened. Though it may not claim any "firsts" in the history of the movies, the Punch and Judy has been a forerunner in many of the trends that have marked the exhibition of motion pictures in the last fifty-five years.

From its inception, the Punch and Judy was noteworthy for both its design and its architect, Robert O. Derrick. Derrick moved to Detroit after World War I and became a popular architect in the city, particularly in the Grosse Pointes, where he designed a number of private homes. His most famous building in the Detroit area is the Henry Ford Museum in Greenfield Village. Designed in the same year that the Punch and Judy was built, the museum contains a theater that is almost identical to the one in Grosse Pointe Farms.

The theater's opening provoked enough public interest for the *Detroit News* to publish an article describing the Punch and Judy three days before its inaugural exhibition.

A few glances are all that are necessary to realize that the Punch and Judy was designed with a home-like comfort as its chief attribute. There is nothing of the elaborate appeal of the standard movie house in its Early American outline. It is more a place to feel at home amid dignified and subdued coloring, modest lighting effects and seating arrangements in harmony with the quiet atmosphere.

The architectural treatment is distinctly Colonial with high roof, brick exterior and shuttered windows. An unassuming sign suspended over the main entrance bearing the name and two quaint marionettes is the only conspicuous indication of its nature. Within, the entire decorative scheme suggests a pioneer stateliness. The walls are plain; the only hint of embellishment being gold borders along the paneling. In the lounge wood paneling, pegged flooring, and spacious fireplaces emphasize the historical impression.[2]

At that time, the theater had 504 seats on the main floor and 96 in the loge. As the same article described them; "The chairs in the loges are really individual parlor pieces, deeply stuffed and having ash trays for the convenience of those who care to smoke." The use of the term "loge," which implies multiple balconies, does not actually fit the Punch and Judy, which had only one. It was the only section of theater seats in which smoking was legally permitted in the State of Michigan. The theater also boasted a full white maple stage behind the screen.

The *Detroit News* went on to describe the care taken by the theater's builders to insure superior sound reproduction.

Acoustical experts of the University of Michigan supervised the insulation of walls and arrangement of the projection and speaking apparatus. A layer of felt in the ceiling and the use of special materials assure the efficiency of the talkie equipment, which is the most modern to be had.

At its opening the Punch and Judy was equipped with both Vitaphone and Movietone sound apparatus, though the vitaphone would most likely have been removed sometime later in that year when nationwide standardization of sound equipment adopted the use of optical soundtracks. According to Harold B. Franklin in his 1929 manual of motion picture projection, this "dual sound projector sys-

Program for opening night at the Punch and Judy Theater, January 29, 1930.

---

[1] *Detroit News*, August 28, 1958. *Detroit News*, May 20, 1959. (Both of these very brief, untitled articles are on file in the Detroit Public Library. They have been pasted onto filing cards, and no other information concerning their publication or sources is listed.)

[2] "Punch and Judy Theater Ready," *Detroit News*, January 26, 1930, sec. 10, p. 1, col. 7.

The Punch and Judy as it looked in its glory days of the 1930s.

tem" originally installed in the Punch and Judy, "was employed in the greater number of installations."[3]

In Charlotte Herzog's article "Movie Palaces and Exhibition," a depiction of the average projection booth in a 1920's movie palace, is also a very close description of the booth at the Punch and Judy.

> *The building codes and fire law, which pertained to the projection booth, were greater in number and more rigid than those governing the rest of the theater because nitrate film was still used. The whole booth and everything in it had to be fireproof; doors had to open outward and be self-closing. The projection and observation portals had to have automatically closing steel plate or asbestos shutters held in place by fuseable links or cords which, in case of a fire, would burn and break, and cause the shutter to slam closed. If one shutter dropped, the rest would automatically follow. Projectors had to have ventilating tubes or flues extending up through the roof to exhaust flames, smoke and gases, and film had to be rewound in a separate room so the only film destroyed in a fire would be that in the projector. Besides the rewind room, there was often a separate fan room, battery room, and a generator room for converting AC to DC current for the carbon arc lamps used in projectors at that time.[4]*

The Punch and Judy's projection booth had two carbon arc projectors, at least one spotlight, and a smaller projector for displaying lyrics on the screen during sing-alongs.

In the early 1940s, the original projectors were removed and two Simplex XL carbon arc projectors were installed. These projectors had Peerless Mag Arc lamphouses, and Simplex ITC soundheads. The amplifiers for the sound system were also replaced with newer models at this time. The next decade brought numerous additions to the capabilities of the Punch and Judy's projection booth. The apparatus necessary for using magnetic soundtracks was added to the projectors. Presumably this addition was made after 1952 when the first feature film with a magnetic soundtrack was released. Though some projectors with this capability could also be adapted to run 70mm film (almost all films in 70mm were also released with a magnetic soundtrack), it is unlikely that the Punch and Judy's projectors were so equipped. The projectors were also wired with a Selsen motor so that they could be run simultaneously for the presentation of three dimensional films. It is probable that this modification also took place sometime after 1952, when 3D started its relatively popular era. The Punch and Judy was also equipped with removable anamorphic lenses for showing widescreen movies. These lens-

---

3 Harold B. Franklin, *Sound Motion Pictures* (Garden City, N.Y.: Doubleday, Doran & Co., 1929), p. 45.

4 Charlotte Herzog, "Movie Palaces and Exhibition," *Film Reader,* No. 2, 1977, p. 190.

es would most likely have been added sometime between the release of the first Cinemascope picture in 1952, and July 1955 when *A Man Called Peter*, a Cinemascope film, was screened at the theater. From that time until thirty years later when the theater closed, only the two speakers behind the curtain were replaced and a 16mm projector, specially adapted to show an entire feature film on one reel, was added, both in 1981.

Throughout its history, the building itself received very few alterations. Perhaps the greatest change occurred in the 1940s when the marquee was added and the original square lobby was changed to a rounded shape. At the same time the orchestra pit was filled in, which facilitated the addition of ten seats to the main floor. Building permits indicate that in 1960 the marquee was lowered and a new awning added. The doors on the front of the theater were replaced and the wood paneling surrounding them covered with brick in 1962. The marquee received new wood paneling in 1964, and in 1969 red draperies were installed, the lobbies were re-carpeted and the red seats were recovered. The Punch and Judy had no concession stand until about 1973, and an arcade installed in the lobby sometime after October 1977 was removed prior to September 1981. Be-

yond these intentional changes, age and neglect also altered the theater. As of September 1984, some of the main floor seats had been removed, the auditorium was in need of painting, the basement restrooms were unusable because of flooding, the upstairs lounge was being used as a storeroom and the balcony was closed because part of the ceiling above it had collapsed.

When the Punch and Judy opened in 1930 there was no indication of the decay it would face fifty-four years later. The program of entertainment instituted by the theater's founding owners was at least as innovative as the up-to-date equipment in the projection booth. Many motion picture theaters of the time, particularly the palaces, downplayed the importance of the feature film in favor of organ concerts, shorts, newsreels and live entertainment, all of which were necessary to subsidize the great expenses to run these huge theaters. The Punch and Judy, however, was one-tenth the size of the largest palaces, and could rely on a much simpler program to draw a sufficient crowd for the theater to remain profitable. The *Detroit News* quoted Arthur Gardner, president of the Punch and Judy, at the opening ceremonies. "The Punch and Judy theater, as you have noticed, has no tinsel and no monkey-business at all.

Looking east on Kercheval, the Punch and Judy in the early 1980s.

The motion picture will be everything and the only thing considered in planning our program."[5]

Furthermore, the paper stated that;

> The idea of presenting "Disraeli" as a trail blazer for the Punch and Judy was an inspired one. Ordinarily a motion picture theater is not a bit choosey about its opening feature film, being content to rely on the colorful nature of the attendant events to make the guests forget. But in the case of the Punch and Judy opening, the finest talking picture produced to date was selected. A beautifully tinted color subject, "The Dance of the Paper Dolls" introducing a score or more of talented juvenile singers and dancers, and a sound news reel completes the first unit.

This emphasis on the feature film was continued at the Punch and Judy, and for awhile it was the only theater in the city which did not rely on double features.

The Punch and Judy was also a leader in the area of matinees specifically designed for children. Saturday and Sunday matinees were certainly a popular aspect of theater-going long before the Punch and Judy was built, but the first matinees tailored for children were not inaugurated until March 23, 1928. The Punch and Judy started matinees, described in the same article quoted above as "selected subjects for children," in February 1930. The Grosse Pointe News reported that; "Janet Mueller, Grosse Pointe News society editor, recalls that in the 1940s, '50s and '60s it was common for children in Grosse Pointe to celebrate their birthdays by first having a party and then going to the Punch for a matinee."[6] Though ownership of the theater changed in 1976, children's matinees continued until 1981.

Aspects of the Punch and Judy's entertainment that did not remain constant throughout its history include the showing of first-run films, weekly program changes, the number of daily performances and ticket prices. From 1930 until sometime before 1936, films were changed two times a week, and there were three performances daily, at 2:30, 7:00 and 9:00 pm. Ticket prices ranged from 25¢ for children at all times, 50¢ for adults for matinees, 75¢ for even-

ing performances and $1.00 at all times for the reserved seats in the smoking "loge." Though the Detroit News article describing the opening events called these prices "popular" they were far from the average movie price at the time, which was 25¢. By 1936, prices at the Punch and Judy were lowered to the national average of 25¢, at least for the mainfloor, though the balcony seats were 40¢ and still had to be reserved in advance. Programs at this time were changed three times a week, and there were two performances daily. Sometime between 1936 and 1977 when the Punch and Judy was converted to a repertory house, it began to exhibit first-run pictures, which had previously been reserved for the large palaces downtown, and programs were changed only once a week. The switch to classical films saw film prices of $2.50 for double features in 1977, while in 1981 the same price was good for a single film, with double features at $3.00. Programs during this period were changed sporadically, from as frequent as a new movie every other day, to films which ran for two or more weeks at a time.

The type of films shown at the Punch and Judy was strictly regulated, first by the theater's owners and later by the Grosse Pointe Farms City Council. A footnote at the bottom of the opening night's program and signed by the managers was quoted in The Detroit News article of the next day:

> Here on the screen and from the perfect sound apparatus there shall never assail you a subject which may be out of accord with the high purpose of those who make the Punch and Judy possible. We pledge that we shall afford you the finest in pictorial dramatizations and the most aesthetic as well as the most constructive in music. For it is and shall be our policy to maintain at all costs the high intentions of those who built this theater.

By 1978, however, the Punch and Judy was no longer owned by those who built it and complaints from neighboring residents, concerning noisy late night crowds leaving the theater prompted the city council to demand a contract with the management which promised that what the Detroit News termed "smutty entertainment"[7] would

". . . it was common for children in Grosse Pointe to celebrate their birthdays by first having a party and then going to the Punch for a matinee."

5 "Punch and Judy Theater Opens," Detroit News, January 30, 1930, Vol. 57, n161, sec. 1, p. 2, col. 1.

6 Pat Paholsky, "Film Group Pulls Out Sans Notice," Grosse Pointe News, September 27, 1984, Vol. 45, n38, Sec. 1, p. 1, col. 3.

7 "Theater OK's Farms' Pact Barring Smut," Detroit News, February 9, 1978, Vol. 105, n171, Sec. B, p. 3, col. 1.

not be exhibited at theaters in Grosse Pointe (the Punch was the only theater in Grosse Pointe at that time). At the same meeting a resolution was also passed that would require that all future operators of the theater sign such an agreement.

The rowdy crowds the residents complained about were at the Punch to attend late-night screenings of cult films, most notably *The Rocky Horror Picture Show*. The crowds received considerable notoriety, as well as coverage in the press.[8] While screenings of the film led to problems with the city government, the manager Larry Lyman, in an article in the *Detroit Free Press*, explained why they were continued. ". . . quite frankly, *Rocky Horror* is the film that has paid the bills, the one that has allowed us to bring in the old musicals and the classic comedies. . . ."[9]

The change in management in 1977 also brought live entertainment to the theater for the first time since its opening. It was an attempt, as outlined in the *Grosse Pointe News*, "to make the Punch the focus of cultural activities in Grosse Pointe. That group's goal was to attract prominent patrons of the arts, restore the building to its original splendor and establish a cultural center for the Pointes similar to Orchestra Hall in Detroit."[11] Despite these grand intentions, however, complaints were raised in city council meetings concerning the type of artists performing at the Punch and Judy. Council members were concerned with the type of crowds shows featuring acts with "punk" musicians might draw, and made several attempts to stop the performances.[12] In 1981 when the theater management again changed hands, live shows were no longer offered, with the exception of a four-month run of locally produced plays for children on Saturday and Wednesday afternoons.

One feature of the Punch and Judy's entertainment potential which received even less use than the stage was its Wurlitzer organ. It was one of only six theater organs left in Detroit, and after 1967 it was maintained by the Motor City Chapter of the American Theater Organ Society in exchange for occasional use of the building. The organ was first used in the Wurlitzer building downtown as a model and was installed in the theater just before opening night. Arthur T. Pugsley was organist at the debut where he played two selections; "Potporri" and "Punch and Judy March," which had been written for the occasion.

Due to the fact that the theater was not built for silent films, the organ was rarely played after that, except to accompany sing-alongs and occasional church services held in the building in 1940. Mrs. Krueger, wife of the manager and organist at the Alhambra theater on Woodward, sometimes played the organ at the Punch and Judy, though not in public. It was restored by the A.T.O.S. in 1967, at which time it was noted for being in remarkably good shape despite so many years of neglect.

One more area in which the Punch and Judy was a precursor of trends that would shape motion picture history involves the people who built it. The significance of the theater's original owners was noted in the *Detroit News* article which described the Punch and Judy before its opening.

> *Representing a project in which many socially prominent residents of the Grosse Pointe Villages are interested, the Punch and Judy is the first concrete expression of the popularity of movies among the wealthy. Ever since their inception, pictures have been predominantly the amusement medium of "the man in the street," and remain so today, but the fact that members of the city's foremost families would sponsor a venture of this nature bespeaks the ever-widening sphere in which the movie is operating.*

The lively interest of Grosse Pointers in motion pictures was further evidenced by the considerable recognition given the debut of what was, in fact, a small neighborhood theater. The *Detroit News* devoted two articles to the event: one, on the society page, listed many of the prominent area residents who attended the premiere,[13] while the second listed other celebrities in attendance and described the national attention given the affair.

> *All the brilliance and gaiety of a Hollywood first night, or even the premiere of one of those giant cathedrals of the motion picture engineered by a Fox or Katz, featured the dedicatory festivities of the little Punch and Judy. . . . A dozen or more distinguished actors and actresses from the stage and screen came in from New York and Hollywood as guests for the opening night and Graham McNamee, nationally-known announcer, dashed away from the National Broadcasting Co. headquarters in New York long enough to give a running account of the opening over station WWJ.*

---

8 For instance: Michael McWilliams, "Midnight Madness," *Detroit News,* April 9, 1982, Vol. 109, n230, Sec. D, p. 3, col. 1.; Eric Sharp, "Bad Taste Attracts Film Cult," *Detroit Free Press,* July 17, 1978, Vol. 148, n74, Sec. A, p. 3, col. 2.

9 Susan Stark, "From Arnold Schwarzenegger to 'Z' On Film," *Detroit Free Press,* September 6, 1978, Vol. 148, n125, Sec. B, p. 14, col. 1.

10 "Theater OK's Farms' Pact" p. 3.

11 Paholsky, p. 1.

12 David Kramer, "P&J Problems Cause Concern in GP Farms," *Grosse Pointe News,* May 31, 1979, Vol. 40, n22, Sec. 1, p. 1, col. 6.

13 "Grosse Pointe's Society Attends Theater Opening," *Detroit News,* January 30, 1930, Vol. 57, n161, Sec. 2, p. 35, col. 4.

Punch and Judy Building under renovation, 1987.

All of this interest in a relatively obscure little theater becomes understandable when reading the names of the Punch and Judy's directors. All were listed in the social register, some in *Who's Who in America*,[14] and many of their names are still well known in Detroit. The directors were: Wendell W. Anderson, Lawrence D. Buhl, Roy D. Chapin, Robert O. Derrick, J.B. Ford Jr., Arthur Gardner, M.J. Kavanagh, John Kerby, Norbert Neff, Phelps Newberry, Wesson Seyburn and Charles Wright, Jr.

Mr. M.J. Kavanagh and his wife were the original managers. In 1931 Carl L. Krueger took their place, and he in turn was succeeded by Frank Krueger in 1933. Some of the extravagance of the opening continued at the Punch and Judy, for as Frank Krueger reminisced in *The Detroiter* in 1975,

"chauffeured limousines used to pull up in front and drop elegantly dressed people off. We catered to the top of snob hill. You needed reservations to sit in the loge back then, and when we presented something like Gone With the

Wind, *we actually had a man with a microphone announcing the theater guests as they arrived."*[15]

Ownership and management of the Punch and Judy did not change hands again until 1976, but the sketchy records found seem to indicate that some internal changes did take place. The owners of the theater went under the name of the Grosse Pointe Theater Co. in 1935, Community Theaters in 1960, and the Punch and Judy Theater in 1964. Polk's *Detroit City Directory* for 1936 listed the theater as vacant,[16] though a Works Progress Administration history of the Grosse Pointes compiled in the same year describes the theater as operating at the time and even mentions the assistant manager as Fred Smith.[17]

In April 1976, the theater was sold to Robert D. Edgar and Richard S. Crawford. A 1983 *Detroit Free Press* article quoted Edgar's claim that the theater had not been profitable for the preceding twenty years, which, along with the deaths of almost all of the Punch and Judy's founders in previous years may explain its sale.[18] On January 16, 1977,

---

14 *Who's Who In America*, XXI (Chicago: A. N. Marquis Co., 1940).

15 "Notes," *The Detroiter*, October 1975.

16 *Detroit (Michigan) City Directory* (Detroit, R.L. Polk & Co., 1936).

17 Maude Johnson, from an unpublished WPA history of the Grosse Pointes, dated February 17, 1936, on file at the Grosse Pointe Historical Society.

18 *Detroit Free Press*, November 24, 1983.

Entrance to the Punch and Judy Building, 1996. Photograph courtesy of Glen Calvin Moon.

the new owners closed the theater due to increasing finan- -cial losses. The Unity of Infinite Presence Church, origi- nally from Detroit, attempted to buy the Punch and Judy in June 1977 for use as a house of worship, but the city council would not pass the necessary zoning changes. The city of Grosse Pointe Farms considered purchasing the the- ater at one time, but did not go through with the idea. After that, the theater had six different operators, among them Lou Bitonti and Larry Lyman from October 27, 1977 until April 1979, and Tom Shaker sometime between then and September 1981. That same month the Classic Film Theater took over operations at the Punch and Judy, open- ing with the film *Casablanca*. They ran the theater until September 16, 1984.

In 1984 co-owner Robert Edgar proposed that the build- ing be renovated into office space. His plan was approved, and the Punch and Judy theater was demolished as part of the renovation in 1986. In 1987, the Punch and Judy Building opened its doors to new tenants.

Today, this small neighborhood theater, considered by many as just a comfortable or convenient place to watch movies, is just a memory. But the Punch and Judy had a

history which may well deserve a place in motion picture annals along side the "firsts" and the famous.

———————————❦———————————

SOURCE: Originally titled, "Small In Size, Not In Im- portance: A History of the Punch and Judy Theater, Grosse Pointe Farms, Michigan, 1930-1985."

———————————❦———————————

Grosse Pointe resident Carrie Jones researched and wrote this paper while a student at Wayne State University. She later donated a copy to the Grosse Pointe Historical Society.

———————————❦———————————

CREDITS: All illustrations and photographs courtesy of Robert G. Edgar and Lakeside Investment Company.

Cumulative Index Volumes 1 & 2

The Cumulative Index lists people, places, and subjects discussed in both volumes of *Tonnancour*. Entries in each volume of *Tonnancour* are indicated by boldfaced type. Italicized page numbers indicate a photo or illustration; a lower-case "n" or "f" following a page number indicates an endnote or footnote.